*After reading* "Stop the Wheel I \̶̶̶̶ *one girl could accomplish so much ir ̶̶̶̶ up, to help less fortunate people, to ̶̶̶̶ ̶̶̶̶ ̶̶̶̶. ̶̶̶̶ ̶̶̶̶ ̶̶̶̶ ̶̶̶̶ well with this most unusual book.*—**Dick Van Patten,** actor

*It's difficult to describe Susan Stafford—a most diversified woman of God, a minister dedicated to helping those in need—with an incredible gift for bringing people together. She has traveled in all circles of life, and with God's help, she has raised herself up from deep despair, to glorify Him as you will see in her book.*—**Rhonda Fleming Carlson,** Classic film star

*When Susan and I met, I was dazzled by her zest for life. I soon loved her and realized she is an extraordinary caretaker who makes good things happen. Susan has a place in my heart and soul. She makes a difference. Thank you, God!*—**Dom DeLuise,** actor

*It's wonderful!*—**Jimmy Hawkins,** producer, *It's A Wonderful Life* child star

*What a fascinating life Susan Stafford leads. Every time I see her, I learn about some new facet or experience—from holiday adventures to working with Mother Teresa. Susan has enough material for 10 life stories!*—**Mandy Evans,** author of "Emotional Options" and "Traveling Free: How to Recover from the Past"

*Susan Stafford is the Ambassador of Entertainment for the Palm Springs, Las Vegas and Anaheim Walk Of Stars. She is the true epitome of a real STAR. No one is more qualified and she will always be my friend.*—**Bob Alexander,** President/Palm Springs, Las Vegas, Anaheim Walk Of Stars and the Motion Picture Hall of Fame

*Susan was the first hostess to turn letters on* Wheel of Fortune *and today she turns hearts with her commitment to help others. Susan is proof positive that one person CAN made a difference. Her book will inspire you and serve as a reminder of what is really important in life.*—**Al Kasha,** not one, but two Academy Awards as a composer

*Susan is a beautiful person inside and out. I met her some 20 years ago and she has always been there for my family through the good times and the bad. That smile of hers lights up any party we've had.*—**Billy Burnette,** former lead guitarist for Fleetwood Mac and son of Dorsey and Alberta Burnette

"Stop The Wheel I Want to Get Off" *is the story of my friend's amazing spiritual journey and those she shared her life with. From the heights of the powerful people of Hollywood and her decision to leave* Wheel of Fortune, *to her quest to find happiness and to help those who are suffering, her dauntless spirit is a shining light of hope and dedication to causes more important to her than self. A life of dedication she continues to lead today. Many of us thank God for bringing you into our lives. We know God has and will continue to bless you, Susan.*—**Fred Travalena,** friend, impressionist, comedian

*I have known Susan for 30 years. She is one of the most devoted, honest and inspirational people I have ever met. I know that her book is a true reflection of herself.*—**Victoria McMahon,** friend and courageous survivor

# Stop the Wheel, I Want to Get Off!

Susan Stafford

**To order additional copies of this book, contact:**
Xlibris Corporation
1-888-795-4274
www.Xlibris.com
Orders@Xlibris.com
51988

# CONTENTS

# DEDICATION

**TO DAN ENRIGHT.** The only man I would ever jump for, though he never asked me to do so. Even when he was silent, he taught me so much. Dan was the kind of man you wanted to wrap your arms around and never let go. All of us make mistakes in life, however few of ours are headline news. Dan learned his lessons well and had compassion for others needing a second chance. Without fanfare, Dan gave everyone who knew him an example to follow. His work ethic was amazing and he was known as the kindest of men, leaving a wonderful legacy. Discovering my faith allowed me to survive. Finding Danny made that survival a joy.

**TO MURRAY SCHWARTZ**, a former agent at William Morris who collaborated with Merv Griffin to form Merv Griffin Enterprises. Murray was President of this successful conglomerate for over 25 years and it's my opinion that without the expertise of Murray Schwartz, Merv Griffin Enterprises would have never happened.

**TO ALL MY BOOBALAHS** whom I've offended as a born-again fanatic. Thanks for hanging in there with me until I found the answers I was seeking. I was also able to find my purpose.

**AND TO THE BABY BOOMERS!**

# FOREWORD

## by Carol Arthur DeLuise

*The comic genius, Dom DeLuise, is known worldwide, but did you know his wife, Carol Arthur is very accomplished in her own right? Carol was an actor, singer and dancer on stage, screen and television. She and Dom met during a summer production in Massachusetts. Carol's professional break came while performing with Buster Keaton in a national tour of* Once Upon a Mattress. *As her career progressed, Carol performed with Elliott Gould in London's first production of* On the Town.

*As Carol says, her favorite productions are Peter, Michael and David and her grandchildren. She is also passionate in her support of the Pearl S. Buck Foundation and received their International Woman of the Year award in 1988.*

*Throughout Dom's career, Carol was truly the wind beneath his wings. She also happens to be one of my most trusted friends.—Susan*

I am honored beyond the stars being asked to introduce "Stop the Wheel, I Want to Get Off!"

Susan brings new meaning to words like *generous*, *genuine*, and *gracious*. One smiles just thinking about her. Those of us, who are blessed to have been in her company, feel her contagious joy, benefit from her thoughtfulness, feel her care and concern, and admire her courage. She is a rare person! When challenged, Susan always meets the expectation. She truly participates in life—no phoning it in!

And she's all about honor. A description of Susan would have to include one listening to the most moving symphony ever heard, bursting with emotion hearing it. Or the inspiration and exhilaration one feels in viewing a masterpiece. The feelings she evokes in us will give you a glimpse of Susan's charisma and what she is all about.

She warms your heart and touches your soul. What emanates from Susan is sacred, beautiful, and lasting. We thank God that she is here, truly because she knows *why* she is here! And it wasn't just to spin a wheel!

*With dear friends—Fred Travalena and Carol and Dom DeLuise in their backyard*

*"In each of us, two natures are at war—the good and the evil. All our lives, the fight goes on between them, and one of them must conquer. But in our own hands lies the power to choose—what we want most to be, we are."*

—Robert L. Stevenson

# INTRODUCTION

## by Susan Stafford

This book is written from *my* perspective. I'm sure some who are mentioned have their own version of certain events and you may be able to read that when they write their books. I have been given countless opinions on how to write this book. Everyone I talk to seems to have one . . .

*"Sex sells and your life has been as spicy as anyone I know. If you want people to read it, you have to give details and the names."*

or the other extreme . . .

*"Be careful what you write. You don't want to reveal too much."*

When anyone discovers I'm the predecessor to Vanna White, they often look puzzled and ask, "You gave up *Wheel of Fortune* to help complete strangers! *Why?*"

This book is more than an answer to a burning question. It's a diary of my unorthodox, yet very fortunate life and career with all the twists and turns along the way. All of the experiences in my life have been used to transform me and shape my way of thinking. I truly hope my story will bring some measure of hope, comfort, and insight to all who choose to plunge into this magical journey with me.

11

I know you've heard the phrase "All that glitters is not gold." Well, I'm living proof of that. Heaven and hell aren't just places you go when you die. They exist in our own lives on a daily basis and are played out according to the choices we make.

My life has been very eventful to say the least, from working with leprosy patients in India to AIDS with Rock Hudson. Although I've had the privilege of knowing the rich and famous, I've also been close to the down and out. Regardless of a person's station in life, I've always been more intrigued with their character than the size of their bank account.

This journey we call life is a long series of lessons. If we listen carefully, and sometimes, that's a big "if," we can learn. I usually learn best by example—the good, the bad, and the ugly. If a new challenge presented itself, I would give it a try. I learned early on to face my fears and that is probably one of the best life lessons I know. Someone shared this acronym for FEAR—**F**alse **E**vidence **A**ppearing **R**eal. When you look at it that way, it deflates the negative impact of the word.

People talk today about living outside the box. Well, I've been doing that for a long time. My early years were not what you would call conventional and it's not likely that my latter years will be either.

One of the highlights of my life was becoming the original hostess of Merv Griffin's *Wheel of Fortune*. Merv was great to work with—more than fair and very charming. I was able to break new ground as the pioneer in game shows for women. I was the first woman to have a microphone (that meant more money, folks), and the first woman to make my own clothing deal with Fred Hayman of Giorgios. The gowns were absolutely gorgeous. Having a parking space with my name and star on the curb next to Johnny Carson—I felt like I had *arrived*!

Our success with the number one daytime television show allowed me to provide a home for my parents in Grandview, Missouri, which was like a dream come true.

I was the hostess for seven years with Chuck Woolery and for seven months with Pat Sajak. I was happy to pass the baton to Vanna, and she and Pat have continued with great success. Most people thought I had it made and wondered how I could even *consider* leaving the show. I have wondered at times too, however the truth is, success is not always what it seems.

I had no trouble being a professional at work, however as Nancy Jones, then producer of *Wheel*, said, on my time away from the set, I was a wild child. When your personal life is out of balance as mine was, you get caught in a downward spiral and something has to give.

Looking back on my life, even I am shocked that a country girl from Kansas City could dabble in so many arenas—gain so much, lose so much, and yet find so much. I never intended to be a Hollywood girl. Never! Imagine my shock to wake up and find I had become just that.

Living the high life, it was easy to get caught up in the escapades of La La Land. I had been taught that sex was wrong outside of marriage and it was never easy for me to go to bed with someone. Basically, I wanted to be held, I wanted to be loved and being vulnerable can make you an easy target. The world in which I found myself was one in which being desired

*Here I am with Nancy Jones, my producer on* Wheel of Fortune

was everything, and seduction became a fun part of the game when the drinks kept coming. I always felt guilty afterwards. It happened a lot less than you might expect, however much more than I ever thought it would. When you don't remember who you slept with, that can be messy. And when you *do* remember, that can be even messier. It took many years to realize what my father said is true—"If you lie down with dogs, you'll wake up with fleas."

My Jewish and Christian friends may be offended by this part of the book while sharing my *new* life may seem preachy to others. Who knows, the atheists may even learn something. I don't share the low times with any sense of pride, but rather a warning that a life focused merely on pleasure can never satisfy the soul.

I have often talked about living *in* the moment—that part has value! Living *for* the moment with no thought of the future was not bright. I've taken paths that led to places I never intended to go and ended up staying far longer than I planned to stay. Coming out alive was the real miracle!

No sugarcoating—just the bare truth of learning the hard way, reaching for a new high when the last one didn't satisfy. Money, fame, success—this girl had it all, so what was the problem? It sure *looked* like I was having a great time, yet no one knew the struggle I faced. My heart was torn apart as I cried out to God for help, if there was a God.

*It was difficult to know which person I wanted to be*

There were two Susans inside, and it wasn't long before one reached for another drink, trying to ease the pain and emptiness for both of us.

In the social whirl of show business and black tie events, even if drugs weren't accepted by some, drinking helped everyone loosen up. I always thought it made me more entertaining. That's a typical alcoholic excuse if I ever heard one.

One of my most embarrassing times was going home with a famous actor after a night of drinking, not on my best behavior, and seeing the look on his little girl's face when she walked into the bathroom and saw me throwing up. I was so ashamed of myself, but not ashamed enough.

In the midst of it all, while unable to handle my own life, I continued to reach out to help others with their problems. It takes effort to listen, to take on yet another human saga. Once someone knows you care, it's hard for them to let go. Abraham Lincoln wisely said "Most folks are about as happy as they make up their minds to be." So many don't *want* to move on—they stay stuck in their problems, and it gets maddening to listen politely to the same old story over and over. At times, I felt sorry for them and became too helpful, however I don't respect those who *choose* to stay stuck.

I don't think there's a script written that I haven't lived in one fashion or another. Which one do you want? Just out of high school, I was in love with a handsome highway patrolman and busy planning my dream wedding. *Staying* married was the challenge when it didn't live up to my expectations. My next wedding was in Acapulco to millionaire and radio giant, Gordon McLendon, "the Old Scotsman". The jet-set lifestyle was part of this package and more than exciting. Later, getting married in eighteen days to Dick Ebersol to keep my promise of celibacy may have held some honor, however it's a poor basis for marriage when you hardly know the person. When at last, I found the true love of my life, Dan Enright, I chose *not* to marry for very unselfish reasons which you'll read about later. Would I ever get it right?

*With the love of my life, Dan Enright*

It's painful to dig down this deep and pull up all the memories. No one wants to show their faults by stripping naked and being judged by all. Frankly, it's only through the grace of the Lord that I'm still alive to tell the story.

After three DUIs, it was embarrassing to have my license taken away. I ended up visiting with people I never wanted to know just to get a ride home. It was such a lie to my soul. If life was too easy, it wasn't challenging enough for me. Learning to be a good friend to yourself is a real art and it has taken me a long time to learn.

I have wanted so much to channel my energy into something productive, but before I can get one project completed, I'm drawn away by another demand or crisis. Gilda Radner, whom I knew from *Saturday Night Live,* titled her book "It's Always Something". I love that title because that's how life is.

I've broken ranks so many times. I don't want to play politics or religion or celebrity. I can only be Susan. Getting comfortable in this skin is quite a task in itself . . .

Having ADHD (Attention Deficit Hyperactive Disorder) doesn't help. We didn't even know the term when I was growing up. You can grab my attention pretty easily—*keeping* my attention is much more difficult. The channel changer was a great invention for TV, and I sometimes think there must be one built into my psyche that I use on life. Friends have often called me a butterfly—flitting to a pretty flower . . . and the next . . . oh, there's another one. Not knowing where I belonged as a child had something to do with that I'm sure.

I've moved so much that Patty Van Patten said she writes my address and phone number in pencil. Because of my experience with such a vast array of lifestyles, people seem to be my strong suit—figuring them out, feeling their hearts, noting their spirit, and helping them in their journey—I've realized it's a gift and that's *living* for me. One of my favorite quotes is by Eleanor Roosevelt, "No one can make you feel inferior without your permission." I believe that each person is important and I try to communicate just that.

When David Rockefeller Jr. attended one of my parties, he gave this toast, "To Susan, I've never seen anyone who could gather so many lions and lambs in one room." It has been my joy to know so many colorful people and count them as friends. I've heard it said that to *have* friends, you must *be* a friend, and I have certainly found that to be true.

While appearing on Oprah's show (now, there's a great gal!), she asked if I'd ever wanted to go back to *Wheel of Fortune*. I thought about it for a moment and said, "I can't go back . . . have to go on because that's the choice I made."

*David Rockefeller Jr. with Dan and I on our Penthouse deck.*

On a human level, the timing didn't make sense because Merv Griffin's top game show was getting ready to go nighttime. Wasn't this what I had worked for the last 7 1/2 years? A larger viewing audience would mean a lot more money, however I had come to a crossroads in my life. No matter *how* successful I might become, I realized I could no longer "turn letters", when I felt called into a life of service. Looking ahead, I saw one road sign marked FAME AND FORTUNE with all the bright lights beckoning. The other one said FOLLOW YOUR HEART and I knew that was the path I had to take.

The truth is, there is no way I can go back and change anything—none of us can. There is no rewind button on life. This is not a dress rehearsal.

Someone said, "If we don't learn from our mistakes, there's no sense in making them." I want to accomplish so much in this life, learn from my experiences, and continue to grow. We are all like snowflakes and only have so much time before we hit the ground.

As corny as it sounds, I am so proud to be an American. When I returned from working with American Leprosy Missions in Ethiopia, I literally got off the plane and kissed the ground. With all its faults, this is still the best country in the world, even though much has to change to keep it free.

I often wish I had a soapbox to stand on to warn people of some dangers out there. I want to make everyone aware that Human Trafficking is the second biggest moneymaker in the world next to illegal drugs. Human trafficking is modern-day slavery which preys on the poor, women and children, luring them with false promises of a better life and it enslaves more people than prior to the Civil War. That was the most useless war with brother fighting against brother. Now we're dealing with the most dangerous war because this battle is for our little ones. More often than any of us realize, they are abducted from neighborhoods across America and never heard from again. Nearly 800,000 children a year are reported missing in America. Extremists are using pornography to advance their plans and Traffickers use gangs for protection and witchcraft to dominate and intimidate their victims. The average age of a prostitute when starting is 12 and getting younger. Most prostitutes come from broken homes where they have been molested or abused. The key elements fueling the demand for trafficking victims is the sexualization of the culture via pornography. The entertainment industry treats sex as recreation and the standards of right and wrong have been greatly compromised. One important element helping protect children is the intact traditional family.

I'm privileged to be on the Advisory board for Tony Nassif and Cedars Cultural and Educational Foundation which focuses on this problem. Keeping informed is essential in today's world and what I'm learning is devastating. The Internet pornography industry makes 12 billion dollars a year. Child pornography has become a commercial enterprise and is one of the fastest growing industries on the Internet. Although you may find me in different arenas of life, it's always with the same goal—to make a difference with the opportunities I'm given.

So many have asked me to tell my story, and the only way I know is to share from my heart. Kierkegaard said "Life can only be understood backwards; but it must be lived forwards." The opinions expressed, which I happen to respect, are mine alone.

So tighten your seatbelts and hang on for the journey. I've had to kiss a lot of frogs along the way and a few toads as well. This is my life as I lived it . . . and the only one I can tell . . . A girl has to leave something to the imagination.

*You can't prevent a bird from flying over your head, but you can prevent them from building a nest in your hair.*—A Chinese proverb

# CHAPTER ONE

# IF YOU WANT TO WORK IN THIS TOWN AGAIN

As any actor or actress will attest, each new script we receive holds the anticipation of being the "big break," the one that can catapult you to the top. I was already in a good position, with a one-year term contract at 20th Century Fox when a special messenger delivered the script titled *Beyond the Valley of the Dolls.*

Turning off the stove, I ripped the envelope open. Grabbing a glass of milk and a handful of cookies, I snuggled into my favorite armchair with the big soft cushions.

My heart was racing as I started to read. About then, my friend Jimmy Hawkins called and asked if I wanted to go with the USO to entertain the troops. I said, "Gosh, Hawkins, I just received my script from 20th Century Fox. I would love to go, but it looks like I'll be acting in a new film."

After finishing our conversation, I eagerly read along as the storyline captured my attention. I kept thinking, *This is good . . . what a great part . . . wait a minute, I didn't expect that . . . my character has a nude scene? . . . this isn't going to work!*

Nudity was not my thing, and my hopes sank as I remembered the term contract I had signed. If I refused a part offered to me, the contract would be canceled. I had been told the studios were strict about complying with their rules *to the letter.*

With some apprehension, I called my agent, Maury Calder to see if he could help.

"Maury, I'm sorry to bother you at home, but this script includes nude scenes, and as much as I want the part, I can't do it."

Maury didn't offer much hope. He said, "You know how these guys operate, Susan. Actresses are expected to take the parts offered or get off the lot. It's that simple."

"That's blackmail!" I shouted.

"It's the business you're in, Susan. While you may not want to hear this, there are plenty of actresses who will do it at the drop of a hat."

"Then why did they send the script to me?" I asked.

"I'd like to tell you it's because you're a good actress, however that's not the whole truth. Let's face it, you're under a term contract, and legally, they have to ask you first. On the business side, it's cheaper to hire you than going outside the contract player list. That's just how it is."

"Maury, you're my agent. Can you at least call the producer, Russ Meyer, and see if he will compromise? I *really* need your help."

Maury promised to try. He called me back in a few minutes to say that Mr. Meyer would like to see me. Maury had already scheduled an appointment for the next day at 3:00 PM.

Arriving early, I looked around the elaborate office which featured expensive reproductions of the Masters. The executive secretary was very officious, noting my name without so much a glance in my direction, just one more starlet on her list. As much as I love people, it's difficult to connect if you can't even make eye contact with someone.

When I was finally ushered into Mr. Meyer's office, he was seated behind a massive oak desk with his back to me, talking on the phone. I heard my name mentioned in the conversation and was hoping my agent had already explained my dilemma.

When Mr. Meyer hung up the phone, he slowly turned his chair around; his eyes were piercing as they seemed to look right *through* me.

"So . . . it seems we have a little problem, Susan. I'm sure we can come to an agreement acceptable for all concerned."

"Yes, sir, I'm sure we can." (I had gone over this in my head all morning and found myself talking very fast.)

"I think it would be much more exciting if I play the entire scene with a sheet wrapped around me, just a little skin showing from time to time. Leaving a little to the imagination is more sexy, don't you agree?"

"I appreciate your comments, but I have a picture to make and I'd like you to be a part of it. Now here's what we'll do, Susan. It will be a closed set so you're more comfortable . . . just the director, cameramen, and essential crew. Hell, I'll even stay outside if that will make it easier for you. See, I knew we could work it out."

Suddenly, I felt like a helpless little girl. All my years of voice training went out the window as I tried to explain about my mother and father back in Missouri. "I couldn't stand to embarrass them. I could never do this to Mama."

The short bald man with the beady eyes just smiled tightly. "Come on, you're a beautiful girl. You'll do 'em proud."

Obviously, Mr. Meyer was used to getting what he wanted. The twinge of sarcasm in his voice, however, only served to strengthen my resolve.

Feeling the fire burning inside, I refused his offer with all the pride I could muster. Keeping my Irish, Italian temper in check, I quietly said, "Mr. Meyer, I want to thank you for the opportunity and trying to make it work, but I simply can't." (Good, I said it. How in the world did I get it out so calmly?)

We had come to an impasse, and since there was nothing more to be said, I stood up to leave.

I noticed that Mr. Meyer's jaw was clenched as he came quickly around the desk. My heart started beating rapidly, seeing the angry glint in his eye. Taking my arm firmly, he walked me to the corner of the room.

His voice was cold, "Susan, I want you to watch very closely and never forget what I'm about to show you."

He directed my attention to two beautiful fish tanks. Picking up a tiny net, he scooped up a goldfish from the small tank, holding it up for me to see.

Dramatically, he plopped the goldfish into the larger tank. There was a swirl of water, and in an instant, the little goldfish was gone.

"Piranhas! This is Hollywood and the goldfish, my dear, is you. That's exactly what will happen if you don't do this film. Have I made myself clear?"

Feeling my determination grow by the minute, I turned and walked out of the office as quickly as I could with my head held high, knowing my father would be proud. As I reached the car, my legs started shaking and reality set in. I was going to lose my first contract by refusing to cooperate.

Could this really be happening?

Sure enough, the word was out and they wasted no time. By 5:30 that evening, my term contract with 20th Century Fox had ended. Although this was a strategic blow to my career, I learned for myself what my dad meant when he talked about standing behind your principles.

I was brokenhearted, but I was not broken and there *is* a difference!

*A mother is a person who seeing there are only four pieces of pie for five people, promptly announces she never did care for pie.* —Tenneva Jordan

# CHAPTER TWO

# WHERE DO I BELONG?
# MUSICAL HOMES: TAKE ONE

It was a cold and blustery winter morning when I came kicking and screaming into the world. I made my entrance on a Thursday, January 27, into "Lynn Lynn, the city of sin—they say you don't go out the way you came in". I was the sixth child of Louise Vignone and George W. Carney, two people who may as well have come from different planets.

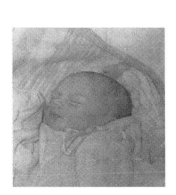

*Here I am as a newborn baby plus a picture with Mama*

Mama was born to a pair of star-crossed lovers from vastly different backgrounds who met at the turn of the century. The blue-eyed, blue-blooded lady named Katherine Kornack moved to America with her bridegroom, Joseph Vignone. Her noble Austrian family disowned her when she fell in love with an Italian. Italy and Austria were not good neighbors at the time, and class distinction meant everything.

When Joseph brought Katherine to his sister's home in Boston, *his* family was equally displeased by the union. While they did not disown Joseph, they did their level best to run Katherine's life. The couple traveled the vaudeville circuit under his stage name, Joe Pino. He changed his name to protect his family because Anti-Italian sentiment was very strong following the trial and execution of Sacco and Vanzetti in Massachusetts.

My grandfather was a top musician who played several instruments and opened for Jack Benny at The Palace.

As an entertainer standing in the footlights myself later on, thoughts of my grandfather have danced through my mind, wondering what he must have felt while waiting in the wings for the show to begin. Slender threads reached to a third generation, and although we never saw each other face-to-face, there is a connection that tugs at my imagination.

*My Granddad, Joseph (Vignone) Pino*

Joseph and Katherine had three daughters: Ida, my mother Louise, and Geri. There are times in life when a sad turn of events changes the course as it did with Katherine when Joseph died at the tender age of thirty-nine. He was performing onstage at The Palace theatre when his life was cut short by a heart attack. Better a heart attack than unending cancer treatments like so many today. Still, it was a sudden end to a life lived with such courage and determination to enjoy his music and provide for his family.

Something devastating happened to my grandmother after his passing. She went into shock and became unable to cope without the husband she loved so much. That same night, she was found with her three young girls, all walking barefoot in the snow. Instead of trying to help her through a most difficult time, my grandfather's family immediately took advantage of the opportunity and had her put away in a mental institution. Hope is as essential as food and water, and when it is destroyed, the soul withers and dies, and that is exactly what happened to my grandmother.

In those early years, with their father and mother both gone, the three girls were shuffled back and forth from place to place. When my aunt Ida contracted polio as a small child, she was placed in a special school. Mama and her little sister, Geri went to live with Joseph's sister, who proved to be a cruel taskmaster. Her ways were harsh, and she knew next to nothing about nurturing children. When she tired of them, the girls were sent to an orphanage.

Mama was a sweet, devout Catholic, strikingly beautiful, and a romantic at heart. At the age of sixteen, she met Bill who seemed to provide a way out. Marrying young was very common in those days, and the decision was clinched when he agreed to have her sister Geri come and live with them. Mama saw this as the answer to her prayers, and they began a family right away, with two daughters in close succession. Unfortunately, he did *not* turn out to be a man of character and Mama finally found the courage to leave. She picked up the pieces and set out to make a new life for Jackie and Carol. Geri, a real beauty, had already fallen in love with a wonderful man and soon married my uncle Walter.

The financial difficulties faced by a single woman without a trade or education in the 1930s were tough, however Mama was determined to make it. The biggest challenge she faced was the stigma of being a divorced woman with two small children. Her bravery and strength of character have been the highest example for her children to follow. (Even though I didn't know everything about her background when I was younger, I couldn't miss the special glow she seemed to experience with each success in my life. I don't know if all mothers are that way, but mine certainly was, and it meant everything to me.)

Mama was a waitress at a popular Chinese restaurant in Lynn, Massachusetts, where Daddy often stopped for dinner. My dad was instantly smitten with her. When he asked her out, the owners of the restaurant overheard. They thought so much of Mama and said because she was divorced, it would not be appropriate for them to go out alone. The owners acted as chaperones and kept their eyes on this dashing young man, who obviously knew the ways of the world. Boy did he!

Daddy came from a strong Irish family which prided themselves on their Southern gentility. They lived in Knoxville, Tennessee and had a summer home in the Smokey Mountains. As a young man, Daddy's maternal grandfather worked in a print shop in Hannibal, Missouri, with Samuel Clemens, better known as Mark Twain. I would love to know more about that story myself. Later in his life, Grandfather Van Valer became a bishop in the Methodist Church and still was when he died at 92.

*My Great Grandfather
Van Valer*

Daddy's father, Clyde Carney, was a banker, and as was the custom in those days, my dad was raised with the help of a mammy named Lally whom he loved very much. Daddy's elder sister Anna Marie doted on him as did Grandmother Van Valer and many others who were to cross his path. Admittedly, my dad fit well in the category of spoiled, charming, and rakish young gentlemen and was what we would call today, a real ladies' man.

Daddy was a keen observer with a quick wit, an avid reader who had an informed opinion on most every subject. He was noted for his conversational expertise . . . some call it the "gift of the blarney". No one who met George Carney walked away without knowing where he stood. After a conversation with him, each person was challenged to know *what* they believed and *why*. I adored his personality and so did he.

Mama was drawn to this man who exuded confidence and knew his way around. Daddy was drawn to her beauty and exceptional sweetness. While he may have been outspoken, he was also very kind to the womenfolk and gave her daughters special attention as well. To Daddy's credit and his family's chagrin, he readily embraced Jackie and Carol and adopted them when he and Mama married. His decision was truly an honorable one, however Daddy was the only one in his family who saw it that way.

Although taking on the responsibility of a wife and two daughters was not a difficult choice for Daddy, his family was mortified by his decision. They expected him to marry a debutante and keep the family name in the society pages.

How could he expect his proper Southern family to accept a divorced Yankee from humble beginnings with two daughters? Especially if that someone was also Italian and Catholic. Yankee/Confederate matches were not made in heaven, not in those days. The staid and proper Irish Methodists took great pride in their standing in the community and refused to bend by welcoming Louise as George's wife. That would mean making her part of their family, which was simply not acceptable.

The consternation and condemnation from Daddy's family set up walls that were never broken down. They held Mama at bay, even after fifty years of marriage and seven children. Of course, if the truth were known—in their eyes, *no one* would have been good enough for my father, George. They were Southern and wonderfully charming, what was then called the "upper crust".

This proud family, bound by tradition, was convinced that Mama was just out after Daddy's position, although their own wealth since the market crash had lain mostly in attitude and not in cash flow. So many were hit hard in the Great Depression, and my grandfather Clyde Carney who owned a bank in Tennessee was no exception. He was an honorable man and that became difficult in a time when so many were facing great loss. Even though it took time and hard work, he paid back all of his patrons. I have always admired his integrity and honor.

Daddy's mother and sister held the Carney banner high with great dignity. They were accustomed to a certain social status, and as they looked down from their pedestal, Mama could not match up. As time passed, Mama proved herself as a wonderful wife and mother, yet the stern Carney clan held their ground. She had to learn how to protect herself when they were consistent in excluding her from family pictures, even at Christmas. Finally, the damage was irreversible, and Mama remained aloof from her husband's family for the rest of her life.

Despite the increasing disrespect which most certainly placed pressure on the marriage, George and Louise moved to Rolla, Missouri, where his family had relocated. Rolla was near the army base, Fort Leonard Wood, and Daddy was hired to run the base commissary. He and Mama also became the proud owners of the C & B Café, and some of their best customers were the boys who attended the Rolla School of Mines. While the students never had much money, that didn't stop my parents from making sure they were well fed.

Mama's home cooking kept them coming, and Daddy kept them entertained. Jackie and Carol helped out at the café too. In the mornings, the boys came early before the regular crowd. They didn't want to miss out on Mama's huge cinnamon rolls which she served warm from the oven, dripping with icing. Mmmm—I can close my eyes and taste them even now. The boys would come back early for lunch. Mama's tender fried chicken was a favorite, and her biscuits melted in their mouths. They were nicely browned, yet wonderfully soft inside and served with her delicious chicken gravy. The meal was topped off with a large piece of three-layer chocolate cake and fudge icing or banana cream pie with mounds of golden meringue. Makes my mouth water just to think of it.

My parents provided the locals with great food and warm hospitality. When times were hard and some were unable to pay for a warm meal, my ever dear mother and my outspoken, charming Daddy gave what they could, even to the hobos who waited outside. They never hesitated to share their food, seasoned with kind words. That strongly influenced my own attitude about what it means to truly "serve" others and to be a giver. I do believe there are two types of people in the world—givers and takers. As you read this, you might think about which category describes *your* life.

My father was quite the diplomat, however his own integrity was about to be tested. Missouri was one of the states which discriminated against Negroes during those difficult days in our nation's history. They had to sit at the back of the bus and only drink from the fountains marked "Colored". One day, a Negro gentleman came in and sat down at the counter of the C & B Café. The regular customers grew quiet, waiting to see if George would serve him. Although a law had just been passed that restaurants had to serve Negroes, white customers were not comfortable with that yet.

My dad quietly said, "I need your help," asking that they speak in private. Daddy gave him a cup of coffee and told him that he was happy to give him whatever food he needed at half price, but if he were to serve him in the café, no whites would patronize it again and his own wife and children would go hungry. The man understood and cooperated because Daddy treated him with such decency and truth. After the word spread about my dad's kindness, all the black airmen at the nearby base got their coffee free and food at half price

I have appreciated the wisdom Daddy used, as well as the genuine compassion he showed. Martin Luther King Jr. said, "The ultimate measure of a man is not where he stands in moments of comfort and convenience, but where he stands at times of challenge and controversy." My dad stood very tall on this important issue.

When WWII ended, people tried to gather the pieces of their lives that had been torn apart. The Academy Award for best picture went to *The Best Years of Our Lives*, and "Zip-a-dee-doo-dah" was on the lips of millions. Every teenager was listening to Frank Sinatra crooning "Come Rain or Come Shine" on the jukebox.

The entire family pitched in at the C & B Café, and even at the age of two, Mama said I always enjoyed greeting the customers. I had a little play area by the front door, and I'm told that my smile through the window beckoned people to come in for my mama's great cooking. I showed a natural enthusiasm for this task and thus began a lifetime of reaching out to love people and make them feel special. It made me feel good as well. You've probably heard it said, "If you see someone without a smile, give them one of yours." That not only produces a nice chain reaction, it's rewarding to the one who gives it as well.

Some of my favorite customers were the town physician, Dr. Davis and his wife, Laura, who dined out at the C & B on a regular basis. At that time in rural America, the position of doctor was equal to that of minister in the amount of trust and respect afforded by the townspeople.

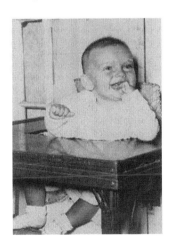

Rolla, Missouri, was no exception. The town was growing and the locals were proud to have their own doctor. Dr. Davis and his wife Aunt Laura, as I came to call her, seemed to live the storybook life. The Davises had the whole *white picket fence* package—social position, power, beautiful home, everything except the child they had wanted for so long.

*Happy in my highchair*

They began to pay more attention to me at the café, and I rewarded them with all the smiles and hugs a toddler has to give. Even now, I can recall the clean smell of the doctor and his soft, gentle hands. He was a bit roly-poly which gave me the feeling of cozying up to a soft cushion when held on his lap. I called him Snookles, and he seemed to like that.

Mama told me later that I was on my *job*, greeting people as usual, when the good doctor and his wife came in one evening. After Snookles hugged me, he put me down to play as the Davises stepped over to the kitchen area to talk with my parents. The doctor said he noticed I had a fever, and Mama agreed that I had not been feeling up to par. It was a very busy dinner hour, and the Davises offered to take me home with them. My parents obviously knew I would be in good hands. After all, he was the town doctor and took care of all six children when we were sick—Jacqueline Louise, Carol Ann, Catherine Marie, Chloe Jane, George Junior, and me, Susan Gail. It was common for good Catholic women to have large families and Mama was no different. She would eventually end up with seven. My little brother, Bobby John, had not yet been born.

Willing to trust them, my parents gave their consent, and off I went to the big beautiful brick house at 616 Salem Avenue. I was all eyes as I walked on the thick green carpet and looked around at the colorful paintings on each wall. Aunt Laura fixed me some cream of tomato soup which tasted so good. I fell asleep in no time by the warm fireplace and then she tucked me into a big bed upstairs with thick comforters. I woke up the next morning to sunlight streaming through the white lacy curtains.

I was feeling better soon, however Dr. Davis and Aunt Laura asked if I could spend a little more time with them. It was a very busy season at the C & B Café, and I was very active and needed constant supervision. When my older sisters weren't in school or doing homework, they were waitresses at the café. This *arrangement* became very convenient, and before long, the days had turned into weeks and the weeks into months. Every so often, Mama would tell them she thought I should be coming home, but the Davises assured her I was no problem at all. That gave my mother a lot of comfort with all she had to handle.

The contrast was dramatic. At home, I had been sharing a bedroom with four older sisters and a constant level of noise. At the Davises, I had my own tranquil room, filled with toys and stuffed animals.

There were fancy lace dresses that Aunt Laura sewed just for me, with miniature versions for my dolls. When Mama saw the delight in my eyes, she thought back to her own childhood in the orphanage and how difficult life had been. By now, she had six children to take care of besides working full time at the café. Mama wanted the best for me which is why she let me stay. I only realized in the last few years how much love that actually took.

As time went by, I remember when I was 3 or 4 coming down for breakfast where Aunt Laura would have a beautiful tray prepared with fresh oranges and bananas cut up so pretty. There was also a thick slice of bread with homemade strawberry jam and a big glass of milk. I especially liked the beautiful yellow rose in a small vase which she had picked, just for me, from their backyard.

People started calling me the Davis girl. To Dr. Davis and Aunt Laura, I was the proverbial gift from heaven. Everything a little girl could dream of was provided, but no matter how much you have, you can only play with one toy or sit in one cushy chair at a time. What I really wanted was to share them with my sisters and brother. At that time, women like my mother did what had to be done, and I don't remember ever hearing her complain. Down deep, Mama must have seen this as an opportunity to give her baby daughter a lifestyle she could never afford. *Why me?* I believe it was the timing and the fact that the smallest one gets more attention. When people look for a dog at the animal shelter, puppies are the hardest ones to resist.

The Davises always enjoyed showing me off to their friends and acquaintances. One of the best places to do that in Rolla was the one and only restaurant in town, the C & B Café. When we stayed home for dinner, Aunt Laura would cook a nice tender steak and soft baked potatoes with sour cream. As a breakfast treat, we would go out to the backyard to pick fresh strawberries.

At the C & B, I got to enjoy Mama's great food, so I had the best of both worlds. These visits to the café became a weekly ritual. Dr. Davis would call ahead and reserve one of the five booths which had window seats. That allowed us to be seen both from the tables inside and by those walking or driving by. The good part for me was being able to see Mama and Daddy and all the kids.

*Catherine, Jackie, Chloe, Daddy, that's me laughing, Carol, and Georgie*

One of my older sisters, Jackie or Carol, would meet us at the door, show us to our table and recite the specials of the day as we got comfortable. I didn't think about it until I was much older, however these weekly visits had to be difficult for Mama and Daddy, seeing their youngest daughter sitting so proudly with the Davises. They were always kind and welcoming, never giving a hint of how this really affected them. On the other hand, I'm sure they were relieved to see that the Davises were taking such good care of me.

After the soup was served, my parents would come out of the kitchen for a brief visit. Mama would pick me up and hold me close, with Daddy holding my hand and softly stroking it. Two things would be accomplished during this time. It would give the Davises a chance to finish their meal in peace, and my mama got a little extra time with me which I longed for as well.

"You look so beautiful," Mama would whisper in my ear. Then she would hand me over to Daddy as she hurried back into the kitchen, holding back the tears. This was the beginning of the constant tug which I felt so deeply.

While Mama searched for a handkerchief in the recesses of the kitchen, Daddy would hold me a little longer, quietly stealing a glance into the kitchen, to make sure Mama was okay.

I learned later on that all was not peaceful at the Davises' table. Aunt Laura would lean over the table and whisper to Dr. Davis, "I don't know why you let him do that. It just confuses her." Patting Aunt Laura's hand, he would say, "Dear heart, we must not forget, Susan is not our child, at least not yet." Dr. Davis always called his wife "dear heart" when things got difficult.

Dr. Davis and my father were very different from each other. Dr. Davis was extremely warm and kind. In Rolla, he was everyone's friend, as a caring doctor should be.

My father was a wonderful storyteller with strong opinions who wrote great letters to the editor about his concerns. He was the most honest of men in that area and could be a little gruff at times.

My dad would eventually bring me back to sit in the booth with Dr. Davis and Aunt Laura. After we ate, Dr. Davis would carry me out of the restaurant as I looked over his shoulder, searching for another glimpse of Mama and Daddy. When I caught Daddy's eye, he would wave as Mama bravely tried to put on a big smile. I wanted to get my sisters' attention; but they always seemed to be working, talking, and laughing with the customers. The Carney kids were all hams, and watching them, I followed right along. I loved them so much.

I'm sure it was hard for them to understand why I continued to live at the Davises' home. Things were not discussed so openly then. If an elephant were standing in the living room, people tried to ignore it. I can't help wondering what the people of Rolla thought about this amazing charade.

As I got older, I became more aware of the differences in the two households. I remember going to our Carney family barbecue on one of my visits home. Everyone was in their Sunday clothes and looked relaxed and comfortable, everyone except for me, that is. I felt very uptight, like I didn't belong there. I was overdressed, like a little princess. I wore a frilly summer dress made of satin with patent leather shoes. My hair was tied back with a matching shiny ribbon and I clutched a precious doll which I named Laura. She had eyes that moved up and down when you tilted her head. I looked over at my brother, Georgie, and saw him adjusting the cardboard in his shoes to keep the hole in the bottom covered. While I noticed it at the time, I didn't realize the significance. I was too young to understand it all, however I knew something was out of kilter.

I know my parents had my welfare in mind, yet as a young child, I felt confused and devalued by being the only one separated from my family. This arrangement set up abandonment issues which I would deal with for the better part of my life. The hurt was so deep and the pain unexplainable for someone so small. At such a young age, I couldn't understand why Mama and Daddy had "given me away" even though I never used those words.

Although I had everything a child could hope for in my second home, including my very own pony named Trixie, there were more than a few nights when I secretly cried myself to sleep, vainly wishing Mama were there to hold me. The hurt was so deep, and I missed her more than I can possibly express.

Yet somehow when the next day came, I found myself enjoying all the niceties and attention the Davises could offer. Who wouldn't? Each morning, I walked down the driveway to get the newspaper, feeling a sense of pride as I turned back toward the house. I always felt special when neighbors saw me walking in and out of this beautiful home. It was a tug-of-war that my soul couldn't resolve. Along with the enjoyment, it was difficult to ignore a nagging feeling of guilt just below the surface.

Although Mama and Daddy always met me with hugs and kisses at the café, I still went home with the Davises. The truth was that Mama's pillow held its own share of tears over the same issue. Her heart ached with longing to hold her baby girl, and her soul was pained by a mother's need to gather her children together. I can only imagine how difficult this situation was for Mama.

Early on, Daddy's mother and sister, my Aunt Marie, started vying for my allegiance which already belonged to Mama. I think in the back of her mind, Mama felt I was one step removed from their clutches by being at the Davises. This river ran deep and there was a lot going on behind the scenes.

I believe Mama also allowed the arrangement to continue because it gave me what she had only dreamed of in her own childhood. With her sister Geri, she shared years of deprivation at the orphanage and servitude at their aunt's house. While Mama welcomed the opportunities opening up for her youngest daughter, she felt distraught at not being able to offer the same luxuries to *each* of her children. She was a terrifically wonderful, caring mother as all of my sisters and brothers will attest. Can you imagine bearing seven children?

For years, I hid a never-ending battle of emotions beneath a veneer of trying to keep everyone happy. I have since learned to have and express my own opinions. In those days, however, I made sure that my face wore "that pretty smile" so pleasing to *both* of my families. At the same time, my little heart struggled to find a way to convince them that we should somehow all live together and be one big happy family. From a child's point of view, that seemed a terrific answer. If we could just make that work, I wouldn't feel so pulled apart.

*Catherine, Chloe, Georgie and I*

I couldn't help but enjoy all the privileges that were part and parcel of the Davis lifestyle, yet I agonized over the guilt of having much more than my siblings on a material level. As I recall specific situations, those feelings rise to the surface even today.

Every Thursday after school, I invited Chloe and Georgie to go along to the drugstore downtown. We would all order our favorite ice cream sundae or soda. It became a habit which continued for four years! I desperately wanted them to love me. Because Dr. Davis had a charge account there, that's what I did, charged it to Dr. Davis. I knew he didn't mind me using his tab.

Even though he really liked my oldest sister, Jackie, Dr. Davis didn't get close to the others. I invited them to come and ride Trixie once in a while, but my sisters and brother were never encouraged to spend the night. As a result, I became quite insulated as the years went by. Except for the weekly visits to the C & B Café, the only time Dr. Davis ever saw my parents was if one of the kids needed medical attention.

Whenever I saw my family, there were a lot of mixed emotions. My need to entertain, make them laugh and be accepted, formed a pattern of behavior evident throughout my life. I loved making others happy because it made me feel good too. However in finding a way to cope with childhood traumas, many of us find ways to hide our pain so no one else is bothered. The challenge comes in recognizing the old unhealed wounds and taking steps to deal with that inner child from the perspective of an adult.

From my vantage point now, I understand my parents' reasons for encouraging my relationship with the Davises, even though a residue of pain is still there when I think back to those days. They had no way of knowing the ensuing repercussions. I learned to play my part early on to make sure people would want me and became a "people pleaser" to the nth degree.

*A grownup is a child with layers on.*—Woody Harrelson

# CHAPTER THREE

# WHERE DO I BELONG? MUSICAL HOMES: TAKE TWO

It took many years for me to grow into an understanding that my parents made the best decision they could at the time. In retrospect, I'm sure my brother and sisters loved me as much as I loved them and didn't realize what I was feeling. We were all caught up in a drama that took on a life of its own. While my adult mind is capable of reasoning, my little child's heart reacted strongly to the loneliness and separation.

While Aunt Laura lavished all the latest styles and fashions on me, the normal sibling rivalries were heightened when my sisters saw me dressed in expensive clothes. They had to learn early to "make do" with what our folks could provide for so many children. The exception was that Grandmother Carney spoiled Catherine because she was *their* first grandchild. Catherine Marie was a doll and since she was named after Aunt Marie, she got some special attention from her as well.

My four sisters shared one room in Mama and Daddy's house while I played with all the newest toys and dolls in the spaciousness of my own bedroom at the Davises. They may have thought I had it made, however everything was not as it seemed. I was only a child, with no power to change anything on my own. **The truth is, I thought about my family all the time and felt guilty every day as I sat there enjoying so much all by myself.**

My older brother Georgie seemed to be a step apart from the tensions shared among the girls, and my admiration for him ran deep. Our mother's dark Italian bloodline boldly showed itself in Georgie's complexion. Living in Missouri in that time period was not comfortable for anyone who happened to be a shade darker than vanilla. Children called him names, repeating words heard at home from the prejudice of the day.

Georgie had such a good nature and it never seemed to bother him. I had always thought of him as my hero, but now it was my turn. Big brother or not, I couldn't stand by silently while he was being harassed.

I have never been good at fighting my own battles, but just give me a cause and I'm ready to go. I appointed myself guardian of our "dark sheep" and at eight years old, enlisted the help of my girlfriends in hatching a plan to put an end to the taunts and insults of the school bullies. Our fearless group pulled a surprise attack one day after school, suddenly charging toward the bullies at full speed, screaming like wild banshees for them to leave Georgie alone. I have always been so proud that Georgie is my brother, and I resolved, at a young age, never to stand idly by and watch another human being mistreated.

As I began to grow past the tomboy stage and into a young lady, Aunt Laura devoted hours to schooling me in the ways of a lady: how to sit and stand properly, how to walk correctly and she made sure I had dance lessons. On the weekends however, we went to the country home at Big Piney River where she taught me farm work—how to plant a garden, dig for worms and sell them, how to shoot, clean and cook a rabbit, bait a fishhook and cut roses properly.

*Yeh, that's me at 5 years old*

I visited the family on holidays and some weekends. When my baby brother Bobby John was born, I was always excited to have the chance to hold him. New babies smell so good, and it was fun to have him chase me around the floor when he learned to crawl. He was like one of my big dolls that had come to life, and I couldn't wait to see the changes with each visit. I loved having a baby brother!

At the same time, I began to learn about some of the puzzlements of the grown-up world. I was about eight when my dad left home and ran off with another woman. Mama was devastated and she came to the Davises' home one night after closing the café. She sat down in the front room with Dr. Davis and Aunt Laura and said, "I need Susan to come home. It's important for the children to be together right now."

There was a moment of stunned silence. Dr. Davis took an extra draw or two on his pipe and spoke softly to my mother. "I quite understand, Mrs. Carney, if you need Susan to come home for a little visit. We will miss her very much, won't we, dear heart?"

Aunt Laura was in turmoil inside, not really *wanting* to understand. How would she explain this? The lease on their "rent-a-child" was up?

"How long is this visit to your house going to last?" asked Aunt Laura. While trying to hide her emotions, her lips were drawn tight as a military drum skin.

"I don't really know," Mama said, not wanting to make it seem like a permanent arrangement. In her heart, she was hoping that was exactly what it would be. "We will just have to wait and see, Laura."

"This is all very inconvenient," mumbled Aunt Laura tersely. "I was taking Susan to buy new clothes next week. She needs them you know. I've already had her measured, so the store won't be able to sell them to anyone else."

"I'm sorry," Mama said, "but I need my daughter to be with the family right now." Standing up, she began to move to the door. "I'm sorry," she said (like Mama needed to apologize!)

There was another moment's silence as the "my daughter" settled deeply into Aunt Laura's thoughts.

Then Snookles saved the day. As my mother stood at the door, he came over and put his arm around her shoulder. "If there is anything we can do to help, please give us a call. Susan has brought an enormous amount of pleasure into our lives, and we both love her very much." With that, he took my mother's arm and walked her to the car to drive her home. Aunt Laura stayed behind. (Mama shared this conversation with me about twenty years later.)

I had been sound asleep upstairs and knew nothing of my mother's visit nor the absence of my father until I came home from school the next day.

*With my favorite doll, Laura—*
*I gave her to my great niece, Analise*

I was busy rearranging all the furniture in my big dollhouse when Aunt Laura came into my room and closed the door behind her. I could sense that something was different; because that was the only time she closed the door.

"Your mother came by last night," said Aunt Laura.

"Why didn't you wake me?" I asked.

"It was very late." Her lips were drawn thin, not wanting to face the hard fact that I was about to leave. "Now, I want you to listen to me carefully."

"Yes, Aunt Laura." I knew something bad was coming, so I got up off the floor, sat on the edge of the bed, and held on tightly to my favorite doll named Laura.

Aunt Laura pulled the white rocker close to me and sat down. "Susan . . . your mother wants you to go and live with her for a while. After talking it over with Snookles last night, we both agreed it would be best."

"Why, what happened?" I interrupted.

Aunt Laura held up a finger to stop me. "Sshh . . . sshh. Let me finish. It's only temporary. Your room will always be here waiting for you. The same goes for your toys and the dollhouse. Your mother will explain more. Now, I'll help you pack a bag, and Snookles will take you to your mother tonight."

I was stunned by this new agreement the adults had made. Didn't I have a say in this? Aunt Laura pulled a few things together, and I helped her smooth them out in the little bag.

One thing I knew for certain, this transition wasn't going to be easy. Living with the Davises, all I had to do was mention something I would like and it was often in my room by the time I got home. That's a pretty heady thing for a little girl to get used to, and now I would be living in a noisy house, having to share a bedroom with no privacy to be sure. (None of us knew at the time that this visit home would last a few months)

Precisely at 6:00 PM, Dr. Davis was ready to take me home to Mama. Aunt Laura gave me a light kiss on the cheek and watched us drive away. She never cried, keeping all her emotions bottled inside. It's interesting that I don't remember Dr. Davis ever turning around to see if she was okay.

When we arrived at my family's house, Mama was still at the C & B Café. Dr. Davis nodded to Jackie, my oldest sister, checked his watch, and bent down to kiss me on the forehead. As I watched him walk back to the car alone, I felt so torn. Why did it have to be like this?

We put my suitcase on the lower bunk in my sisters' room and Jackie took me to the café for dinner where the other kids were waiting. Mama came out of the kitchen and scooped me into her arms. I always loved that part. After we all got settled in a booth, she brought us meat loaf and mashed potatoes which tasted so good!

Everyone was talking at once. I leaned across the table and whispered, "Where's Daddy?"

"Well, he . . . he ran off with this redhead. That's why Mom wanted you home."

"He did *what?*" I asked. "I don't believe you. Daddy would never do anything like that."

"Just go ask Mom," they said.

I ran through the swinging doors in the kitchen and cried out, "Is it true? Is it really true? Did Daddy run off with another woman?"

Mama stopped frying the steaks and smiled sweetly at me. Wiping her hands on her apron, she put her hands on my shoulders and said quietly, "He just went away for a while. It's nothing for you to worry about. He'll be back soon. Now go and finish your dinner, Suzanna."

"So what did Mama say?" asked my sisters in unison as I returned to the table and sat down.

"She told me not to worry. Daddy is gone for a while and will be back soon."

At that very moment, Mama came out of the kitchen bringing us a freshly baked banana cream pie (my favorite). The conversation about Daddy ceased in a flash. Mama knew what we would all be talking about, and she quickly shut the conversation down. That pie kept us occupied very nicely.

When we went home, I had to get used to some new sleeping arrangements. At first, I shared the bottom bunk with Chloe, but the bed was pretty narrow. I even tried the bathtub with two pillows and a blanket. That was fine until someone needed to use the toilet in the middle of the night. It's no wonder that I missed my comfortable room at the Davises'.

Mama had the biggest bed, and since Daddy wasn't there right now, I crawled into bed with her. You have no idea how happy this made me. Although I tried to cuddle close and comfort her, it was difficult to get much sleep when she cried so much during the night. Mama needed her sleep even more than I did. She had a business to run, seven kids to feed, and a husband who was gone to parts unknown.

There was a trade-off in some ways because Mama was a fabulous cook, and every night, the family ate at the C & B. I could handle that with no problem.

The following Saturday, I mentioned something about how great Dr. Davis had been to me. My sisters pulled me aside and one of them said, "Susie Q, even though you think your Dr. Davis is so wonderful, he has a girlfriend, just like Dad." You know how kids always want to be the first one to share the news.

"What? That's not true!" I shouted. I would not, could not believe it.

They said, "Just wait till Tuesday night! You can see him for yourself."

Directly across from our little house was one of the two local movie theaters. When Tuesday night came around, My sisters took me by the hand to the front window. They said we could peek around Mama's lace curtains without being seen. I was practically holding my breath as we waited, not really wanting to be there.

Dr. Davis was my other "dad" and I loved him. There was no way *he* was going to let me down.

We watched patron after patron buy their tickets at the little booth and enter the theatre. As the starting time for the main attraction approached, I began to feel more comfortable about defending Dr. Davis. Then, one of the girls began to point and tug at my sleeve. My heart started beating very fast. There was Dr. Davis at the ticket booth and beside him was a tall good-looking redhead.

"Is that her?" I whispered.

"That's her. She's the nurse from the hospital."

I saw that she was holding on to his arm like I did when Dr. Davis took me skating. I couldn't believe my eyes. Then I remembered seeing this nurse once before when I went with Dr. Davis to the hospital to visit a patient. He had asked me to stay in the waiting room for a few minutes. I saw them laughing and talking together but couldn't hear what they were saying.

One of the girls nudged me. "Do you think Mrs. Davis knows? There he is, right out in the open. I mean, everyone can see them. No wonder she always looks so sad."

I took one more desperate look. Maybe I hadn't seen them clearly. Maybe it was really Aunt Laura in a new coat and higher heels, *but it wasn't!* Even my vivid imagination couldn't stretch that far. There he was in plain sight. It was unthinkable that Snookles could be unfaithful.

As I ran from the room, the girls were still talking. "I bet everyone in Rolla knows Dr. Davis has a girlfriend."

I had to be alone right now and found a spot at the back of the yard to sit. The girls hollered that they were going to the café for dinner. My stomach was tied up in knots, and I couldn't have eaten anything. I stayed right where I was, just looking at the sky until the moon came out.

By the time Mama finished at the C & B and came looking for me, it was pitch-dark. "Why are you sitting out here in the cold?" she asked, sitting down beside me.

"I saw Dr. Davis and his girlfriend go into the movie house," I mumbled. "We were in the front room watching him."

"It's been going on for some time, Susan. A lot of folks in town know about it, but thankfully, they prefer to keep it to themselves. My heart breaks for Mrs. Davis."

"You mean Aunt Laura knows?" I asked.

"I have no idea," Mama said.

I threw my arms around Mama, partly for comfort and partly for warmth as it was getting really chilly out there. We sat in silence for a couple of minutes, then she turned me around so we were facing each other.

"Perhaps it's time you know more about what happened with your father," she said softly.

"Is it really bad?" I asked, holding on to her tightly.

There was a long pause as she summoned the courage to break the news to me. "Your father met a lady at the restaurant supply store and decided he'd like to go away and spend some time with her."

As I looked up at her, she began to cry. I started crying along with her. "Why did you let him go, why, Mama?"

"I couldn't stop him. What was the point? He'd probably have gone anyway. Somehow, I know he'll be back. These things don't last long." She wiped her tears away with a hanky. "It's not that easy to walk away from your family—especially this brood!" She smiled at me through her tears. "I promise you, he will be back."

We had all slipped into a routine once again, trying to be more helpful to Mama.

A few months had passed and I was fast asleep on Chloe's bunk when I heard a big commotion in the living room. "Dad's home, Dad's home, Papa's back!"

By the time I got to the living room, he was surrounded by my sisters and brothers, all hanging on to him at once. He was trying to hug and kiss them all. Mama was standing off to the side, crying and smiling at the same time. He was getting a hero's welcome as if he had just returned from the war. The reason he had been gone didn't seem important now—Daddy was back and that was all that mattered.

Seeing me in the doorway, Daddy held out his arms as I ran to him and he gathered me in close. It was so good to see him again.

Then it was Mama's turn. We all stood back as he moved toward her, holding her in a long embrace. I think if we had been sophisticated enough, we would have given them a standing ovation. We were all excited to see them back together.

The forgiving part was easy, because I loved my dad. Forgetting was a different story, especially when dealing with such a barrage of emotions for him and Dr. Davis at the same time. I decided then and there that when I grew up, I would never let a man leave *me* for someone else, never!

On Monday afternoon when school was over, I found Dr. Davis waiting for me. I was happy to see him, just a little quieter than usual. He took my hand and walked me over to the car. As we drove along, he said, "Your mother and father had a long talk with us last night and they asked if we could take care of you again." (I found out later that the Davises had actually begged Mama and Daddy to let me live with them, now that he was home again.) "How do you feel about coming back to Salem Avenue?"

"I would love to, but what about Mama, Jackie, Carol, Catherine, Chloe, Georgie and Bobby John?"

"I know that's what you've always wanted," he answered quietly, "it's just not workable, sweetie."

We drove in silence the rest of the way home. There was nothing I could do except make the best of it. Frankly, it was nice to get back to my own room at the Davises. Aunt Laura had everything ready for my return. She had kept it nice and clean, and the room was just the way I left it. As I lay in my bed that first night, my emotions were going haywire. Did being back in this room mean I wasn't wanted by my parents any more? That couldn't be true, or could it? How badly did they want me? I would never know since no one seemed to talk to me about the decisions being made.

Even though I knew Aunt Laura was happy to have me back, she seemed a little more subdued than usual. The next afternoon, I came downstairs to get a glass of milk and found Aunt Laura sitting on the back steps of the huge summer porch, my favorite spot. She was crying and smoking the first cigarette I had ever seen her touch. I walked out quietly and sat down next to her. "What's wrong, Aunt Laura?"

"It's good to cry sometimes," she said.

Aunt Laura tried to smile at me through her tears, and I was instantly reminded of my mother when we'd talked that night about Daddy. Aunt Laura had always been more reserved, but now, that proper and disciplined front had cracked open a little. Perhaps not all the way, however I could see she was really hurting. A new and remarkable feeling of closeness began to develop between us. I reached for her hand and held it. It was as cold as ice as her fingers tightened around mine.

"Is it Snookles?" I asked.

She nodded her head, confirming my worst fears. She grasped my hand even tighter.

"I heard that he has a girlfriend. I didn't want to believe it, but then I saw them at the movies together."

I moved closer and we sat in silence for a while, interrupted only by her quiet sobbing.

"It's been going on for some time, Susan. Some days, I just can't accept it. It's too hard. I pray and I try . . ."

"Is today one of those days, Aunt Laura?"

She nodded again, wiping her tears. We sat close to each other for more than an hour. Eventually, the only sound was the heavy rain beating down on the glass roof of the porch.

I had seen those same tears of betrayal spill from my own mother's eyes, however she didn't want to talk much about it. Aunt Laura's situation seemed more humiliating under the weight of their social status in the small town. It was unthinkable that this man of prestige would publicly parade around with another woman, like no one would notice.

As the weeks went by, life at the Davis house was okay, but not the same as before. The closeness I had enjoyed with Snookles was slowly being transferred to Aunt Laura. While I tried not to make it too obvious, I'm sure he realized by now, that I had heard about his girlfriend.

Now that Aunt Laura had taken me into her confidence, she wanted my help. We were all sitting in the dining room one lunchtime during Easter vacation when Dr. Davis asked me to go on rounds with him.

"I'm going to see a few patients in the country this afternoon, Susan. Like to come along?" I looked over at Aunt Laura and she nodded.

"I'd like that."

As soon as Dr. Davis left the dining room to pack his little black bag, Aunt Laura said, "I want you to keep an eye on Doctor this afternoon. Will you do that for me? Try and remember where you went and we'll talk later." (She was in such pain so I agreed.)

We both heard the office door open and close. Aunt Laura stood up and quickly began collecting the dirty plates. She put a finger to her lips and quietly muttered "ssshh" as the sound of Dr. Davises' footsteps came closer.

What could I say? I didn't really want to spy on anyone, even for Aunt Laura. Yet that afternoon, I went along with her request. I hurt for her so badly and have to admit that I was also curious.

There was very little to report that evening when Dr. Davis left to attend a chamber of commerce meeting.

"So where did you go this afternoon?" asked Aunt Laura as she fixed me a cup of hot chocolate.

"Nowhere special. We went over to the Cox's farm. Mrs. Cox has cancer you know. Then to see Mrs. Richardson, to check on her medication. After that, we drove to the railroad station and picked up medical supplies which had come in from Kansas City. Then we came home."

"Did you go to the hospital?" asked Aunt Laura, hoping for a meaningful tidbit of information.

"Not today," I replied.

Dr. Davis taught me about fevers, flu and colds, how to really listen to patients, and how to give an injection. He had even trusted me with confidential information about some of his patients, how sick they were and how some of them couldn't pay and he'd take a chicken or some firewood in exchange for his fees. It made me feel like I had "inside" information—a holder of trusted secrets. He always made me feel special.

The truth is I had spent more hours than I care to remember, sitting alone in the doctor's big white Cadillac, parked outside the nurse's house. Although Dr. Davis always had me work by his side during all of his house calls in the country, the *only* time he had me stay in the car was when he went to the nurse's house. I didn't like being put in this position at all. When I voiced any complaints, he told me that I was simply too young to understand and assured me that I would feel differently when I grew up. If I could, I would hold his hands even now, look deeply into the warmth of his eyes and tell him, "I'm all grown up, Doctor, and I *don't* feel any different now than I did then!"

I slowly stopped going on rounds, telling the doctor I wanted to spend more time learning to ride my pony, Trixie, now that I was getting older. In later months, I only went when it was raining and I couldn't ride Trixie or he needed someone to help with the map when he was visiting a new patient in the country.

We all continued to play our little roles: the loving wife, the adoring daughter, the important doctor, and things seemed to go along as if nothing were wrong. I often thought to myself, *I guess this is what being grown-up means.* You just hit your marks and stick to the script. It was not until many years later that I learned grown-ups *can* rewrite the script if they choose.

On top of everything else, I was about to be caught in another family tug-of-war. Not long after Daddy had returned home from his sojourn with the redhead, Grandmother Carney, summoned him to their house after church one Sunday. She was an opinionated woman who became pretty fierce when she felt strongly about something. (Maybe that's where

I learned it.) Grandmother Carney was generous and great to me, except there was something in her manner that always seemed to scare me.

Grandmother pointed out to Daddy that since I was living back at the Davis house, I was once again becoming "that Davis girl" and she didn't like it one bit. She didn't like Dr. Davis much, and I later found out the feeling was mutual. I think she was one of the few people Dr. Davis refused to have as a patient, referring her to a new doctor in town.

Grandmother Carney told my dad in no uncertain terms that I was to visit her once a week, on Friday nights, and return to the Davises on Saturday afternoon. This was not a request, it was a command. So my grandfather Clyde Carney, whom I adored, would come to pick me up at school every Friday afternoon in his beautiful black sedan. Spending every Friday night at their home was not something I relished. Once again, I was involved in an emotional dilemma without anyone asking what I wanted.

I remember that when Grandmother talked up a storm, Grandfather would shut off his hearing aid and just nod and smile. She did not like that a bit. I suppose it didn't help that I found it so amusing and would giggle behind the book I was supposed to be reading. Other than that, my visits felt like a duty which I did not enjoy. I was always a little scared of Grandmother. She was a pretty, charming woman, I just felt so trapped in having to go visit them.

I had to admit the unqualified warmth I felt for Dr. Davis had diminished. In my eyes, Snookles wasn't the same man anymore. I didn't feel like holding his hand and hugging him like I had always done. Knowing about his secret bothered me immensely.

At least Daddy had been honest. He told Mama he was leaving, with whom, and he made his exit. Dr. Davis was so well respected in town, thought to be above reproach, and yet he was courting another woman openly. This early experience with the two most important men in my life caused me to mistrust men in general.

The one I did look up to, who was not yet a man, was my brother, Georgie. This friendship had been encouraged by Mama as she felt he got left out with so many girls in the house. The more I was with him, the more I laughed at his antics and began to see how much wisdom and kindness he possessed.

I will always remember the time I had to go to the Rolla Phelps County Hospital for an emergency appendectomy. I shared a room with a wonderful lady, Mrs. Springs, who was nearly ninety-six years old. It's amazing how I can remember her name and sweet face after all these years. She was not well, and one day when she called and called for the nurse, no one came. She needed the bedpan badly, so I decided to get it for her. My surgery had been two days before, and I wasn't that steady yet. In my struggle to hurry and get out of bed, I fell and busted the stitches open. When the nurse came running in, she was none too happy, but I didn't know what else to do. When the doctor fixed me up, he told me to stay in bed as well.

Due to hospital rules, my brother, Georgie, was too young to come into the room, so he stood outside in the hallway and entertained us both by dancing and making funny faces and cute noises. Each day, the nurses would eventually lead him away with the promise of a candy bar. I don't think it was because of the noise—they were probably worried Mrs. Springs might have a heart attack or something. She laughed so hard at Georgie, she almost split a gut as we say back home.

Despite the pull and confusion I felt about the Davises' situation, my nine-year-old head was full of happy dreams and my future looked bright. I spent countless afternoons at the movies, torn between wanting to be Esther Williams, Rhonda Fleming, Annie Oakley or Doris Day; and my favorite song at the time was "Once I Had a Secret Love". I had finally reconciled myself to my dual existence, never imagining more upheaval was to come.

One evening, I had just settled into the soft cocoon of my big comfortable bed when I heard the doorbell. Knowing from experience what an unexpected guest at the doctor's door could mean, I quietly crept out to the staircase and peeked down at the foyer below, eager to hear the visitor's tale.

When Dr. Davis opened the door and my dad stepped in, my heart leapt with the joyous thought that perhaps my real family missed me so much and Daddy had rushed right out to bring me home again. A split second later, my heart plummeted when I thought he might have come to get the doctor because someone in the family was desperately ill. My father had never come to the Davis' house before. They always came to the C & B Café if anything needed to be discussed.

Aunt Laura joined the men as the doctor greeted Daddy in his usual friendly manner. Seeing the serious look on my dad's face, he realized this was no social visit. Dr. Davis showed my dad into the library, motioning for Aunt Laura to come along. Their voices were too muffled for me to distinguish most of the words, however I kept hearing my name mentioned. I squeezed my eyes shut, straining to hear more.

The doctor's voice increased in volume, and I had a sinking feeling in the pit of my stomach. "You have six *other* children, George," I heard the doctor pleading. "We only have Susan!"

"Look, Susan is *our* daughter, and she's coming with the family. There is nothing further to discuss."

I could hear Aunt Laura crying and trying to calm the two men. Shortly thereafter, the heavy wooden doors to the library swung open.

As my dad made his way to the front door, Aunt Laura grabbed his arm, pleading with him. Daddy paused in the doorway and turned to face Aunt Laura. He was firm, unsmiling.

"I have to do this, Laura, for my wife and our family. I'm sure you understand."

"No, I don't. She's like my daughter, George! You can't just move her around like this every time it suits you. Susan needs a home, a place that's secure."

He said, "I agree, Laura. That's why she's coming home—to *our* home. You may not want to hear this, but Susan's still a Carney, and she always will be."

Dr. Davis appeared in the hallway, waving the checkbook in his hand. He was frantically searching his jacket for a pen. "I'm sure we can work something out here. Let me give you a check for $10,000, George. Raising a large family is an expensive business these days."

Immediately, Daddy bellowed, "My daughter is NOT for sale! Do you hear me? Susan is not for sale."

Aunt Laura ran from the hallway, crying and sobbing uncontrollably.

Daddy was obviously touched with the gravity of the situation. "I'm sorry it has to be this way, Harry. Give my apologies to Laura. I do appreciate what you've done for my girl, however I want you to have her ready to leave by next week. Susan can visit you during the summers, but she's moving with the family and that's that!" My dad walked out and closed the door firmly.

Dr. Davis turned and glanced at the staircase. I wasn't sure if he had seen me in the shadows. If so, he chose not to speak. He walked on down the corridor toward the kitchen, hopefully to comfort Aunt Laura.

I scurried back to bed and crawled under the covers. Devastated by the shocking announcement, I lay awake for hours, staring at the ceiling with my favorite doll, Laura, clutched tightly while I whispered promises that we would always be together, no matter what.

The next day, I found out my dad had obtained a new position, managing the cafeteria and PX at Whitman Air Force Base near Salina, Kansas.

Although I was always torn between being with my family and the Davises, as long as we all lived in Rolla, I could enjoy the best of both worlds.

Now everything was going to change! Hearing my father refuse the money gave me a new feeling of importance to the family, but it didn't resolve what was raging in my heart. Where *did* I belong and why did I have to leave Aunt Laura and Snookles when they needed me so much?

At nine years old, no one bothered to ask what *I* wanted. Although I would greatly miss having my own room and my very own pony, I knew I would be giving up much more than that by moving to Kansas. I would be giving up a way of life as "the Davis girl." How could I go back to living full time in a large family after being the center of the universe for seven years?

There was no time to get used to the idea with such an abrupt change. Daddy had made up his mind, and we were moving.

Making matters even worse, my oldest sister, Jackie had met and married a student from the Rolla School of Mines, Robbie Robertson, and wouldn't be moving to Kansas with us. She had always been so loving to me, showing how much she cared, and I hated the thought of not being with her. Later in Salina, my sister Carol met the most wonderful man, Leo Normoyle and married him. They were grown and moving on with their lives. In my case, the grownups were making the decisions they thought best and I was given no choice in the matter.

There was so much sorrow wrapped up in the move. Seven people crammed into one car with everyone talking at once and the smell of bologna sandwiches filling the air. It was all I could do to hold back the sobs. I could still see Dr. Davis and Aunt Laura waving good-bye, fighting back their own tears as we drove away. I wanted desperately to jump out and run back to them, back to the orderly and secure existence I had come to love.

How I wanted to, but I couldn't bear to hurt Mama's feelings. Going back and forth was too much for someone so young to understand. Keeping my thoughts to myself, I remained transfixed on the figures at the curbside as they got smaller and smaller, finally fading from sight. I wanted to die.

Even though I was glad to be back with my mother and father, the life I had come to enjoy was back in Rolla. The pull on my heart was agonizing. Please, God, take this pain away. I began to wonder if it would *ever* end. It was so hard to think that I wouldn't be able to see Doctor and Aunt Laura every day. They always made me feel so special and I was going to miss it . . . a lot. This new reality was almost more than I could bear.

*Front row—Catherine, Chloe and I*
*Back row—Bobby, Daddy, Mama, Jackie, Carol, and Georgie*

*Challenges make you discover things about yourself that you never really knew.*
—Cicely Tyson

# CHAPTER FOUR

# A TASTE OF SUCCESS AND A FEW DETOURS

It took quite a while before I could finally settle into life with my family. We moved around to some of the smaller Kansas towns where my dad ran the commissaries and PX stores at nearby military bases. In 1958, tired of the continual packing and unpacking, Daddy and Mama leased a small family café in Grandview, Missouri, a suburb of Kansas City.

Coach McCrary, who was also the school principal, told me that my parents often brought a hot meal for him and Mary after work since they just lived across the street. After a long day, they said that kindness meant so much.

In the eighth grade, I began dating the nicest guy—Sam Wilkens Westbrook III who as a senior at the time. Sam was not only good-looking; he was from a military family with a lot of polish and had some big goals of his own.

I worked as a waitress at my folks' café after school for a couple of hours every day. Before the women's movement hit its stride, winning local beauty pageants could lead to opportunities in larger cities. Local girls entered Miss National Dairy Queen or Miss John Deere contests, whatever was available.

The commander at Richards-Gebaur Air Force Base was Colonel John Ripple, and his wife took a personal interest in me. It was probably a result of trying to make my customers feel special and Mama's good home cooking. I have to admit it was pretty exciting when Mrs. Ripple told me she had entered my name in the pageant for Miss Richards-Gebaur Air Force Base. I was only fifteen when I won the title and it was quite a thrill.

Up to that point, my only performance in front of a crowd was as a high school cheerleader which I thoroughly enjoyed with Erna Land and Jane Hennen.

Before Sam graduated, he received an appointment to the Air Force Academy. This was an exciting time. After he became a cadet, we were "pinned" which made me feel very special. Sam always treated me like a lady. Not only was he wary of my dad, who was always watching when he came to visit, he truly *was* a gentleman. This was a time in Midwest America when being a virgin meant something. For that matter, so did being a gentleman.

Daddy and Mama had a pretty good vantage point from the kitchen to see everyone in the café. When a dish was completed, my dad took a look around through the food service window as he placed meals there to be served. Since his daughters were the waitresses, he was able to keep an eye on us too. A couple of times, a drunk got past the entrance and into the center of the café, trying to make trouble. Daddy hurried out of the kitchen and quietly walked the offending drunk to the back door before anyone knew what was happening, giving him a cup of coffee and a sandwich to go.

Beneath that keen eye, my dad had a compassionate heart, a people person who loved to have friends around him of every age.

Mama had a heart bigger than her smile. Besides her great cooking, she handled the cash register and greeted everyone warmly while watching out for us girls, just like Daddy.

I knew Sam really cared, I just didn't know he had taken my picture with him for a special purpose. Sam entered me in a contest at the Air Force Academy in Colorado Springs. After a few weeks, I was the happiest girl in the world when I was named "Sweetheart of the Air Force Academy, Ninth Squadron". This picture was taken at a parade in Kansas City.

*Sweetheart of the Air Force Academy, Ninth Squadron*

At sixteen, I was a very small fish in a big pond, and while Sam was already respected by the guys in his unit, being the "sweetheart's" boyfriend didn't hurt either. While my dad was upset that he hadn't been consulted, when friends started calling to congratulate him, any apprehension quickly turned to pride. When I went to Colorado Springs for this honor at the Air Force Academy, my parents were assured I would be properly chaperoned for the entire weekend, and Sam and I certainly were. It was such an exciting time!

One beauty contest led to another until I was up for the big one—Miss Kansas City Photographer! This contest was a preliminary event for the Miss Universe Contest.

I will never forget the day of the competition. We were asked to bring our bathing suits with us. Being quite shy, I wore mine under my clothes to the Kansas City Convention Center. I didn't want to worry about changing clothes when I got there.

We were instructed to walk onto the stage when our names were called and do a little turn when we reached the center. There were thirty of us competing. As the girls got in line, I looked around and saw they were all wearing black bathing suits and high heels. Why hadn't anyone *told* me? How could I compete with that? I had never seen anyone wear heels with a bathing suit before.

I only had one suit that I wore in the summer. It happened to be lavender and white striped, and I was barefoot. I never wore shoes with a bathing suit and my tennis shoes wouldn't have looked right. As I watched the other girls take their turns in front of the judges, I was feeling pretty embarrassed. Then I remembered what Daddy had said. "When you go out there, Susan, just hold your head high and give them a big smile."

When my name was called, I stood up tall, walked on my tippy toes, acted like I was wearing the most beautiful bathing suit in the world, and gave the judges a big smile. At least I had given it my best. I looked around at the others, wondering who the winner would be.

There was a buzz in the room as everyone waited for the judge's decision. When they announced *Susan Carney*, I felt like I was floating. My dad jumped to his feet, cheering loudly, and Mama sat there beaming. As they placed the crown on my head and presented the trophy and prize money, I felt like the luckiest girl in the world. I had actually won!

Very early on Monday morning, I was the first one at the café, mopping the floors before getting ready for school when I heard a slap on the sidewalk outside the front door. The paperboy was pedaling away as I went out to pick up the *Kansas City Star*. I unfolded the paper like always, placing it on the counter for Daddy to read when he came in. I couldn't believe my eyes! I looked at the headline on the front page

*Kansas City Star newspaper photo*

again—*Susan Carney Wins Miss Kansas City Photographer Pageant.* There was my picture in the faded bathing suit!

I finished mopping as quickly as I could and locked the door. Running home with the paper, I burst into the house. When I showed them, Daddy twirled me around the living room and Mama was jumping up and down. She cut the picture out and said she was putting it right by the cash register where everyone could see it when they came in. It was such a thrill for all of us!

A week after the event, someone from KCMO-TV in Kansas City called the café and asked for me. Mama answered the phone and continued to listen on the extension as they asked me to come in for an interview on a local television news magazine show.

"You really want me to be on TV?" I asked as my heart jumped several beats. I could hardly believe it.

"Sure thing, Miss Carney. Can you be here by ten tomorrow morning? We'll be in Studio 3."

"I'll be there," I said, bursting with excitement. As soon as I hung up, I realized I'd forgotten to ask for the address.

Mama told me not to worry. She called the station back to make sure this wasn't some practical joke. They assured her everything was on the level. Daddy went out to buy a bigger TV and had it installed above the counter where everyone could see it. I don't think either of them realized I'd only be on for a couple of minutes, sandwiched between the weather forecast and a live report from a dog show.

I was so nervous as I sat in the makeup chair at the studio. (Little did I know this would be the first of many times in the years to come.) My hands were freezing and felt clammy at the same time. When they took me into the studio set, I sat down in front of the interviewer. She could tell I was petrified.

Leaning forward, she patted me on the knee, and said "Relax, Susan . . . everything's going to be just fine. If you make a mistake, we'll simply stop the tape and start again."

"Okay, Ma'am, no problem."

As a voice from the shadows began the countdown, I quickly asked, "Which camera do I look at?"

"The one with the red light on top," whispered the interviewer.

The voice continued, "5 . . . 4 . . . 3 . . . 2 . . . 1," and I saw a hand point to the interviewer.

I was so proud to represent Kansas City, but as she began to ask questions, my hands were so cold I was shivering.

"So tell me, Susan, how did you feel when you discovered you had won?"

I looked at the camera in front of me, but the red light wasn't on. so I looked at the other one. It didn't have a red light either. Just then, I saw the red light flash on the first camera.

"Shocked," I said. "It was a great surprise."

"I understand you won the pageant barefoot and wearing a used swimsuit."

"Well, yes, ma'am," I told her, "but I was the only one using it."

From beyond the lights, I heard several people laughing. I froze! I had screwed up my first television appearance in less than twenty seconds.

I looked around, panic-stricken. The interviewer touched my knee to get my attention and she was smiling. "Susan, what are you going to do when you graduate from high school?"

"I don't know yet. I've got another year to think about it."

There was a moment's silence as I waited for the next question. By the look on her face, there wasn't going to *be* another question. She just leaned toward the nearest camera and said, "We'll be right back."

Someone shouted, "Hold it right there," over a loudspeaker and everything stopped. The overhead lights came on and suddenly, without a word to me, the interviewer stood up and walked off the set.

As I waited for someone to tell me what was going on, I saw several people disappear behind a closed door. The only ones remaining in the studio were two cameramen and the boom operator who huddled together lighting their cigarettes.

I sat quietly, not knowing what else to do. Then I noticed the makeup lady walking toward me. She didn't look too happy. "Excuse me, ma'am, could you tell me what's going on? Is it something I said? Why won't anyone speak to me?"

She said, "I'm not really sure. Why don't you take a short break? There should be some sodas in the greenroom. I'll show you the way."

I followed her down several corridors wondering what in the world a green room was. When I got there, it wasn't even green which really threw me. I walked into a small room with a few green chairs and orange walls. An automatic coffeemaker was at one end of a long table, near the soda machine with paper cups stacked nearby.

The makeup lady said, "If you'd like to make a phone call, dial nine first and then the number you want."

As soon as she closed the door, I called Daddy at the café. I was almost in tears when I heard his happy voice.

"How's it going, sweetheart?"

"I'm not sure, Daddy. Something's wrong. They asked me what I was going to do after high school and I told them I hadn't made up my mind yet."

He said, "Well, that was a good answer. So what's the problem?"

"I don't know. The interviewer just stopped. She walked off the stage and left me sitting there."

Daddy was upset. "That's terrible! Do you want me to come and get you?"

At that moment, the door to the greenroom opened; and the interviewer, accompanied by several men in suits from the Kansas City Committee came into the room. They stood around me, none of them smiling.

Then the interviewer spoke, "Susan, how old are you?"

I still had the phone up to my ear. Daddy was very clear, "I heard them, Susan. Now listen to me. Just answer the question honestly."

"Okay, Papa, I'll call you later," I said, placing the phone back on the cradle.

The interviewer asked me to sit down, and she pulled up a chair facing me. The men remained standing behind her, just glaring.

She tried her best to be nice. "Susan, I have to ask you again, how old are you?"

"Seventeen. I'm in my junior year at Grandview High."

There was a long pause. The interviewer got up and walked with the men to the other end of the room. My heart was in my throat as I watched their frantic, whispered conversation with a lot of arm waving and finger-pointing.

After a couple of minutes, one of the men in suits broke away from the group and stood over me. My heart was pounding so hard, I didn't know if it would stay inside my chest.

"My name is Mr. Peters. I'm the head of the Kansas City News Photography Awards Committee. I'm sorry we had to stop the taping, however I have to inform you, Miss Carney, that we have to disqualify you from the pageant because of your age. The official rules state that you have to be over eighteen to win the crown. We should have checked everything more thoroughly before the pageant. Unfortunately, you do not qualify to win this competition, nor are you entitled to represent us in the Miss Universe Contest."

I looked down at the floor, fighting back tears, not quite believing what I'd just heard.

Everyone in the room took a step back and stared at me. The silence was broken by Mr. Peters. "If you have any expenses in getting here today, we will of course, reimburse you."

"Just a dollar fifty for the bus, that's all," my voice was barely audible.

He nodded to the rest of the group and they began to file out of the room, including the interviewer who never looked my way again. Mr. Peters stopped at the door and turned toward me, "I'm truly sorry, Miss Carney. Come and see us next year, okay?"

He closed the door and everything was silent.

Before I had time to absorb all he had told me, Mr. Peters opened the door again and stuck his head in long enough to say, "I'm sure you understand you'll have to return the crown, the trophy, and the cash prize. They will go to the runner-up now."

When he closed the door, the tears rushed in like a flood. I couldn't hold them back any longer.

I called Daddy again and all I could get out was, "Daddy, please . . . come and get me."

It took my dad just twenty minutes to get to the studio. He held me while I sobbed in his arms, telling me it would be all right, I would see. This wasn't the end of the world.

When we returned to the café, I got my second dose of reality as I grabbed an order pad and began telling customers the special of the day. My dad was very smart, not letting me dwell on it. So was Mama. She insisted my picture stay by the cash register and the patrons who loved sports made sure the new TV stayed right where it was.

About the time I was getting over the pain of losing the title, three officers from the Missouri Highway Patrol came into the cafe. They looked so sharp with their polished boots, crisp uniforms, and bright yellow badges. Gosh I love uniforms!

My dad greeted them and poured their coffee. When I walked over with my order pad, they already knew what they wanted. "Two eggs over easy, hash browns, and sausage," said the officer in the middle. As I was writing it down, I felt his eyes focused on me. "And I'll take a double order of wheat toast with plenty of jelly, strawberry, please."

"Sure thing," I said, continuing to write, keeping my eyes on the pad.

"What's your name?" he asked. Why, I don't know, but my mouth felt dry as a bone. He was good-looking all right, but so were many others who came into the café. While I couldn't put my finger on it, something felt different about him.

"Susan Carney," I managed, trying to appear nonchalant while waiting for the others to order.

"Oh, you're George and Louise's daughter. Better watch it, guys." The officer held out his hand to shake mine.

"Hi, Susan, I'm G.K. and these two patrolmen are Tom Ferguson and Lloyd Quinn. We all work together."

"Hi," I said, shaking their hands too. "Let me put some music on."

I walked over to the juke box, put a quarter in and pushed "You're 16", "Blueberry Hill" and "Only The Lonely".

When I came back to the table, Officer Ferguson said, "We'll all have the same."

"No problem, I'll get the order in right away." I left in a hurry, put the order on the peg, and rushed into the kitchen where I could get a good look without appearing too obvious.

"What's going on out there?" Daddy asked, filling ten orders at once.

"Oh, nothing special," I said, trying to act casual.

"Someone giving you a hard time?"

"No, Daddy, I just needed a cracker to nibble on."

Giving me a quick wink and a pat on the arm, Daddy said, "It's okay. I understand." He knew what was going on. He'd probably seen G.K. giving me the eye long before I realized it.

Back in the café, G.K. and his friends were talking.

"Man, that's some doll," said G.K.

"Too young for you, G.K. my man," Lloyd told him.

"Hey, good things are worth waiting for," G.K. replied.

Not long after meeting G.K. I felt I had to write a "Dear John letter" to Sam Westbrook III at the U.S. Air Force Academy. During all the time we dated, Sam had treated me so well. He was scheduled to leave for another base, much too far for weekend visits. Seeing each other on a regular basis was going to be impossible. Writing that letter was very difficult for me because I really did care about Sam. I like to believe that Sam understood and also wished our romance didn't have to end. (Sam became a Rhodes scholar and married a beautiful lady in Alaska. He eventually rose to the rank of Major General. I will always consider him a friend, one I greatly respect.)

After the *Kansas City Star* reported that I won the title but had been disqualified because of my age, the ensuing result was better than anything I could have expected. I began receiving offers for modeling at clothing stores and a car show. I also had my first appearance on television. Art Linkletter came to Kansas City to tape segments for a show called *Homeowners Mart.* I got paid $75 to walk on stage in a mink coat and deliver a small basket of promotional goodies to Mr. Linkletter. Not exactly Oscar material, however it paid more than I could earn at the café in three weeks. That was quite a start, sharing camera time with Art Linkletter. He is still one of the most respected and loved men in the business.

G.K. was eight years older than I. My dad was definitely not pleased with the idea of my dating an older man; however, G.K. was persistent, old-fashioned, and respectful. He told my dad he was willing to wait and do this right. He asked Daddy for permission to date me and said Mama could be our chaperone if it would make Daddy feel better. It did. Those dates mainly consisted of endless cups of coffee at the café when my shift ended and a couple of drive-in movies which Mama enjoyed from the backseat. G.K. won my parents over as he was winning my heart.

Tongues were wagging unjustifiably, unless of course there were some way for a young girl to get in trouble playing footsie in a café with the glare of fluorescent lighting overhead and my mother nearby, ready to run interference if she saw hands begin to wander. Talk about safe sex! Needless to say, my virginity remained firmly intact. Daddy really hammered that into all of us.

Not long after the show with Art Linkletter, I was approached to do PR (Public Relations) work for some men who said they were in the encyclopedia business. I was asked to go to their office in downtown Kansas City to finalize the deal.

I borrowed G.K.'s car for the drive from our suburb in Grandview, Missouri. The two men I met had an impressive office with a paneled library. Before we started, I asked if I could use the ladies' room. One of the men pressed a button under his desk and part of the library wall slid back to reveal a passageway and he nodded in that direction.

As I walked through, I noticed both men watching me, exchanging smiles which made me a little uncomfortable. Once I reached the ladies' room, I saw a beautiful young blonde woman sitting in front of the mirror, holding a syringe. I couldn't figure out what she was doing with one in the ladies room. She looked up at me rather strangely, made a fist, and started to put the needle in her arm.

"Are you okay?" I asked.

"Just vitamins . . . got to take them any way you can. You want some?" She held up the dripping syringe, then sank back in the chair, her eyes starting to close.

"No thanks," I said, edging toward the door, ignoring the urgency of my bladder. As I entered the main office again, one of the men offered me a large drink.

"Did you meet Tricia?" he asked, moving closer.

"Yes, she's nice," I said, refusing the drink and looking around. "Is there a phone I can use?"

"Oh yeh, honey, you'll find one at the bottom of the stairs."

The first man spoke up, "Come on, where you goin'? I have a drink you're gonna like, sweetie pie." He kept coming closer.

I quickly made a side step, opened the door, and ran down the stairs. I didn't stop running till I saw the phone. I quickly called G.K., telling him what had happened.

"I know where you are," he said. "I'll be right over. Just wait for me outside."

I went out the door, terrified the "book men" would come after me. To my relief, they didn't.

It took G.K. just five or six minutes to get there in his patrol car. He gave me a big hug and said, "Get in my car and go home. Now!" I was so scared, I completely forgot I had driven G.K.'s car to the meeting.

"What's going on up there?" I asked.

"Susan, those guys have mob connections. One of our patrolmen saw my car and called it in to the main station. They ran a check on the address, and I was on my way over when you called in. Those are not the kind of people you should be associating with, job or no job, okay?"

"I'm sorry, I had no idea. I won't go near them again."

G.K. kissed me on the cheek and waited for me to drive away. A couple of days later, one of the "book men" called my father and threatened him if I didn't come back for the job. He told them in no uncertain terms to "go to hell!" The episode was over, however it was a big wake-up call for me not to be so trusting. I think I've been on the alert ever since. I learned to always sit facing the door in a public place so I can see who is coming and going. It was a great lesson for me!

I graduated from Grandview High School the end of May and started preparing for our wedding on June 30th.

Before I knew it, the day had arrived. Wearing a borrowed white wedding dress, my heart was pounding hard as I gripped Daddy's arm tightly. I was on my way to happily ever after with the man of my dreams.

"You've got yourself a beautiful bride, G.K. old buddy." The guys laughed together at the reception and I pretended not to hear them. I really was a blushing bride.

A report in the local Grandview newspaper read like this:

*Susan Gail Carney married G.K. a highway patrol officer, at the Grandview Methodist Church on June 30th. Susan Carney is the youngest daughter of Mr. & Mrs. George Carney, well-known local restaurateurs. G.K. is the only son of a lawyer and senior Judge in Jefferson City. As a wedding present, the groom's parents purchased property in Lee's Summit, Missouri, where G.K. and Susan will build a three-bedroom house, a barn, and some stables.*

G.K. told me we were going to Las Vegas for our honeymoon. I'm not the only young bride who was so caught up in the wedding preparations, the dress, and the flowers. In the excitement of it all, I didn't think much about what married life would be like. Then I started to wonder, was I really ready for this?

It's embarrassing to admit how little I knew. My only consolation is that I wasn't alone. There was no Dr. Ruth around, and sex education in school was pretty slim and polite families never discussed what went on behind closed doors.

Most of our first night was spent driving from Kansas City to Albuquerque—twelve hours of boredom with nothing to see. G.K. told me to go ahead and get some rest while he drove. He was so anxious to get there, I think he would have kept driving till we reached Las Vegas. I was getting so tired, and after all, this *was* our wedding night.

Finally, about 5:00 AM, G.K. pulled over and checked us into a motel. The room was nothing fancy, but that didn't really matter. Here I was with my husband and the very idea was exciting. We quickly got ready for bed, and when the moment finally arrived, it wasn't quite what I had in mind. I'm not sure what I expected . . . however that wasn't it. I buried my face in the pillow and started crying. G.K. asked what was wrong and I gave the typical answer, "Nothing."

G.K. rolled over and fell right to sleep. I had always heard so much hoopla about the excitement of waiting for your wedding night. As I lay there staring at the ceiling, I remembered a story someone shared with me and kept trying to figure it out. I thought there must have been a pony in there somewhere.

When he woke up a few hours later, G.K. seemed even more determined to get to Las Vegas. I thought we had come for our honeymoon. I soon learned G.K. had chosen Las Vegas so he could gamble.

G.K. spent so many hours leaning on the casino table, his elbows became swollen. I began feeling pretty insecure since he seemed to prefer gambling to spending time with me. G.K. was a wonderful man, but I didn't know how to tell him how miserable I was and he apparently had no clue.

How did I deal with this bizarre situation? I spent the time walking around the casino and hotel and began talking to people. I got to know the security men, pit bosses and cocktail waitresses by name.

I recognized Telly Savalas at one of the tables. When I stopped to watch, he grinned at me and said, "Hi, beautiful!"

Every four or five hours, I'd walk back to see how my husband was doing. He would look up and smile, show me what he had won, and then it was back to the game.

---

Since we had just gotten married, I was kind of hoping for some attention. Then I felt guilty, thinking maybe I was acting selfish myself. After all, this was apparently something he enjoyed and Las Vegas *is* a gambling town. Maybe he thought it would bring him bad luck if I looked over his shoulder. I was hurt and didn't know what to do.

On the third day of our honeymoon, G.K. came up to our room to get some rest. When he told me he had lost all our money, I couldn't believe it. We were about to be stranded in Las Vegas. I was feeling desperate, so far away from home. I decided to have a little talk with the pit boss who had witnessed G.K.'s losing streak. His name was Jerry and he'd worked at the casino for a number of years. He had seen everything from large wins to total wipeouts and was very kind to me the last few days as I wandered around the casino.

I waited for a moment when he wasn't busy and pulled him to one side. "Jerry, would you be willing to trust me?" I asked.

He looked at me very quizzically. "Why would I?"

"Because it appears that my husband has just gambled away all our money and we can't get home to Kansas City. Would you consider lending me $200 and let me mail it back to you?"

Jerry looked at me for what seemed like an eternity. "In all my years of working Las Vegas, I have never done anything like this," he said. Then Jerry put his hand in his pocket and pulled out the money. "Whenever you can," he said and kissed me on the cheek.

The drive to Missouri was long and silent. I spent most of the time staring out the window. I think G.K. was genuinely sorry about what had happened and was also embarrassed to talk about it. At the same time, I was busy trying to prepare myself mentally for life with G.K. I vowed that things would have to get better if this marriage was going to work.

So much for driving across country in the heat of the summer—there were mirages everywhere, including the one inside our car.

When we arrived home, I opened the drawer where I had tucked money away from my last modeling jobs. I mailed Jerry the $200, and we wrote to each other for quite a few years. I was so grateful he agreed to trust me, and he was surprised to get his money.

Back at work, G.K. was assigned to the graveyard shift from 12:00 midnight to 7:00 AM, so he slept most of the day. While he was out chasing the bad guys all night, I tried to sleep; and while he slept during the day, I did the housewife thing: wash and fold laundry, clean and cook G.K.'s favorite meals. I was determined to be the best wife I could be. I even went to Tupperware parties and took time out for a cup of tea when the Avon lady came to call.

One thing we both agreed upon was not to have children until after our first year of marriage. Daddy had made me promise we would wait, and G.K. did not object. In retrospect, it was one of the wisest decisions I ever made.

I was like a lot of hopeful young newlyweds, learning as I went. All across the heartland, young brides of eighteen and nineteen were trying to cope with leaving home for the first time, trying to adjust to marriage with very little preparation to know what it takes. Being a virgin wasn't so unusual at that time. Most guys wanted to marry one and most girls tried to hold to that standard.

Since G.K. usually worked while I slept, I really looked forward to the weekend nights when he would be home. Following a nice home-cooked dinner, he would come to bed with me. After we made love, he would say, "Some of the guys are getting together for a poker game. Since you're going to sleep anyway, I think I'll join them, okay?"

What could I say? If I insisted, he might have stayed, but the last thing I wanted to be was a nagging, clinging wife, so I always told him that was fine. It never took him long to get dressed and out the door. I cried myself to sleep, not understanding what I was doing wrong.

The first lesson I caught onto real quick was that married life can be boring. I finally told G.K. we needed to talk.

One sunny afternoon before work, we went to a local eatery. "G.K., I need to get out of the house more. Now, I don't want to do anything that would embarrass you as a highway patrolman and all, but I've had a few calls asking me to model again."

G.K. just looked at me without smiling or saying a word for the longest time. Then he spoke like a policeman. (Once a cop, always a cop.) "Who called?"

"Thelma Weir. She was my agent and booked some shows for me before we were married. She said a couple of the department stores in Kansas City where I worked last year are asking if I'm still available."

"What exactly do they want you to do?" G.K. asked.

"Photography layouts for the Fall sales that are coming up," I explained.

GK. leaned over the table toward me. "What kind of layouts?"

"You know, bowling shirts, the Gas Company, Buick car lines, pots and pans, that kind of thing."

G.K. thought about my answer for a few seconds. "How much?" he asked, still in the questioning mode. Highway patrolmen didn't make large salaries but he was an only child and his dad was a judge.

"I have no idea. I didn't want to discuss money with Thelma until I had a chance to share it with you. If you say no, I won't do it."

Suddenly, his face broke into a big smile. He reached over and held my hand. "Honey, I think it's a great idea." G.K. got up to pay the bill. "Call her and see what she has in mind."

"Could we finish our dinner first?" I asked.

G.K. had eaten while we were talking, but I had been too nervous to even start. He smiled and sat down beside me, putting his arm around my shoulder. "Sure thing, honey."

While I adored G.K., I don't think he ever looked at me in quite the same way again. I'd hoped he was proud of his wife appearing in a few photo spreads, however I believe it had a lot to do with the extra money I was starting to bring in.

If you're married to a highway patrol officer, some things that go with the territory are the war stories. The guys worked all night, often wondering if the next driver they stopped for a traffic violation would blow them away. G.K. told me that putting on his uniform was the same as strapping a target on his chest. There were too many crazies out there who liked to shoot cops.

In spite of the difficulties in our marriage, G.K. was my husband, and I loved him. I used to lie in bed at night, often wondering how I would deal with it if he got shot. That's scary stuff for an eighteen-year-old newlywed.

—

Sometimes after their graveyard shift, G.K. invited Tom and Lloyd over for breakfast and they would talk—all morning if I'd let them. They talked car chases and drunks, victims and arrests, accidents and the "looky loos". They were always talking about the "looky loos".

I would often cook omelets and hash browns. If they were cooked to perfection, which they were 99 percent of the time, the best compliment I might get from the guys was a thumbs-up or a kiss on the cheek as they strapped on their gun belts and headed home to sleep.

One night, G.K., Tom, and Lloyd approached a fatal traffic accident up on the interstate. As usual, people gathered to see how bad it was. The "looky loos" had once more come out of the woodwork. "If this mess was any place else, they'd run so fast, you couldn't catch them," Tom said. "Out here on the highway, they gather like flies around fresh horse pucky."

There was a lapse in the conversation. They all looked at each other and then at me.

"So what happened?" I asked, turning the pork chops.

"Well, this woman kept asking me questions," said Lloyd. 'How many people were killed? What happened? Was someone drunk?' She kept crowding me and was really pissing me off with her nonstop questions."

He paused. I could tell Lloyd was uncertain about going on with the story.

"Don't worry about me," I said, dishing up the last plate.

Lloyd took a deep breath and continued. "We'd been at the accident scene almost five hours. This dingbat got fed up with me stonewalling her, so she went after one of the other patrol officers and started pestering him. After telling her once more to please clear the area and let us work, he threw up his hands. He reached into the demolished car and held up a man's severed head by the hair. He swung it around right in front of her. 'What does this look like, lady?' he shouted. 'Now, will you get lost?'"

The guys collapsed with laughter. The officer in question was suspended for two months. After being around them for some time, I learned they used humor to take the sting out of dealing with such catastrophes. Most of us will never know the enormous pressure law enforcement faces on a daily basis. I'm so grateful for those who put their lives on the line to protect us.

While G.K. continued with the Highway Patrol, I began getting calls to work hospitality suites at local conventions. I took the job seriously, learning how to deal with many different personalities as I went along.

*I'm third from the right—Head of Hospitality hostesses nationwide for*
*National Screen Service at the Theatre Owners of America hospitality suite*

*Working the hospitality suite at Showarama in Kansas City -*
*pictured here with John Ashley, actor from the* Beach Party *films*

In the late '60s, Melvin L. Gold worked for NSS, National Screen Services, a company that produced trailers and commercials for the movie industry. Over six months a year, he traveled to various cities, running sales pitches in hotel meeting rooms. From Peoria to Houston, from Albany to Kansas City, Mel Gold was a skillful salesman who knew how to make a pitch with the right amount of Hollywood insider knowledge. He was the consummate professional—"Mr. Smooth".

Wherever he traveled, Mel Gold hired local girls with big smiles and great figures to work the hospitality suites. They were expected to serve drinks and snacks while handing out flyers and putting the customers in a receptive mood. If his girls did their job right, the customer would be like putty in his hands. Selling to the theater owners was his main goal, and all he cared about was getting the job done. Behind the scenes, he had a habit of being harsh with the girls. He didn't have time for whining or complaining.

When he came to Kansas City, he set up his NSS booth at the annual Theater Owners of America Convention. I was working another hospitality suite down the hall and had just finished closing everything up in that room. I was on my way to the elevator when I heard a man frantically barking orders at the local girls. I stopped at the door for a moment and looked in. He seemed to relish playing Simon Legree, cracking the whip as the women grew increasingly frazzled. It was obvious the suite had not been organized efficiently.

The man in charge was rude and offensive in the way he talked to them. His brash manner and bluster only made matters worse. I felt sorry for some of the girls he'd hired for the event. Not used to his "big city" no-nonsense approach, they weren't responding as he wanted. He hollered a few more choice words and stormed down the hall.

I knew some of the girls since we had worked together at previous functions in Kansas City, and I took it upon myself to pitch in and give them a hand. After about fifteen minutes of trying to soothe the girls' jangled nerves, everything had smoothed out and the patrons were happy. About that time, the man came back in and looked around the room. He could tell that things were in good order, however something was out of place. He walked straight over to me, took me by the arm, and ushered me to a corner.

"Who are you?" he demanded angrily. "I never hired you, and I don't like people interfering in my business!"

Smiling at him, I said. "I was just lending a helping hand to some friends of mine. We sometimes work together, and they seemed to be having a hard time in here."

"Yeah, well," he said, calming down a little, "we were swamped with people and these broads aren't up to scratch."

"These <u>what</u>, Mr. . . . ?"

"Gold, Melvin Gold," he said unsmiling. "Broads, girls, hostesses, whatever you want to call them," he said, still peeved at my being there. "It's been a long day!"

"These young ladies have always done well when I worked with them in other hospitality suites. Next time you come to Kansas City, Mr. Gold, I would suggest you tell the girls exactly what you require of them a couple of hours before your clients arrive and everything will work out the way you want it to."

As I turned to leave the room, he stopped me. "Is that so?"

"Yes, it is, Mr. Gold," I said firmly. I was getting tired of his attitude.

"And what makes *you* such an authority, Miss Know-it-all?" his voice was curt as he followed me to the door.

"I run a lot of hospitality suites during the year and it's not brain surgery, Mr. Gold. I handle car shows, boat shows, home shows, and Buyer's Market four times a year plus conventions."

I turned on my heels and left the suite, heading for the elevator at the end of the hall. Mr. Gold followed me. *Oh, no,* I thought. *Here we go again.* I reached the elevator and stood there waiting when he caught up to me. The darn elevator never arrives when you want it.

A little out of breath, Mr. Gold just looked at me for a moment. "Would you like to have dinner with me?" he asked, attempting a smile.

Dinner! I'm a type A personality and was seething inside. Fortunately, the manners Mama and Aunt Laura had drummed into me from an early age forced my brain to give him a civil reply. "No, thank you, Mr. Gold. I have to go home and cook dinner for my husband."

"Then I have a better idea. Go home, get your husband, and bring him back to the hotel for dinner. Let's say an hour and a half. Does that give you enough time?"

Placing my hand on my hip, I asked, "Now why would I want to do that, Mr. Gold?"

"Because I have a business proposition for you, and I want your husband and you to hear it together. That way, there's no confusion. Understand?"

At last, the elevator arrived and I stepped inside. Mr. Gold placed his arm across the door so it wouldn't close. "See you at eight thirty, Mrs . . . ?"

"My name is Susan. I'll see what my husband says and call you."

"I'll be waiting for you in the lobby," he said, moving his arm to his side. As the elevator door closed, I could tell by the old goat's smile, he wasn't just thinking about business.

When I got home and told G.K. what happened, he was understandably reluctant, but he certainly didn't want me going back there by myself. As we met Mr. Gold in the lobby, the men warily shook hands. Based on what I had told him, G.K. was suspicious of his motives, and I wasn't sure what to expect either.

Mr. Gold got right down to business, directing his comments to G.K. "I'd like to offer your wife a one-year contract with National Screen Services to run our hospitality booths at all the Theater Owners of America Conventions across the United States. She would supervise all aspects from the catering to hiring and training the girls. I saw her in action today, and in just a short time of working with the girls, she turned what had been chaos into a smooth operation. I'm a businessman and when I see talent like that, I want to make an offer you can't refuse. Your wife knows how to make this a success and the girls listen to her."

G.K. was impressed on two counts—first, that Mel Gold appealed to his business sense, *and second,* he honored the fact that G.K. was my husband. As I sat there listening to them talk, I realized nothing had changed much since the Stone Age!

Mel Gold continued with his sales pitch. "I've made a few inquiries since you left to get your husband, and everyone tells me you're the best hostess in town. I'm very impressed by the way you handle things and though I didn't like it at first, even the way you stood up to me when you were right. Along with being my top hostess, I want you to hire and train the girls for all the hospitality suites around the country."

I listened to him in amazement. As Mr. Gold continued to talk about the offer, I realized it would mean I'd be away from G.K. for three to four days at a time, something I had never done since we were married. Then Mel Gold started talking money. For a young woman in Missouri, it was big time.

G.K. and I sat there in silence, trying to assimilate all that was involved. Then G.K. did the police thing—he started asking detailed questions about National Screen Service: how the business operated, were travel and clothing expenses separate from the salary? Mel Gold answered every question in a clear and concise manner.

Then came the question I knew G.K. would ask. "You gonna try and make a move on my wife while she's on the road with you?"

Without a moment's hesitation, Mr. Gold said, "Absolutely!" and then roared with laughter, slapping G.K. on the shoulder.

After traveling with Mr. Gold to the smaller markets for a few months, I made my first trip to New York. It was in the Catskills of Upstate New York, the world of "Borscht Belt" humor. It was an adventure and a culture shock all rolled into one. I was a conservative, Gentile Midwestern girl thrown into the deep end of traditional Judaism. It was the first time I had mixed with people totally open about expressing every inner feeling they had with such passion and enthusiasm. I loved it and I loved the Jewish people!

The Theater Owners of America Convention (TOA) was held at the famous Concord Hotel. The clothing I had been modeling in Kansas City ranged from bowling shirts to conservative dinner wear. I wasn't prepared for the kind of fashion I encountered at the Concord.

After checking in, I wandered around the lobby, looking in the shop windows. Mr. Gold walked up as I stood there, transfixed, looking at an incredible green cocktail dress. I had never seen anything so elegant.

"Would you like to have that dress?" he asked.

"It's beautiful, but it must cost a fortune. I could never buy anything like that, Mr. Gold."

Brushing aside my protests, he said, "Listen, Susan, you're working for me now and I want you to look your best. I'll be the judge of what you should be wearing. If you feel uncomfortable, just think of it as a bonus for three months of good work. You deserve it! And please, call me Mel."

For a moment, memories from my childhood with Dr. Davis and Aunt Laura flashed through my mind—the days when I was treated like a princess and made to feel so special.

Mel took my arm, and we went into the store. He asked the clerk to show us the dress. She said, "This is one of our finest and it's four hundred fifty-eight dollars."

Hearing the clerk state the price startled me back into the present. Again, I tried to protest, however Mel was adamant about buying me the dress.

"Hey, G.K. will love it." The mention of my husband put me at ease—something Mel had become quite adept at doing. In spite of whatever designs Mel may have had on me at the outset, he treated me with the greatest respect. In time, I learned that he really only wanted what was best for me.

Leaving the dress shop, we bumped into two up-and-coming comics who were performing at the Concord: Marty Allen and Steve Rossi. Marty greeted Mel with what was to become his trademark, "Hello 'dere!"

Steve Rossi was one of the most gorgeous men I had ever seen. (I saw him in Palm Springs recently and he still looks great.)

Mel invited them to join us for dinner which was a unique experience. The conversation was fast-paced, hilarious, and exhilarating. Everything was discussed—politics, show business, philosophy, and they treated me as an equal. I wanted desperately to fit in and hoped nothing I said would give me away as a "country bumpkin". Mel had become my Henry Higgins, and I was doing my best not to embarrass him.

I couldn't help remembering that shortly after I started working for Mel, he took me to dinner and ordered vichyssoise for our first course. When it arrived, I whispered to the waiter that although the potato soup was very good, it was a little cold. Drawing himself up and tucking his chin, he said "It's supposed to be, madam." I told him that I preferred my soup hot and asked if he would mind warming it up for me. Mel remained silent during this exchange, trying to hide his amusement.

It was difficult to keep up, particularly when others at the table expressed themselves in a strange language that I hadn't heard before. They kept bursting into gales of laughter; and while I had no idea what it was all about, I laughed right along with them, giving the impression that I understood it all.

When I stepped into the ladies' restroom, I had to go back and look at the sign again to make sure I was in the right place. Everything was gorgeous with different sizes of gilded mirrors decorating the walls and ornate furniture, covered with heavy damask upholstery.

After washing my hands, I looked around for a paper towel. I was taken aback when a woman in a white uniform stepped up, offering me a fresh hand towel. It wasn't until another lady took one of the towels that I got the idea. She reassured me that everything was "kosher". That was a new word I had just learned at the dinner table, and I was relieved—I knew it meant everything was okay.

Feeling more comfortable now, I turned to the lady who had just rescued me. "You know," I beamed, "I love your dress. It's really 'schmuckie.'"

The lady was horrified at first, then she began to laugh uncontrollably. She turned to leave, still laughing, and left me standing alone and confused. I looked at the ladies' room attendant who was trying desperately to suppress a laugh. Finally, I caught a glimpse of myself in the mirror and could swear a bit of hayseed was stuck in my freshly coiffed hair.

Needless to say, a few years later, when a book came out titled "The Joys of Yiddish", I was the first to buy a copy.

Though I tried to maintain my composure when introduced to a big movie or recording star, inside, there still beat the heart of a little girl who had years earlier been star struck upon meeting the famous George Nader and Art Linkletter. Now, I was meeting Sean Connery; Shirley MacLaine; Peter Fonda; Dale Robertson and Miss America, Mary Ann Mobley—the list is impressive to me, even now.

*With Mel Gold, and Shirley MacLaine*
*This is the first of several poignant times spent with Shirley MacLaine.*

I attended an elegant dinner party for TOA at the Mayflower Hotel in Washington, DC and was seated across from a beautiful new actress. Her name was Ann-Margret. I have always admired her talent. Perle Mesta was the Hostess of Washington, DC at the time. The place settings were extravagant with more forks and spoons than I had seen before. I remembered what my dad told me and carefully watched Ms. Mesta to see which fork she used for the various courses. I didn't want to embarrass myself and found that this saved me. I was only 18 years old.

Exploring the world outside Kansas City was very exciting, yet there was still the Susan who loved her husband in spite of our difficulties. Looking back on it now, my real life's education began the day I stepped off the plane in New York where I met Larry Burrell who became a fabulous friend and Mel Gold took me under his wing. He taught me so much and introduced me to a world where the opportunities were unlimited. Later, I met Annick DeLorme who felt the same way about gaining knowledge from Mel. She's still a friend today.

With Mel introducing me around, I gained a lot of knowledge from the theater owners and their wives. I also perfected the art of getting those who had too much to drink discretely out of the hospitality suites without embarrassing anyone.

Every time I came home from a trip, G.K. met me at the airport and took me out to dinner. He'd always ask about the famous people I'd met and if everything was going well. Then we'd go home and make love and I'd be happy. I think he really missed me when I was away. He seemed to appreciate me more, however unfortunately that didn't last. Old patterns would soon weave their way into the fabric of our lives. Lovemaking was still a puzzle that continued to leave me feeling empty. After just a short time together, G.K. would leave for a late-night game of cards with the guys.

Sometimes, he would ask if I minded. It seemed easier to let him do what he wanted and I would just say, "Have fun." When I was away, he had all the freedom in the world. I had hoped he might want to spend our evenings together. The rejection I felt was unbearable at times.

One of my biggest fears was being alone at night. Perhaps I had a fertile imagination, but there were times I was really scared. Especially when a storm was brewing and huge gusts of wind rattled every part of the house. I'd take the dogs into the bedroom and lock the door, tucking my gun under the pillow.

Sometimes I'd keep the television on for company, but when a scary late-night movie came on, I was more frightened than ever and changed the channel quickly. With nothing to occupy my mind except fear of the unknown, I'd lay there in the dark, counting the hours until the sun came up. In the summertime in Missouri, the nights never cooled down, but I would close all the windows and turn off the air conditioner so I could hear every little noise. I didn't want anything to catch me by surprise.

When I felt really low, I'd sometimes call Mel in New York, just to hear a caring voice. One night in the middle of a summer storm, he said, "I have an idea. You sit tight and don't go to sleep. I'll call you back."

"I promise," I said, hanging up the phone. I snuggled down under the covers and began to cry. For some reason, I've always seemed to cry when people were especially nice to me.

Unbeknownst to me, Mel had raced over in the pouring rain to his favorite nightclub in Manhattan just as they were closing. Twenty minutes later, he called me from the nightclub.

"You still awake?" Mel asked.

"Yes, why?"

"Press the phone up against your ear and listen to this," he said, placing the receiver toward the band. Led by Bobby Short, they not only played my favorite song, they continued on with the great standards for thirty minutes.

Each time a song ended, Mel would shout, "You like that one?" Before I could answer, another song would start.

I lay very still with the tears rolling down my cheeks in Lee's Summit, Missouri, the phone clasped tightly to my ear, listening to a band 1100 miles away in New York. Finally, Mel came on the line again.

"Are you okay, Susan?"

"Sure," I whispered, not wanting him to hear me sobbing.

"Because I'm always here for you, I hope you know that."

"Mel, how can I possibly thank you?" I mumbled.

The band was still playing as I put the phone back on the hook.

I sometimes wonder if getting married is too easy while divorce is too difficult. Perhaps there should be a grace period, where each of the newlyweds is given time to evaluate their respective mate in real-life situations.

It would be easy to lay the blame on G.K for the problems our marriage had from the outset. In looking back I believe he was behaving exactly as he thought he should. The sexual revolution and

*Susan Stafford*

the women's movement had yet to register on the Richter scale of our consciousness, and sensitivity training for men would have been scorned as "sissy stuff".

So along with making dinner, I chose to make do. I wanted my marriage to work and spent more time in Kansas City. Modeling and the hospitality suites soon became not just a way to make extra money, they also built my self-esteem. Models like Shirley Pike, Marion Green, and my dear friend even today, Connie Hancock, were my fellow professional models in Kansas City. We had such fun working together.

Before I met Mel Gold, modeling had already begun to pay dividends. Thelma Weir had taken me under her wing, and I began selling everything from bowling equipment to frying pans. Before long, I was a partner in the modeling agency, Monza, where my career began.

I tried to be the perfect wife, but it was difficult to build a relationship with someone who spent so little time with me. On the other hand, my presence and talent were now in demand and as often happens, I gravitated to where I was appreciated. As G.K. and I drifted apart, I began to take control of my life, and yet the tug in my heart to be the good wife competed with the longing to grow and be all I could be.

G.K. and I made plans to take a short vacation to visit my sister Catherine and her family in California. He wasn't particularly excited about the trip until I enticed him with an offer I had received from Dale Robertson whom I met at one of the TOA Conventions. At the time, Dale was starring in a television series called *The Iron Horse*, and he graciously invited me to visit the set when I came to California. While G.K. was not impressed with Hollywood in the least, he loved to watch Dale's show and was so excited to meet him.

When we arrived in California, I took it all in—the palm trees, the Pacific Ocean, endless sunshine, lavish cars—it was very hypnotic. In my heart of hearts, the moment I saw Los Angeles, I knew it would be a part of my destiny.

During our brief stay, we visited Dale Robertson and G.K. was duly impressed. Dale was wonderful and greeted me like an old friend. After showing us around, he took us to lunch at the studio commissary. He and G.K. hit it off and couldn't stop talking about their horses and the bloodlines. That was the *only* part G.K. liked about the trip. I was *drawn* to California and gently broached the idea of moving, suggesting that I could make more in commercial work there. As far as G.K. was concerned, it was *full of faggots*, and he had no interest in setting foot in California again. *Move* there? Forget it!

G.K.'s implacability was infuriating. It was obvious there would be no discussion about the matter. I was just as stubborn and chose to "suffer in silence". After all, I was a Carney woman, and my mother set a high standard. She never left her man.

After we returned from our California trip, my work for National Screen Service consumed my life. When I traveled on business, I started staying away for longer periods of time. G.K. never questioned the length of my trips. While I didn't really enjoy being home, I grew to resent his indifference in not asking me to spend more time there. We had placed ourselves in a terrible double bind.

Finally, a second California visit to see my sister, Catherine was planned. I would be going alone this time and not surprisingly, there was no protest from G.K. In my heart, I knew I wouldn't be returning. By this point in our marriage, we were just going through the motions. If G.K. had tried to stop me from leaving with real passion and conviction, I might have stayed. I wanted to be wanted, *especially* by my husband. I just didn't know that being married meant spending most of my time alone. When I arrived in California and unpacked, I almost missed the piece of paper hidden under my clothes. It was a note from G.K.—the message was simple and direct. "Dear Susan, I know you won't be coming back. I'm sorry. I'll always love you, G.K."

I stored my suitcase under the bed. And the note? I ended up using it at Lee Strasberg's Actor's Studio in a class taught by Jack Garfine. When he asked us to dig deep for an emotion to fit each scene—excitement, sadness, longing . . . they were all there. All I had to do was glance at the note and the feelings came rushing back. They call it acting, but it was also my reality.

*It' is never too late to be who you might have been.*—George Elliot

# CHAPTER FIVE

# THE REAL DEAL, LIFE IN HOLLYWOOD:

I soon learned that in Hollywood, it's not always easy to discern the difference between real life and playing a part. I began sending postcards to all the agencies and calling to get appointments. Little by little, I started getting offers of work.

Thanks to the trailers I had filmed for National Screen Services and the commercials I made in Kansas City, I soon found my first agent, Robert Longnecker. He was a solid, hard-working man, married to actress Ruth Hussey.

I was blessed with some very marketable assets which were soon to be tested. That first summer in California, I was cast in national commercials for Alberto V05 and Borden's Milk.

When I was selected for a Hamm's Beer commercial, I was instructed to meet the crew at Huntington Beach at 7:00 sharp on Tuesday morning in a bikini.

The first question the director asked when I got to the beach was simple and direct.

"You can surf, right?"

Brought up in Missouri and having only seen the ocean twice, what was I supposed to say? I had *seen* people surf. How hard could it be?

Without hesitating, I said, "Sure, no problem!"

It was then that I noticed the waves were pretty high. So much so that I didn't see anyone in the water.

I wasn't too worried. After all, I was pretty athletic and a good equestrian. I could handle this! __

A production assistant handed me a nice new surfboard which was freshly waxed. Carrying it confidently toward the water, I acted like I did this every day.

I was told to stay outside the surf line until the director had all the foreground action ready to go. Then the first assistant director would wave a green flag, and I would stand on the board and surf in toward the beach.

Although the water was freezing, I kept paddling, ignoring the chattering of my teeth. Somehow, I managed to get out beyond the surf line. I kept moving around to keep my blood circulating, waiting for the green flag.

There it was! I knew what to do. I'd watched surfing movies when I lived in Missouri, and it all looked pretty easy. Wait for the right wave, paddle like crazy, kneel on the board, and when you reach the crest of the wave, stand up, use your arms for balance, and go for it. I kept telling myself, "You can do this! You just need to stand on the board long enough for them to get the shot."

Okay, everything was going according to plan. I got my footing, and the wave carried my board swiftly through the water. What a rush! I was sailing along for about ten seconds when suddenly a monster wave crashed and flipped me beneath the water. Struggling to know which way was up, my head finally broke the surface as I looked around to get my bearings. Just then the board slammed down, striking me on the cheekbone, knocking me under once more. Before I could get any air, a churning wave tossed me around and finally washed me toward shore.

As I crawled up the beach on my hands and knees, I was choking on salt water and spitting out seaweed, but the "thumbs up" told me they had gotten the shot. Can't tell you how relieved I was that we didn't have to do another take.

The director walked over and said, "Thanks. What's your name again?"

With a hand clamped over my eye, I started to tell him when my nervous stomach started acting up.

He motioned to the second assistant director who walked me over to the production trailers. He hollered at someone to bring me a towel and sat me down on a prop box.

"You okay?" he asked. "You look a little green around the gills. Should I call a doctor?"

"No, I'm okay. Just nerves, I guess. The waves are pretty big."

"You're not kidding!" he said. "The lifeguards wanted to cancel the shoot before you got here."

"Why?" I asked, wrapping the towel tightly, still shivering.

"Well, I shouldn't be telling you this," he confided, "but the producer had to grease a few palms so we could get the commercial finished in time for airing on national television next weekend. He was keeping a wary eye on the high waves, but when you seemed so confident, he decided to get the shot in one take."

When my sister, Catherine, came to pick me up, she took one look at my shiner and was more than concerned. When she heard how the shoot had been bulldozed through because of time constraints, she was all for suing the production company. Catherine's caring meant a lot to me, but after much persuasion, I managed to talk her out of it. I needed the work, and if word spreads that you're a complainer, they don't hesitate to call someone else!

La La Land is all about contacts and being in the right place at the right time. Of course, now I know it was more than luck, I was truly blessed.

As my bank balance improved, I moved from Catherine's house in Long Beach to Hollywood. The year before, when G.K. and I visited with Dale Robertson, I noticed a number of apartment buildings that looked nice beneath the large HOLLYWOOD sign. I drove to that area and found a small place with one bedroom, a tiny kitchen, living room, and one and a half baths. (The half bath bit has always amused me. Who takes half a bath?)

There was a little swimming pool for the residents surrounded by giant ferns and palm trees. I would sit out there, sometimes reading a book or hopefully, a script and imagine I was in some magical, tropical paradise. The illusion was so vivid until I was rudely interrupted by all the horns when rush hour started.

One person who turned out to be a real friend in Hollywood is Jimmy Hawkins, a child star from the classic film *It's a Wonderful Life*. Jimmy played Shelly Fabares' boyfriend on *The Donna Reed Show* and co-starred in films with Elvis. When we met, he had become a producer and won an Emmy for the *25th Motown Anniversary Special*. He also produced *Love Leads the Way* with Timothy Bottoms, a wonderful story about the first seeing-eye dog. Jimmy continues to be a dear friend to this day.

When my divorce from G.K. was final, I began dating. This was quite a change from Kansas City. I was taken to parties by a young Lee Majors and dated some great actors such as Ben Murphy; Clint Ritchie; Anthony Hopkins; Scott Wilson; Robert Lansing; MacLean Stevenson; Freddie Prinze; Robert Forster; Harry Gardino and Maximilian Schell, just to name a few. It was a fun time.

When Clint Ritchie and I were riding horses in the desert, we came across a

*With Jimmy Hawkins*

wonderful dog that had just been left in the middle of nowhere. He was so friendly and warmed up to me right away. I named him Butcherman, took him home and learned to trust his instincts even more than my own.

Later on, I had been seeing Maximilian Schell for a while, you know for coffee, before he actually came to my home. That night I learned something very important. He didn't like my dog and my dog, Butcherman, didn't like him. Needless to say, that was the end of our relationship.

I think any woman would be smitten by the greats like Frank Sinatra Jr., Jack Jones, Trini Lopez, and David Clayton-Thomas from Earth, Wind and Fire. It was a whirlwind, and I was enjoying every minute.

Stuntman Bob Yerkes and Richard Gesswein, son of Rev. Armin Gesswein, were also a part of my growth in Hollywood, for the better, I must say. They became good and faithful friends.

"Starmaker" Jay Bernstein who was responsible for the careers of Farrah Fawcett and Suzanne Somers was such a dapper escort, and we had a great time together. Jay is truly missed by a long list of beautiful companions.

Two very successful attorneys Arthur Crowley and Greg Bautzer—both so intelligent and charming—were wonderful to me. There were times knowing a good attorney came in very handy. Ed O'Sullivan (Bing Crosby and Senator Goldwater's attorney) has been the most loyal friend, very Irish and is someone I truly appreciate.

Composer Paul Hampton, terrifically talented on his own, used to write with Burt Bacharach, and while we were an item at one time, he is still my friend and still composing some great music.

Jeffrey Hunter was one of my favorite human beings. He had the most gorgeous eyes! We were so attracted to each other, however after seeing him portray Jesus so effectively in *King of Kings*, the romance we both desired was difficult when I couldn't get past that image.

Jack Palance, a great actor and friend, taught me how to make Hungarian-stuffed cabbage but he never did one-armed pushups in my presence. I spent a lot of time with George Peppard and his kids who were wonderful. George was so bright and talented. Remember *Breakfast at Tiffany's?* George was different.

While I've never had children of my own, I often enjoyed spending time with some special kids. When I was dating Sen. John Tunney, he told me Senator Ted Kennedy's son and his buddies were coming for a visit. I knew Ted through my friend, Rosey Grier and offered to take the boys swimming at Hermosa Beach. Ted Kennedy, Jr. had lost his leg to cancer when he was just 12. As I watched the guys run together on the beach, Teddy stooped down and removed his leg before jumping into the ocean. I really admired the way he handled it without any embarrassment. When I saw him speak at his dad's memorial service, I was really proud of the man he has become. He's an attorney now, specializing in healthcare as an advocate for cancer patients.

I have to admit it was a very exciting time . . . then came the slump. Everyone goes through one of these times and you have to learn how to deal with it. I had experienced rejection being shuffled back and forth between my parents and the Davises and with my husband. But in Hollywood, rejection can hit you full force without mercy. They seem to eat their young. All the more reason to have friends who only want the best for you, just as you do for them.

When you're constantly told you're not right for a part, you can easily begin to believe there must be something wrong with you. One has to realize that casting a movie, a TV show, or a commercial is often based more on someone's opinion rather than talent. They see the character one way, the director sees it another way, and you're caught in the middle.

You also have to learn the part about spending time alone, waiting by the phone. I was used to being alone while married to G.K., but I had family close by and that made all the difference in the world.

This was a new challenge. Those early days, living on my own in Hollywood, not knowing where my next paycheck was coming from, was one of the hardest things I've ever had to do.

When people who were so friendly and claimed to believe in you, quickly move on to someone else who catches their eye without so much as a backward glance, that's difficult to handle. You overhear bits of gossip that are very hurtful and mean. It doesn't take long to discover you were being used for work contacts that might be available. The right contacts can make or break you, and when you can't readily supply those nuggets of inside information, they dump you real fast.

*Modeling and Commercial days*

*Wearing a gown designed by Edith Head*

Tinseltown with its bright lights continues to draw the youth of America like a magnet and I guess it always will. It's really one of the few places in America where you can be starving one month and a celebrity the next, earning huge bucks with no training about how to spend them, or even more importantly, how to keep them.

For the long haul, Hollywood was pretty good to me. Sure, I felt rejected and insecure at times, however that's part of the package. It comes with no guarantees, living on hope and on the edge.

I honestly believe my Midwestern upbringing gave me a good foundation, even though I made mistakes along the way. I think my biggest problem has been trusting too many people and leading with my heart and not my head. I can't blame Hollywood for that. I believe I would have been basically the same even if I'd spent my life waiting on tables in Rolla, Missouri. There is an inner core to our being and it tends to show up, regardless of what playing field we're on.

The funny thing is—acting was never my goal. My interest was in national commercials. I had enjoyed good success with Sheraton Hotels, Alberto VO5, Borden's Milk and Eastman Kodak. I actually got into acting because of people's kindness. My first television drama was courtesy of a friend of a friend who sent me to meet producer, Perry Lafferty at CBS. He asked me to do a small part on *Hawaii Five-O*, produced by Leonard Freeman and Tony DiMilo. It was being shot in Hawaii and I couldn't wait! CBS arranged the airline ticket, and I was on my way to the tropical isles.

When I arrived, I was informed the part was a non-speaking walk-on! This was a long way to come to simply *appear* on camera. Still, I had to realize Perry had gotten me a "network" show, so I didn't want to complain. I had been taking acting classes at the famed Estelle Harmon Studio and thought I was ready for more. I had told all my friends I would be on *Hawaii Five-O* and they were so proud of me.

Once on the set, I got lucky. When I met the director, Abe Biberman, he changed his mind and decided to give me a couple of lines to say. I was to play the part of a nurse and he sent me to wardrobe to be fitted for a uniform.

This was not a lavish Hollywood set with tall rooms and a grand staircase. It was just three painted plywood walls of a hospital room. The star of the show, Jack Lord, was already in position and waiting to get on with the scene. Although it may have been easier to meet him as my character, the nurse, I was still nervous. This was a very successful show and I didn't want to blow it.

Walking me over to the set, Abe began giving me instructions. "Now, here's what I want you to do . . . I want you to walk into the room, go up to the hospital bed, and say to Jack, 'Hello, I'm Janet Feinberg. It's time to put your slippers on.' That's all you have to do. Okay?"

"Do you want me to close the door behind me or leave it open?" I asked.

"It will swing shut on its own, dear. Okay?"

I walked over to a dark corner and stood quietly, waiting for my cue. Everything was very quiet as they ran the camera up to speed.

"Action!" shouted Abe. Opening the door, I walked up to Mr. Lord and said, "Hello, I'm Janet Feinberg. It's time to put your slippers on."

I gave Mr. Lord a sweet smile and turned to leave the room.

"Cut!" screamed Abe. There was a moment of silence.

"Where are the damned slippers?" he shouted. "You're supposed to bring the slippers into the room and give them to Jack."

"Nobody game me any slippers," I tried to explain. I could hear some of the crew whispering in the background.

"C'mon, will somebody give this girl the slippers so we can get on with it?"

Slumping into a chair, I heard Abe's icy voice again. "I *hate* television!"

I looked at Mr. Lord for possible support, but he was sitting on the bed, thumbing through a newspaper. I was feeling so insecure. Little did I know that after coming up the hard way, Mr. Lord was tuned in and very aware of how important this part was to me.

One of the prop men handed me a pair of slippers just as the first assistant director put a marker board in front of my face and shouted, "Roll camera!"

The commands were coming rapidly.

"Speed," the camera assistant hollered.

"Sound rolling," called out the sound mixer.

"Mark it," barked the first assistant.

"Scene 23, take 2!" the assistant cameraman yelled.

"Quiet on the set!" shouted the first assistant director.

Mr. Lord folded the newspaper and tucked it under the pillow.

"Action!" Abe roared.

I walked briskly into the room, this time carrying the slippers and walked up to Jack Lord. "Hello, I'm Janet Feinberg. It's time to put your slippers on."

I placed the slippers on the floor by the bed, gave him a sweet smile, turned and walked out of the room. I rushed down the corridor to the restroom where I promptly got sick. I didn't even hear Abe shout "Cut!"

By the time I came out of the restroom, the crew was moving on to the next scene and my job was done.

My television debut was over and it took less than a minute of screen time. I was searching for my purse in the darkness when Mr. Lord came over and held out his hand. He was a true professional.

"Hi, I'm Jack Lord. Nice bit."

I shook his hand; he smiled at me and was gone, leaving with me an intense desire to run back to the restroom.

I was so frightened I would screw up and cost the studio money. They could replace me so fast and I'd never get my face on the screen. Fear is such a killer.

My queasy stomach

*Steve Lawrence and I co-starred in*
Police Story

continued to be a problem; and as my career progressed, I lost my lunch immediately after co-starring roles on *Marcus Welby* with Robert Young and James Brolin; *Police Story* with Steve Lawrence; *Love American Style* with Bill Bixby; *Ironside* with Raymond Burr and *City Beneath the Sea,* Irwin Allen's two-hour movie. William Shatner was in that film as well.

By this time, I'd also started to drink a little. I was tired of being the only one *not* drinking at a party and I found it helped to steady my nerves.

I was given a leading role as an alcoholic in *So Near, So Far.* For the first time in my career, I was at ease on camera and didn't get sick afterwards. I really identified with this role.

As my finances slowly improved, I was able to buy a beautiful house in Encino and my parents came for a visit. At every opportunity, I took them around town to see the sights like everyone does. Mama knelt on the concrete outside Mann's Chinese Theatre and compared her hands with Judy Garland! She said *The Wizard of Oz* was about Kansas and Grandview, Missouri wasn't that far from Kansas—almost walking distance!

During their visit on the Fourth of July, I had been invited to a party at Fred Jordan's home. Naturally, I asked my parents to go along. I didn't know my sister Catherine, had already invited them to her home, and while Mama went there, Daddy came with me. When we arrived, Jack Lemmon struck up a conversation with my dad, who kept him captivated with his stories. When Jack Lemmon got up to circulate among the guests, he walked over to me and said, "That guy is amazing. You introduced him as your dad, but I just know you got him from Central Casting." Jack's comment didn't surprise me at all. Not only was my dad a fantastic conversationalist, he loved color, and always dressed sharply. That day he was wearing all red, white, and blue including white shoes and red socks. He loved America. I always enjoyed having Daddy and Mama with me and my friends did as well.

Between these excursions, Daddy sat in my tiny garden and snoozed in the warm sunshine. I loved watching my dad sit out there under the bougainvillea, his eyes closed, quietly snoring. He was at peace. I felt it was a small payback for all he did for me and the family—work, work until he dropped. Now, I could give him a little space to relax. Mama, as always, was cooking. There was no way you could stop my mother from spending her time in the kitchen. It made her happy and kept us well fed, so it worked well for all of us. I went to auditions, worked on television shows from time to time, met friends, and tried to help people as I could.

Helping people is a trait I inherited from my parents, all the Carneys seem to have that. In all the cafés they were involved with, Mama and Daddy were constantly on the lookout for someone who needed a little help. Not with money, because they didn't have any to spare, but a free meal or a friendly chat. I remember way back when we lived in Rolla and ran the C & B Café, seeing an old man burst into tears because they gave him a free meal. He had a hard time believing someone could be so kind to him. They helped so many people out, their business actually lost money, however their hearts were full and satisfied.

It was on one of my "helping" days that I met Rick. I'd had lunch with a friend of mine at Butterfield's on Sunset; and as we walked outside, I saw this guy sitting at a table in the patio. He wore a Hell's Angels jacket, had a black patch over one eye and his head was shaved. He looked very depressed just sitting there, staring into space. After my friend saw me to my car, I sat there for a moment, gazing at this strange young man and had a tremendous urge to talk to him.

As I approached him, I quickly discovered two things. His name was Rick and he wasn't playing with a full deck. I think he'd lost a lot of brainpower due to drug use. Even though he seemed to have a lot to say, the words that came out didn't always connect. He was lonely and seemed grateful to have someone willing to listen to his story.

Four cups of tea later, I was inviting him to my home. I must have been nuts. I actually said, "Hey, Rick, you look like you need some TLC. Come on home with me, meet my mom and dad, have some dinner, and I'll make a bed for you in the garage, if you don't mind."

"What's TLC?" he asked.

"Tender Loving Care," I explained.

"Screw the TLC, but the free dinner sure sounds good."

When I arrived home with Rick, Mama and Daddy gave me some questioning looks, but God love them, they welcomed Rick into the house with open arms. Mama cooked a great dinner as usual while Daddy and Rick talked in the backyard.

One of the by-products of running restaurants is talking to people. You seem to always be meeting new people and trying to put the world in order with your customers. Making them feel special is the goal. If you're good, it becomes an art form and my dad was a true artist; however, if he didn't like you or you annoyed him, you would know it.

One time I remember walking home with Daddy from the garage in Grandview where he'd left his car for service when one of the local politicians crossed the street to greet him.

"Hello, George," the politician said brightly.

"Don't 'Hello, George' me," said Daddy. "All you want is my vote."

"Now, George, that's not true," sputtered the politician, still trying to shake my dad's hand.

"Well then, why is it you've been in my restaurant every week for the past two months and never said 'hello' before now?"

As the politician struggled for an answer, Daddy took my arm and we headed home. "He's a bag of hot air," he mumbled, "full of ego and self-importance."

Anyway, back to Daddy and his conversation with Rick. I kept glancing at them from the kitchen window as Mama and I were fixing dinner. It was fascinating to watch them. Daddy was using his hands as always to make a point as crazy Rick listened to every word. If I'd had a camera handy, it would have been a Kodak moment.

Before dinner, I managed to persuade Rick to take a bath. I found some clean sweats and a T-shirt for him to put on. I don't think any of us could put up with the smell for much longer, certainly not while we ate!

When dinner was ready, Rick sat down, gazed at all the food on the table, and after a pause, he looked at Mama and Daddy. "You know, I think everyone over fifty should be killed."

My dad was totally unfazed by his remark. He'd probably heard more of this lunacy in the garden before dinner. Daddy looked kindly at Rick and in a gentle voice told him, "I think we'd better pray for the food first and see what God has in mind for us."

After the prayer, Daddy said, "Tell me, Rick, how do you plan to go about this? Do you think we should be killed right now or after we eat?"

"Let's eat," said Rick, and without another word, he ate until not one morsel was left on the table. It was hard to know when he'd had his last meal.

After dinner, I made up a bed in the office/garage. He thanked us all, and in a few minutes, we were relieved to hear some loud snoring.

As Mama and I washed up the dinner plates, she whispered to me. "Listen, Susan, there's no lock on our bedroom door, so please ask God to protect us. I mean Rick might get up in the middle of the night and call some of his gang members to join him. Who knows what could happen?"

As I went back into the living room, she grabbed my arm. "He might be planning to kill Dad and me tonight. We're both over fifty you know."

Hugging her close, I said, "Mama, it will be okay. I promise."

As I started to think about the conversation, it hadn't even occurred to me that I might have put my parents in danger by bringing Rick home.

Before turning in myself, I prayed real hard and asked the Lord for some serious protection. About midnight, I woke up and thought I'd better check on Mama and Daddy. *The Tonight Show* starring Johnny Carson was still on in their room, and I gently opened the door to check on them. I could see they were sound asleep and tiptoed in to turn the TV off.

Little did I know that besides praying, they had also set up a little barricade with a large suitcase which I didn't see until it was too late. I tripped; and before I could catch myself, I fell flat, my knee and shoulder hitting the floor hard. I lay there, trying hard not to laugh.

The only other sound besides Johnny and his guests were Mama and Daddy, snoring in unison. I spent the next hour sitting in a chair with ice on my bruises, keeping an eye on the office door to make sure Rick didn't start wandering around.

Rick stayed for three days, and in spite of his strange dialogue, we all laughed a lot, especially my dad. I don't think he'd ever met anyone like Rick in his entire life. Eventually, the visit had to come to an end, and I drove Rick to the Vineyard in Hollywood where they specialized in helping those who were down and out. I never saw him again, but on reflection, I realized my guardian angels had to work overtime with some of these situations.

I took some very outlandish people under my wing during those years, often from Hollywood Boulevard or Sunset. I often talked to prostitutes, trying to let them know they didn't have to sell themselves short. It's a small wonder I was never raped or robbed.

Some people are willing to be helped and some are not. I have to believe that many are touched when they know someone truly cares and is willing to help. "There, but for the grace of God go I," is not just a phrase to me. I happen to know it's true!

Many of us remember the frightening headlines about the activities of the Black Panthers. I was attending a large church picnic when Dr. Robert Schuller introduced me to Eldridge Cleaver. Dr. Schuller told me that Eldridge had become a Christian and he and his wife needed a safe place to stay. Eldridge was one of the founders of the Black Panthers and became their spokesman. Since becoming a Christian, the Panthers wanted nothing to do with him and most Christians were very reluctant to trust him.

Since he was not welcome in either camp, these were extenuating circumstances and someone needed to step up to the plate. I felt the Lord could use me and without any hesitation, I opened my home to them. It was only later when I started receiving death threats that close friends insisted I ask them to find another place to live. I hadn't even considered that I would be in danger, nor was I aware of his background of raping white women.

I believe the Lord did change his life and I have to say Eldridge was always respectful to me and grateful for my willingness to help. After a few weeks without me saying a word, they moved on. As you can see, my life has seldom been predictable.

My home on San Ysidro was near Benedict Canyon. It was a pretty quiet area, so one afternoon when I heard two motorcycles stop outside, I checked to see who it was. To my surprise, Pat and Shirley Boone were waving at me. The most shocking part was seeing Shirley on her own motorcycle. They called out, "Come on and go for a ride with us, Susan."

As I ran out to join them, another rider turned around in the drive. Pat said, "Susan, I'd like you to meet Evel Knievel."

I think if you looked up daredevil in the dictionary, you would see a picture of this man. Here he was with my dear friends, saying, "Hi, Susan. Hop on and I'll give you a ride."

It was a beautiful day and I was sure it would be a leisurely ride. Wrong! I had barely gotten seated when Evel took off up the canyon at full speed, leaning into the tight turns. He left Pat and Shirley in the dust as they followed from a distance. Holding on for dear life, I closed my eyes and held my breath. I have *never* been so terrified and my life did indeed flash before me. As he kicked it into high gear, I never expected to see my family again, much less Shirley or Pat. Up and down the hills he went, leaning into the curves, almost parallel to the ground. He yelled for me to lean with him and I was too scared not to do just that. With my eyes closed tightly, I had no idea we were back on my street until he came to a screeching halt in front of my home.

My legs literally felt like jelly as I got off the bike, trying to act so brave. When Pat and Shirley drove up, I was shaking as I walked over to them and said, "Never again!" They felt badly and had no idea I would be so terrified. I think I've always been a little wary of motorcycles ever since.

*Lindsay Wagner's reaction after a wild motorcycle ride with Evel Knievel*

No one took a picture of me that day, however one was taken of my friend, Lindsay Wagner, after her own experience with Evel Knievel. One look at Lindsay's face will give you an idea of how I felt. A picture *is* worth a thousand words, no doubt about it.

During my time in Hollywood, I was most fortunate to meet a number of famous people, movie and television stars, producers, directors, writers, and the financial wizards who make it all happen. Actually, it started long before that.

When I was in the seventh grade, I met my very first movie star. My best friend at the time, Sherilyn Smith and I were so excited about seeing a premiere film. When we heard that George Nader would actually be in Kansas City, we had to be there. Mr. Nader was promoting his latest release, *Away All Boats* with Jeff Chandler. Sherilyn's father agreed to drive us downtown so we could get a glimpse of this famous movie star. George Nader was one of the most handsome men ever created.

The Grand Theatre had one of those spacious entrances with gilded ornate trim and tall ceilings. There was a giant white organ which rose from the orchestra pit for the live intermission music. Sherilyn's father bought our tickets and made sure we were seated before leaving to meet friends for dinner. He made us promise we would meet him in the lobby at 9:00 PM sharp, no later.

During the film, we were ecstatic every time we saw Mr. Nader on the screen, and we couldn't wait to see him in person. When the film came to an end, Mr. Nader walked onto the stage. If it were possible, he looked even more handsome in person. After giving a short speech about the movie, he thanked everyone for coming and the curtain came down as the thunderous applause continued.

Sherilyn hurried out to the lobby, hoping to be one of the first to get his autograph. My dad had instructed me not to ask for one for myself. By the time Sherilyn got there, at least a hundred women had the same idea. They were elbowing each other out of the way, pens at the ready as Mr. Nader was seated at the table.

I ran up the staircase to the observation area where I could see well. The ladies must have thought it would be their only chance to get this close to a movie star and they weren't going to lose out. In the midst of all the pushing, Mr. Nader was very patient, smiling and signing each autograph book and program offered to him.

I must have been on the observation level watching for probably fifteen minutes when Mr. Nader looked up and saw me. My heart began to beat faster and I thought, *Is he really looking at me?* I held onto the railing, frozen in place.

Mr. Nader excused himself from the crowd and started up the stairs. I must be dreaming! When he got to the second level, he walked right toward me. My feet felt like they were set in cement. He was so handsome and I was so young.

Mr. Nader walked up to me and asked, "Would you like an autograph?"

"Oh, no, sir, I promised my father never to bother a celebrity by asking for an autograph," I blurted out.

"It's no bother. I hope you enjoyed the movie."

I was dazzled by his smile. He was wonderful! He walked back down the stairs, and when he got to the bottom, he turned and waved. I stood there beaming—I had actually spoken to a real live movie star!

Many years later when I was living in Los Angeles, my boyfriend, Clint Ritchie, star of *One Life to Live* introduced me to George Nader and his partner Mark Miller, who was Rock Hudson's

*With Clint Ritchie*

assistant. I told George that he had made two young teenage girls very happy in Kansas City many years before. I know it must sound like glib showbiz talk, but George said he remembered coming up the stairs to meet me. He said he was mystified as to why the young girl watching from the balcony wasn't downstairs with everyone else. That's what caught his attention. When I got home that evening, I called Sherilyn and we relived the excitement of that special time together. What a wonderful memory, even now!

Since that second meeting with George, he and Mark and Rock and I remained close friends. Go figure. They were homosexuals, and I was a Jesus freak—but friendships don't always follow a set pattern. We all had fears and hopes as well as a willingness to set aside our differences to truly care for each other.

I felt so privileged to be asked to give the eulogies for both Rock and George. Per my request, when I was honored on the Walk of Stars in Palm Springs, my Star was placed between those of Rock Hudson and George Nader. Thank you, Mark Miller, and another thanks to Bob Alexander, his wife Janet and the board of the Walk of Stars for making that possible.

I've met many wonderful people since living in Palm Springs. As Congresswoman Mary Bono Mack said, when you're coming from L.A. and take the 111 turnoff, as you pass the bend and the mountains rise before you, it's like driving into a different world where you can literally breathe a little deeper. I'm very grateful for the hospitality shown to me there by Charles Dunn and Rob Piepho; Bud Burnley; Sally and Danny Maarsman; Amy and Michael Cohen; Mandy Evans and Clancy and Albeth Grass. Jackie Lee and Jim Houston have been very kind to the Walk of Stars board which I appreciate and so does our president, Bob Alexander. Their parties are always given with care, love and fun—just fabulous!

One of my true friends in the desert was Beverly Rogers. We had known each other from the days in Beverly Hills when she and her late husband, Buddy Rogers lived at Pickfair, the original Mary Pickford, Douglas Fairbanks estate. Beverly and Buddy were so dear to me, rare people from another era.

I had recently gone through a difficult time seeing our close friend, June Haver MacMurray lose her fight with cancer and now Beverly was dying. I wasn't ready for her to leave either. Both of these gracious ladies taught me so much and I cherished our friendships.

When Beverly was so weak, I admired the great courage she displayed by managing to attend the ceremony to honor her dear Buddy as his statue was unveiled at the Mary Pickford Theatre in Rancho Mirage, California. Beverly asked me to give a prayer during the ceremony and I was honored to do so.

It's difficult to see anyone die, however when those who can afford the best health care possible die sooner than necessary like Beverly Rogers, it's very hard to understand.

Life in Hollywood often joins links in a chain with those important connections we all keep hoping to make. In the early days, after my 20th Century Fox contract was terminated, I continued to work in commercials and series television.

My social contacts were taking on a new level as well. At a party in Burbank, I was introduced to Barry Goldwater Jr.—so tall and handsome and a Republican. When we started dating, he invited me to meet his father, Senator Goldwater and his mother, Peggy. They were both such gracious people. The senator's hobby was ham radio, and he spent hours talking to people all over the world. His transmission equipment was in a small room at the back of his beautiful yacht in

Newport Beach, and he loved sharing it with people who showed any interest. I dated Barry Junior for quite a while and spent time with his wonderful family. I adored his father. I guess I've always been fascinated by older men.

*With Barry Goldwater Jr.*          *Sen. Barry Goldwater Sr. and I*

Barry Junior introduced me to a dear friend of the family, Barbara Ford. Barbara was married to Ken Curtis who played Festus on the television series *Gunsmoke.* She was also the daughter of John Ford, the great classic film director with over 125 films to his credit, including *Stagecoach, Grapes of Wrath,* and *How Green Was My Valley.*

Barbara invited me for lunch one day to meet her parents, John and Mary Ford. They welcomed me with open arms and made me feel like part of the family. I had the privilege of calling him "Pappy" which he was called by close friends.

John Ford was a living legend by that time, having won 4 Oscars for Best Director and many famous actors used to come by or call. He enjoyed the company of old friends as they reminisced about the golden age of movies. Pappy's face would light up, and for a few hours, his illness would be forgotten. With that black eye patch and ever-present cigar, he could look scary; however, he was really a pussycat.

What a privilege it was for me to sit in on some of those afternoon sessions where the classic movies came to life before my eyes. Can you imagine what it was like to sit in the midst of Henry Fonda, Joanne Dru, Jeffrey Hunter, Harry Carey Jr., and Maureen O'Hara? Maureen's brother Charles Fitzsimmons, who is a fabulous human being, often came with her.

I would sometimes answer the phone if Pappy was occupied, trying to keep my cool as John Wayne or Katherine Hepburn would ask to come by for a visit. Her voice was so distinctive.

One summer day, Mary Ford had plans for the afternoon and called to ask if I could keep Pappy company. I think it eased her mind to have me there in case he needed medication or help getting up. It was a real treat for me because Pappy was quite a character.

For about three hours, I sat with one of the world's greatest directors whose personality was such a combination of forceful and yet peaceful. He was a terrific human being, and I always enjoyed hearing his stories. This afternoon, he focused the conversation on me!

He asked many questions, wanting to know all about my background. I found myself sharing with him about Dr. Davis and Aunt Laura and some of the confusion of my childhood.

He asked, "Susan, did you ever think about changing your name to Davis?"

"Not really, once a Carney, always a Carney," I said.

"Good for you," he said. "Carney's a good Irish name!"

"I agree, however it's proving to be a little difficult."

"What's the problem?" he asked.

"There's another actress in town with a similar name, Suzanne Charney, and we're often confused by casting directors," I said. "I've been to two of her auditions and she's been to one of mine."

"Then choose a different name, a stage name, something euphonious." Pappy thought for a moment. "Let's see . . . how about Staf-ford? I think that would be a *great* name for you—Susan Stafford. I knew we could get Ford in there somewhere. That way, I could officially be your godfather."

"That's an interesting choice, because the first boy I ever had a crush on was Steve Stafford."

To Pappy, it was a done deal and I liked it too—the name seemed to fit. I informed Equity and my agent of the change within the week, went downtown to change it legally, and that has been my name ever since. Changing it from Carney hurt my mother's feelings at first, but she finally understood.

John Ford, whose birth name was Sean Aloysius O'Feeney, was an Irishman like my dad. What a great name! On the other hand, I'm sure the name "John Ford" was never misspelled on a movie marquee.

The following November, I was invited to stay at the Ford's home for Thanksgiving weekend. I called Mama and Daddy to make sure they wouldn't mind if I stayed in California instead of going to Kansas City as usual. I had to make that call because Thanksgiving is very much a family celebration. My parents responded sweetly and were actually excited for me. Not only were the Fords the kind of people my parents admired, I almost felt like I was entering a Norman Rockwell painting every time I went to their home.

Mary Ford made me comfortable in one of the guestrooms for the holiday and it was a Thanksgiving dinner I will never forget. The table was decorated with an enormous cornucopia. The Oscars on the mantle were shined to perfection, and Pappy was moved downstairs in his wheelchair where he held court like a king. He wore his best black eye patch and an old smoking jacket. There were butlers, waiters, and extra cooking staff to serve the huge feast.

The whole scene has been frozen in time in my memory. Among the guests were Senator and Mrs. Barry Goldwater Sr. and my escort, Barry Jr., Harry Carey Jr. and his mom, Charlie Fitzsimmons, and Joanne Dru who starred in several John Ford pictures including *Red River Valley, She Wore a Yellow Ribbon,* and *Stagecoach.* Peter Marshall who hosted *Hollywood Squares* was Joanne's brother, and they were like little kids who laughed together easily and displayed such love for each other. Peter has a wonderful voice and he and his wife, Laurie have a real love for dogs. Ken Orsati, former president of Screen Actors Guild, was also a guest. He used to take my mother and me out to lunch—such great company!

Gossip was never a part of the John Ford household, only facts were spoken. As impressed as I was in that setting, what really touched me was the tremendous amount of love in the room that night. These people were household names who genuinely loved each other and made me feel like I somehow belonged there. What an honor it was to have Pappy and Mary take me into their fold.

Shortly after Thanksgiving, Barry Goldwater Jr. took me to meet John Wayne and his wife Pilar at their beautiful home in Newport Beach. It was right on the water, and the view from the living room was picture-perfect as yachts sailed into the harbor for a day at sea. The Waynes served a delicious lunch, and then Mr. Wayne took us on a tour of his beloved *Wild Goose*. Looking out over the stern of John Wayne's yacht at sunset with this great man standing next to me, I had to keep pinching myself. He was holding a spare jacket in case I got cold in the evening and chided me for being so formal.

He said, "Now just stop with that Mr. Wayne crap and call me 'Duke'."

This brought to mind my very first meeting with John Wayne years before. He was a generous man who truly cared about people. One Saturday afternoon, I was at USC (University of Southern California) playing in a celebrity baseball game. Afterwards, someone asked if I wanted to ride the USC Trojan horse. That was a special treat! As I was getting down, this voice bellowed out, "Hey there, little lassie. Come on over here and say hello!"

It was Duke. He put his arms around me, lifting me high in a bear hug. He treated me like I was "somebody". Even though he didn't have to do that, I learned what a genuine person John Wayne really was. I loved his sons, Michael, Patrick and Ethan.

The links in the chain continued to connect when two years later, long after my romance with Barry, I found myself standing beside the Duke again at the stern of the *Wild Goose*. This time, I was accompanied by Gordon McLendon, "the Old Scotsman", who happened to be a close friend of John Wayne. Gordon and I were invited to take a cruise on his yacht to Canada, starting in Newport Beach, all the way up the Pacific Coast to Vancouver and beyond. Duke had a big heart and always liked to take food to a group of very poor people who were mute and lived way back in the woods.

During those long days of sailing, the Duke and I became partners in some very serious games of Gin Rummy. We were unbeatable, as it turned out. Hugh O'Brian, who sailed with us most of the way, teamed up with Gordon as they tried to get even with us and failed miserably. I'm quite sure our fame as the team to

*With John Wayne on the Wild Goose*

beat, had been quietly broadcast over the radio telephone. Dan Martin, owner of Martin Cadillac in Los Angeles, had his own seaplane and he flew in to challenge us as well. Our winning streak continued. The Duke was good, and I was lucky. Those are such fun memories.

On one of our trips, Gordon told me that marriage was not in his plans. We had been dating for well over a year with me spending quite a bit of time at his ranch in Texas.

I was reflecting on Gordon's statement when the Duke walked up and asked, "What is it Susan? You seem a little down,"

When I shared what Gordon said, Duke asked me, "Would you stick around even if he doesn't marry you?"

I thought about that for a moment, "I guess so, as long as we're good to each other."

He said, "Then that's your answer. Just enjoy your time together."

I was seeing a lot of George Peppard at the time, going back and forth to Los Angeles and enjoying fun times with his children. (Their mother was his former wife, Elizabeth Ashley.) We were having dinner with Frank Sinatra's manager, Bullets Durgham and his wife, Marian Montgomery when George said, "So when are you and McLendon getting married?"

I told him the way things were going, I didn't know if Gordon would ever ask me to be his wife.

George said, "Tell you what, Susan. You go on back to the ranch. I'll fly out next weekend and I bet you anything, something will happen."

*The real measure of your wealth is how much you'd be worth if
you lost all your money.*—Bernard Meltzer

# CHAPTER SIX

# MONEY ISN'T EVERYTHING, BUT IT SURE DOES HELP

Along with *Top 40 Radio*, Gordon McLendon was instrumental in starting the multiplex theater chains. Some of you may remember the first computerized baseball spot on radio with Dizzy Dean. It was a pivotal point in the history of sports. That was just one small example of Gordon's genius.

The first time I met Gordon McLendon was in 1970. I was in Las Vegas on a public relations job for Bankers of America with Dandy Don Meredith, Bill Dunagan, and Clint Murchison, owner of the Dallas Cowboys.

I liked Gordon right away. He was witty and wonderfully intelligent. He was quite a bit older, however that didn't bother me. The timing was perfect. I was tired of the Hollywood scene and dating all the pretty boys. I wanted to be with someone from whom I could learn. Gordon was a man of wisdom, and I was ready for an education. Who knew he was also one of the richest men in America?

After dating for a year and a half, Gordon proposed to me in a rather unique way. He handed me a plain envelope to open. Inside was a small beautiful card on which he'd written "Marry Me! I love you. Gordon." Attached was a Neiman Marcus credit card to which he'd added an "s" to Mr. Gordon McLendon. It now read *Mrs.* Gordon McLendon. He said, "Well, what do you think?"

It took me all of two seconds to say yes.

This took place the week after George Peppard's visit. Whatever transpired during that visit, George was right.

We were married at the Las Brisas Hotel in Acapulco in a double ceremony with Sy Weintraub who produced *Tarzan* and Linda Ashley (formerly Mrs. Ted Ashley—Ted was the president of Warner Bros).

*Look at the size of that marlin! It was my first catch.*

We had a second wedding in Kansas City at the famous Muelbach Hotel which both sets of our parents attended. We spent our honeymoon in Bermuda with nine of his friends and staff! Typical of Gordon, he made every moment count as I have learned to do.

*Daddy and Mama, bride and groom, Gordon's Mom and Dad*

Gordon provided me with a lifestyle that was one of a kind. We married in Acapulco and visited his bank accounts in Switzerland. We also vacationed in Puerto Vallarta at Liz Taylor and Richard Burton's home. Our travel was so extensive, I began to lose track of all the different countries.

When we were in Copenhagen, Gordon took me to a beautiful harbor. He pointed to a location offshore where he had anchored a ship to receive radio waves. Having it at that distance meant he didn't have to pay for a license for his station. I think the proper term is piracy.

*Mr. & Mrs. Gordon McLendon*

When in Los Angeles, we lived at the Beverly Wilshire Hotel in our eleventh-floor suite. One time I was there while Gordon was in Dallas and the manager Hernando Courtright, called and asked to come up. Mr. Courtright was genteel, much like Fred Hayman with class and style. The suite across the hall was being prepared for a visit by the Japanese prime minister, and in carrying out a security sweep, they had come across three large marijuana plants growing on the balcony. For some obscure reason, Mr. Courtright thought I would know what to do with them! Why didn't he ask Warren Beatty, great actor and a real caring liberal, who also lived there?

"Ask Mrs. McLendon," became a much-used phrase at the Beverly Wilshire. I couldn't very well say, "Bring the plants over and I'll water them," so I suggested they go in the incinerator. You must always burn the evidence. As the pungent smell of burning "pot" drifted down Wilshire Boulevard, I gazed over the balcony to see quite a few puzzled faces looking up from the sidewalk, wondering where that aroma was coming from.

Rita Hayworth attended one of my parties for Robert Graham Paris, our voice coach. Later that evening, I went to get someone's wrap and found Rita sitting in my closet, talking to herself. Naturally, I thought she had too much to drink. I didn't know she was in the beginning stages of Alzheimer's. At the time, I knew nothing about the disease at all. I felt badly, I just didn't know.

In Dallas, we had an apartment at the Dallas Athletic Club (DAC), a most prestigious building in downtown Dallas. Among other amenities was a library wall with a hidden section like I had first seen with the "book men" in Kansas City. When you pushed a button, the wall revolved, revealing a back room. This was designed for a well-known man who was married to a famous actress. This secret room allowed him to move his lady friends in and out as he desired.

Gordon owned a ranch near Dallas, Texas called "Cielo" which means the sky. The main part of the ranch was built between 1935 and 1943 and was intended to be a private club on Lake Dallas. The grounds covered over six hundred acres, one hundred of them were dedicated to beautiful landscaping. It was a ranch that would knock your socks off. Its founder, H. S. Cherry, father of the famous singing act, the Cherry Sisters, started the construction with twenty-six different types of stonework imported from all over the world. Cherry eventually ran out of money and the property was sold. When Gordon bought "Cielo", he added a few special features of his own: a Japanese restaurant, a fully equipped movie theater, a private landing strip, a golf course, a tennis and croquet court, a movie sound stage, and, most important of all, a bomb shelter! Nothing but the best would do. After all, we were living Texas style.

Gordon was very astute; and when he discovered my thirst for knowledge, he quietly set about trying to upgrade my education. He considered reading a very important part of this quest and set up a large library in a separate wing off the main house for me. Gordon had hundreds of books set aside, and as quickly as carpenters could build the shelves, they were full and ready for my reading pleasure. I remember the first present Gordon ever gave me was the book "Atlas Shrugged" by Ayn Rand. (At over 1,100 pages, it was quite a challenge! I'm still looking for John Galt.)

Gordon also built me a chapel so I wouldn't have to leave the property to go to church. In the main house, apart from the many bedrooms, bathrooms, sitting rooms, anterooms and a large Western saloon, was the largest fireplace in America made by the Cherry family. There were also two special rooms—the Ward Bond Room and the John Wayne Room named for Gordon's friends who visited quite often. If there is a more descriptive word than *impressive*, it

*Robert Preston, Actress/Director Ida Lupino and Ben Johnson visiting with Gordon and me at "Cielo"*

would be most appropriate. John Wayne and Chill Wills opened a ghost town, which a lot of people enjoyed exploring. When Gordon and I hosted parties at the ranch, sometimes it was a small private party, more often, the minimum was 1,500 people. It was always great P.R. We even had a printed guide for visitors, which listed twenty-seven separate attractions!

Some weekends, "Cielo" seemed like Hollywood, except there wasn't a high-rise or palm tree in sight. John Wayne, Warren Beatty, Julie Christie, George Peppard, and Clint Eastwood all came to visit, along with George Nader, his companion, Mark Miller, Rock Hudson and Carol Burnett. Gordon loved Hollywood, and it gave him great pleasure to have the stars on his territory. They all wanted their movies to run on the McLendon theatre chain, and what better way to persuade Gordon, than to come to Texas and pay him a visit. It always worked.

Gordon was great with people. He was a wonderful host and having a pretty wife to help him entertain didn't hurt. I loved people, so that part was easy for me. Gordon was considered worthy, and they were assured of a substantial audience for their pictures. It was quite a nice arrangement, like salt and pepper.

I remember one time when Regis and Joy Philbin came to visit us. I walked into our master bedroom and saw them on our bed. What do you think they were doing? Absolutely nothing—just sitting there laughing like two teenagers, looking up at the mirrored ceiling. It was a fabulous ranch, and I loved making sure everyone enjoyed themselves.

*Rock Hudson with Gordon and I*

*Clint Eastwood with Gordon and I at my 25th birthday party at Ambassador Hotel's Cocoanut Grove*

Gordon was also instrumental in furthering my career. He gave me my own radio show called *The Susan Stafford Show* on his McLendon stations. It was syndicated across America and Mexico on KLIF, KNUS and XTRA; and in California, it was KOST. I gave critiques—ninety-six one-minute spots per week of plays, movies, actors, producers and directors. It was like *Entertainment Tonight* on radio. I recorded the show either in Los Angeles or at our ranch in

*With Rod Roddy*

Texas, and it gave me a tremendous amount of self-confidence. I also interviewed stars like Richard Chamberlain during a visit to London. Wherever we traveled, I would take the opportunity to interview someone in that locale for my show.

Thinking back, I realize now it was not the best way for an up-and-coming actress to make friends in the industry. People can get pretty testy when their work is scrutinized and challenged, especially by a young whippersnapper.

Rod Roddy was my producer, and when our show expanded to Hollywood, I wanted so much for Roddy to join us. Gordon and I were living at the Beverly Wilshire Hotel, and I wanted to make Roddy comfortable in his new surroundings. At our studio in Texas, KLIF we had designed a humongous chair for Roddy and that was the first thing I moved to California for him. Roddy was the first radio show host I know who did the show nude. What a character! He always made me laugh.

As I look back on the list of celebrities I had the privilege of interviewing, it reads like a Who's Who guide. I still have the tapes:

EDWARD ALBERT                MITZI GAYNOR
THEONI ALDREDGE             ROSEY GRIER
STEPHEN BOYD                 RICHARD HARRIS
PETER BOYLE                  SIGNE HASSO

GOV. PAT BROWN
HARRY BROWNE
SID CAESAR
GLEN CAMPBELL
RICHARD CHAMBERLAIN
IMOGENE COCA
JACKIE COOGAN
JOSEPH COTTON
BILL DANA
DINO DELAURENTIS
JOSE FELICIANO
EILEEN FORD
BOB FOSSE
BURL IVES
LOUIS L'AMOUR
CAROL LAWRENCE
TRINI LOPEZ
HENRY MANCINI
NOEL MARSHALL
JOHNNY MATHIS
MERCEDES McCAMBRIDGE
GORDON MCLENDON
SAL MINEO
PATRICIA NEAL
ALAN J. PAKULA
BOB RIDGLEY
SUGAR RAY ROBINSON
MAXINE SAMUELS
JOYCE SELZNICK
MAXIMILLIAN SCHELL
RIP TAYLOR
JAN MICHAEL VINCENT
JON VOIGHT
SIMON WARD
GEORGE CARNEY, my father

JIMMY HAWKINS
MIKE HENRY
RORY CALHOUN
JOANNE CARSON
WALTER CHIARRI
PAT COLLINS
HOWARD COSELL
RICHARD CRENNA
MAC DAVIS
TROY DONAHUE
LARRY FINE
CARL FOREMAN
DAVID FOSTER
STANLEY KRAMER
MERVYN LEROY
HAL LINDSEY
PAUL LYNDE
JOHN MANOLESCO
ROY MASTERS
DARREN MCGAVIN
RAY MILLAND
JASON MILLER
HOWARD MINSCKY
GENE NELSON
JULIA PHILLIPS
MARTHA RITT
RICHARD ROTH
KERMIT SCHAFER
ROBERT SHAW
ROGER STAUBACH
RICHARD THOMAS
TOM TRYON
IRVING WALLACE
CHILL WILLS (Kissin' Cousin)
PAUL WINFIELD

*KOST RADIO promotion ad for*
The Susan Stafford Show

I have a memorable quote by Richard Harris. When I asked him about the fighting in Ireland, he said "it's interesting that they're fighting in the name of God over the love of hate." Really makes you think. There were such fascinating interviews with this eclectic group.

Gordon never interfered with the programming. He wanted me to succeed in radio, and in his eyes, there was only one way to do that—learn as I went along. He provided the studio and the airtime, however if my show had been badly produced, he wouldn't have hesitated to pull it off the air.

As enthralling as it was to share Gordon's lifestyle, I learned that material things cannot really satisfy. Many people tell me they would sure like the chance to find out for themselves. It may sound strange, however unless you've been on both sides of the fence, you may not realize that riches can actually rob you.

Gordon was under a great deal of pressure, supervising his vast financial holdings and investments, and he had a continual battle with drinking. There were times when he was "on the wagon" like when I met him, but they were few and far between. Alcohol wasn't good for him, and it certainly wasn't good for me; what happened, happened. Since Gordon has passed away, I feel the less said about this part of our marriage, the better.

There were some very good times when Gordon and I were able to laugh and behave like two kids. I was blessed when my parents came to live near me in Texas. Even when things started to disintegrate in our marriage, I never ran home to my parents. I had the utmost respect for them and never wanted to put them in a bad position. Like most parents, they just wanted their children to be happy.

Gordon was very good to my parents, and Daddy was good for Gordon. After learning about my dad's background, Gordon was astute enough to hire him. He gave Daddy a job running the 153 concession stands at all of his movie theatres. He liked my dad because he knew his stuff and took care of business.

Since Daddy had run his own café plus the army commissaries, he was used to handling personnel and large operations. Gordon trusted Daddy and knew he didn't have to monitor his work. They enjoyed a mutual respect, and Daddy brought in good money for Gordon.

In the early '70s, President Nixon was on a big push to get rid of drugs in America. I will always remember seeing that famous photograph of Nixon shaking hands with Elvis Presley, when he offered his services to help in the war against drugs. It was said that Elvis was on drugs himself at the time, however Nixon was keen to have him aboard. It was a classic case of wanting a "name" to bolster the cause. If Elvis had gotten some serious help instead of all the "yes" men around him, he might be alive today, working at the Hilton in Las Vegas! (If Tom Jones can still perform in Las Vegas at sixty-eight, Elvis could be going strong as well!)

As a man of substance in the country, Gordon was appointed by Nixon to an anti-drug committee and he took it very seriously.

You hear about millionaires being eccentric. Gordon was no exception. He always wore the same jacket until it fell apart. Now these weren't just any jackets. They were the best polyester suits that J. C. Penney could supply. Although they didn't really go with the shirts handmade for him in Hong Kong, that was his preference.

When President Nixon invited Gordon to a demonstration at the newly formed Drug Enforcement Agency in Washington, DC., Gordon was very honored to be there.

Off he went, wearing his J. C. Penney jacket and some lipstick on his cheek. As a Nixon appointee, he was very impressed and enthusiastic about the newest techniques they were using.

Gordon bought me the most gorgeous, most expensive fur coat which I wore with such pride. From what he told me, Barbra Streisand actually wore it first as a promotion for the McLendon theatre chain. For every picture shown, there is often a behind-the-scenes story that is not known. In this case, even though the mink was highly insured by Lloyds of London, Gordon kept it in a vault, and the only time I could enjoy it was when there was a reason to have it photographed.

I was feeling very unsettled and spent time in serious contemplation, thinking about what the future might hold. I had to admit that even though I was greatly stimulated by Gordon's genius, his money and lifestyle had been the bigger attraction. I was no longer content even though I was the envy of so many in the social whirl around Texas. While everything looked good on the outside, I was wilting away, losing my own identity.

This decision was even more difficult since my parents had moved to Texas and my dad was working for Gordon, doing a great job I might add. When I shared my heart with them, my parents just wanted me to be happy. They could see I wasn't, and as always, were there to give me support for the decision I needed to make.

After I told Gordon I was leaving, he told my dad that regardless of anything, he would like him to continue on with his job. Daddy thanked him, but said he "couldn't stand the whispers". With a big staff like we had on the ranch and their longtime loyalty to the boss, allegiance was automatically given to Gordon.

Daddy and Mama didn't think twice about leaving Texas because of their love for me. When the time came, the parting was very sad as we said our good-byes, and they drove back home to Missouri while I returned to Hollywood.

Throughout my life, there have been times when I didn't feel accepted by some of my siblings, however that was never the case with Daddy and Mama. The love they gave me was unconditional. When I didn't experience that kind of love from my husbands, it became difficult to stay.

When I left Texas, the only item I took was the King Louis desk which had been a special gift from Gordon. And naturally, my dog, Butcherman stayed with me.

Years later, it was difficult to read this report from the *Dallas Morning News. September 14, 1986, Gossip Column—Page 11.*

*Dallas is saddened by the death of Gordon McLendon. Among the mourners expected at the funeral service is actress Susan Stafford. Susan Stafford and Gordon McLendon were married for just over a year.*

Unfortunately, I was in Ethiopia when Gordon passed; however, I don't think it would have been a good idea for me to attend his funeral. Since I broke his heart by leaving, it would have caused a stir.

The article continued:

*On September 14ᵗʰ, 1986, Gordon McLendon (known to friends and enemies alike as "The Old Scotsman"), passed away at "Cielo", his home on Lake Dallas after a long battle with cancer. He was 65. McLendon was born in Paris, Texas on June 8ᵗʰ, 1921. He graduated from Yale in 1943 and attended Harvard Law school in 1946. McLendon accumulated a fortune in broadcasting, real estate and precious metals.*

*Upon his death, his estimated wealth according to the Forbes richest men in America list, was over $200 million. McLendon has been credited with founding the Top 40 radio format, the all news format and charting new grounds in the arena of radio promotions. At one time, Dan Rather, Gary Owens and Tom Snyder all worked for McLendon.*

*KLIF, established in Dallas in 1947, was the cornerstone of his Liberty Broadcasting System. His delayed broadcasts of baseball games, with sound effects and commentary added later by Dizzy Dean, were heard on over 400 stations across the Nation. KLIF and the rest of his radio network were sold in 1972 for over $100 million.*

No doubt I would be a wealthy woman today, had I hired an attorney to take care of my interests, but my conscience wouldn't allow that. A lot of people believe if they just had enough money, life would be smooth sailing. If only that were true! Money does take the pressure off, however it can never bring true satisfaction to your soul, believe me.

In 2003, when Rod Roddy lost his battle with colon cancer, I went back to Dallas to remember my friend and gave the eulogy at his funeral. It was such a pleasant surprise to see Bart McLendon, Gordon's son, who showed such class in honoring Roddy. So many memories came flooding back when I saw Bart. He was very compassionate as we spent time reminiscing. My marriage to Gordon seemed like a different lifetime and in many ways, it was.

Anyone who has been divorced knows that friends tend to choose sides when the marriage is over. Many stay close to the person with the money or position, especially when they're in the business, but Roddy's friendship was one that endured from those days. We were still friends when he passed 34 years later. We had come full circle and I'm so grateful to have known him. Roddy was the best thing I got out of our divorce and I was so sad to know of Bob Barker's behavior toward my friend.

Learning when to speak and when to keep silent is a real art. When someone I love is hurting, my compassion is at its peak. Support and understanding are more important than ever when someone is down. Author, Barbara Johnson said, "Patience is the ability to idle your motor when you feel like stripping your gears." I've learned to choose my battles.

Like most of you who lived through the 60's, I remember exactly where I was when JFK was murdered. I was vacuuming the carpet in Lee's Summit, Missouri while watching television. When the program was interrupted by Walter Cronkite's announcement, I dropped the vacuum and for the next few hours, my eyes were absolutely glued to the TV set. None of us could believe it was true—the shooting was such a shock. When we were told our president was dead, we were absolutely numb. The entire country was in mourning with this devastating news.

I saw Oliver Stone's film *JFK* and have heard many conspiracy theories through the years. For me, the theories took on a more personal note after recently reading Barr McClellan's book, "Blood, Money and Power—LBJ Killed JFK". (This is one book I suggest you read.)

Suddenly, memories from my days with Gordon started to surface and pieces of the puzzle made more sense. After Bobby Baker was released from prison, he and his wife, Dottie stayed at our ranch for a few days. Sy Weintraub was the executor of Gordon's estate and he came to join us for dinner. They were meeting about writing the true story of Bobby Baker which Sy was underwriting to the tune of $250,000.

After dessert was served, the phone rang and our housekeeper, Mabel was breathless, telling me this was a call I needed to take. The voice on the other end said, "Mrs. McLendon, this is President Johnson.

—

115

I understand Gordon is in the hospital." (he was on the blood thinner Coumadin and had to be closely monitored. President Johnson seemed to know everything.)

He said, "I hope he'll be all right. I know Bobby and Dottie Baker are there visiting 'Cielo' and I'd like to take a moment to say hello to Bobby, if you don't mind."

I said "Of course, Mr. President."

I called Bobby to the phone and after speaking only a few words, he told his wife they had to go. They were packed and off the ranch in no more than 15 minutes. I have no idea what was said, I just know they left . . . in a hurry.

According to Mr. McClellan's book, Bobby Baker became Lyndon Johnson's secretary when LBJ was the Democratic leader. Within ten years, Baker was secretary to the Senate, keeping track of the schedules and needs of ninety-six senators. The attention he paid to every detail was most impressive and Baker worked himself into a position of power. Johnson began thinking of Baker as "his son" and they became inseparable. When LBJ spoke, Bobby Baker stopped whatever he was doing to comply and I saw that in action after his phone call to Bobby at our ranch in Texas.

"Blood, Money and Power" talks about a couple of million as a payoff to the killers of John F. Kennedy. Gordon and LBJ moved in some of the same circles in Texas politics and business. I remember Gordon telling me about LBJ asking for a loan of a million dollars in the early 60's. To powerful Texans, a million here or there is no big deal. Dealing in cash was pretty standard. In those circles, when a friend needed a loan, you didn't ask questions. Gordon sent over one million dollars in a suitcase which he had his foreman hand deliver.

After a few years when it was obvious that LBJ had no intention of repaying the loan, Gordon lost any respect he had for the man. We had our own box at Texas Stadium and loved to watch the Dallas Cowboys play. Gordon was a close friend of Clint Murchison, and it was always a highlight to be there.

There was only one thing that could put a damper on our enjoyment of the game. When LBJ attended, it was always announced that the President was in the stadium. Anyone sitting with Gordon knew that was the end of the game for us. Gordon would stand up and we would all follow him out of the box and on out of the stadium. We never attended an event where we knew LBJ would be and if he showed up, we immediately made our exit. Gordon had no absolutely no use for him.

His loathing of Johnson ran deep. While we didn't discuss the assassination in this light, if Gordon had any idea that his million dollars may have been used as "blood money", he would have been horrified.

# PICTURE GALLERY

*Sheer Innocence*

*With Santa*

*First national commercial—Pepsi*

*First picture entered in several*
*Kansas City contests*

*First magazine cover at 18*

*The "covers" kept coming*

*On a record album cover—courtesy of MGM Records*

—

*Another cover shot*
*I started out in modeling and eventually opened my own agency*

*Professional pictures for modeling and acting*

*This page shows me in two very different worlds.*
*The first is of my days as a barrel racer with*
*the one of horses I owned.*

*Cover shot for Luzier Cosmetics*

While dealing with so many people who are hurting in various ways, I've always tried to minimize my own pain. Even after falling off horses as a rodeo rider and other accidents including breaking my back, going through back surgery many years later and a knee surgery that went south, I tried to "tough it out". The end of June, 2010, that was no longer possible. With a meniscus problem and arthritis in one knee and bone on bone in the other, plus a painful hip, shoulder and back, I felt like I was on my last leg. The Lord always seems to have another way. In this case, it came in the form of a clinic actually called **AnotherWay** in Little Rock, Arkansas.

It's hard to imagine that using stem cells from my own blood was the answer. As a result of glowing recommendations from Jewel Bregman, Sarah Karloff and Jimmie Rodgers, I placed myself in the capable hands of founder of AnotherWay, Carl Keller, and physicians, Dr. Jay Holland and Dr. David Harshfield. They treat everything from joint pain and trauma to chronic wounds and severe burns with great results.

While some can argue the theory of using different treatments, no one can argue with the success achieved, SUCCESS which I have experienced first hand. I was so touched with the level of caring from these professionals. Not only is my pain gone which was major, the stem cells are continuing their work of regeneration which takes 14-16 weeks. I'm so happy to share this in the event you or someone you love may need their services.

For more information, contact Carl Keller, Jr. at 501-664-2580 www.anotherwaycorp.com

Abrams-Rubaloff & Associates
10 East 53rd Street • New York, N.Y. 10022 • (212) 758-3636
9012 Beverly Blvd. • Los Angeles, Ca. 90048 • (213) 273-6711

**Susan Stafford**

*Composite shots submitted by my agent, Dean Parker*

*Modeling Days*

*I've always loved braids*          *At a speaking engagement*

*Black tie event in Beverly Hills*          *On a safari*

*For Tiffany*

*More modeling days*

*First cover in Kansas City*

*A woman for all seasons*

*Casual*

*Spritual*

*Business*

Scholar— *Ph.D. in Psychology*

*I have learned to be comfortable in any setting*

*Taking some time
for contemplation*

*Speaking at a Chabad fundraiser as
Co-Chair of the Chai Circle which
Dan and I hosted in our home*

*I love to have fun and I love to learn*

*After working with Hansen's disease, I was determined to make a difference along with those who were willing to help me*

*This was Dan's favorite jacket*

*With Fred and Lois Travelena at a Toys For Tots Fundraiser*

*With Marilyn McCoo, Stella Stevens and Carol Connors*

*Palm Springs Walk of Stars ceremony. Front row—Deborah Keener,*
*Marilyn McCoo and Bob Alexander, Walk Of Stars President*
*2nd row—Stevi Goetz, Carol Connors, Pat Van Patten,*
*Suzi Wehba, Palm Springs Mayor, Ron Oden and Dick Heatherton*
*In the back—Rev. Terry Sweeney and Jimmy Hawkins*

*George Barris, Jan and Mickey Rooney celebrating with me as
I received my Star on the Palm Springs Walk Of Stars*

*Pat Van Patten, Georgia Durante, Carol DeLuise and I
with Sherry Hackett in front*

*With Jay Bernstein, "The Starmaker"*

*With Sue Turner, Jay Bernstein and Chuck Woolery*
*I'm reluctantly using a cane following back surgery.*

*Billy Davis, Jr. and Marilyn McCoo from "The 5th Dimension"*
*Now, they perform as a couple and lead "Soldiers of the Second Coming"*

*Dick and Pat Van Patten and I with Martin Luther King III*
*and friend at the World Unity Award Gala*

*Edward James Olmos, Attorney Gloria Allred and I with Rosey Grier at the World Unity Award event*

*With Robert and Rosemarie Stack*

*With Alice Starbuck Sells and JoJo Starbuck Gertler,*
*Olympic ice skating champion in my backyard in Las Vegas*

*With Sybil Brand, the "Golda Meir" of Los Angeles*

*With former Speaker of the House, Dennis Hastert
and California Congresswoman, Mary Bono Mack*

*With Mrs. Bob Hope (Dolores) and Buddy Rogers at
a fundraiser for the Motion Picture Home*

*With the legendary Milton Berle*

*With Martin Luther King III and Edward James Olmos.*
*We were World Unity Award recipients for Humanitarian service.*

*Front—Phyllis Diller, June Haver MacMurray*
*Back—Mrs. Sammy Davis, Jr., Rhonda Fleming and I*

*Cesar Romero and I with Mr. Blackwell (The Best/Worst Dressed List)*
*at the World Unity Awards*

*I'm on the near left and Rock Hudson and
Bob Ridgley are on the right.*

*With Chill Wills and Cicely Tyson*

*With John Gavin and Clint Eastwood at my 27th birthday party*
*It was given at the Coconut Grove by Gordon McLendon*

*With Fred Hayman, former President of Giorgio's*
*The beautiful gowns I wore at the beginning of the show*
*on* Wheel of Fortune *were from Giorgio's*

*Working with Dandy Don Meredith from the Dallas Cowboys*

*With actor, Burt Young from* Rocky

*My favorite shot of Sammy Davis, Jr. as "Mr. Bojangles"*

—

*With boxer, Ken Norton and Marci Weiner in Las Vegas attending the Las Vegas Walk of Stars ceremony for Sammy Davis, Jr.*

*With Mrs. Sammy Davis, Jr. (Altovise)*

*With Carol DeLuise, Pat Van Patten, Altovise Davis, Lois Travalena and Victoria McMahon—attending a baby shower for G.T. Hamilton, the son of George Hamilton and Kimberly Blackford. G.T. is my godson*

*With Billy Davis, Jr., Michael Colyar, Jean and Casey Kasem and Valerie Harper on a trip to Washington, DC to march for the homeless*

---

*With "Fleetwood Mac" stars, Billy Burnette and Stevie Nicks.
Billy is the son of Dorsey and Alberta Burnette*

*With Hugh O'Brian, Buddy Rogers and Gene Autry*

*You remember Shirley Jones from great movie roles like* April Love
*with my friend, Pat Boone, to popular mom on* The Partridge Family

*With Dom DeLuise*

*With friends, Barbara Valentine, Sandy Goldfarb,*
*Stevi Goetz and Mrs. Sammy Davis, Jr. (Altovise)*

*With Jimmy Hawkins, producer—child star of* It's A Wonderful Life

*With veteran newscaster, Eric Sevareid*

*Jack Jones and I in my early Hollywood days.*
*Jack is still going strong.*

*With Al Kasha, two Academy Awards as a composer, a real scholar and Messianic Jew, Shirley Boone—"mother of Israel" and Pat Boone, at the Media Fellowship Brunch. Pat wrote the great lyrics to "Exodus".*

*Fred Wehba, sharing at my Star ceremony in Palm Springs*

*With Lindsay Wagner and Marilyn Ball*

*With Marianne, owner of one of my favorite dress shops,*
*"Marianne of Palm Springs" – a very stylish lady*

*With Pamela and Rev. Terry Sweeney*

*With my sister, Catherine; Palm Springs Mayor, Ron Oden;*
*Patsy Steerman; Charles Dunn and Rob Piepho from* Your Family Name

*When I received my Star in Palm Springs, I arrived in a white fire engine with gold trim and the firemen stayed to enjoy the ceremony. I wanted to honor them for the protection they provide for all of us.*

*Jan and Mickey Rooney at my Star ceremony in Palm Springs Background—Amy Cohen. I performed the wedding ceremony for Amy and her husband, Michael in France at the Christian Dior castle.*

*With Mark and Amy George at my Star celebration*

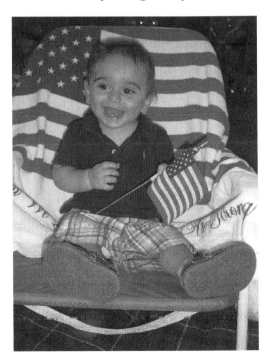

*Mark Minor George II*

*With my dear friend Bob Yerkes—master stuntman
who has doubled for so many stars*

*With Bob Yerkes, Georgia Durante and her daughter, Angie*

*With Dr. Mark and Verena Karalla and Clare Sofia*

*With Tim Cook and John Campbell.*

*I gave a "Welcome To New York" party for my nephew, Russell Kibbee when he joined Goldman Sachs. Interior designer friend, Charles Burke attended.*

*With Zacki Murphy in New York following*
*my speaking engagement at Sardi's*

*With Todd Tomlinson, friend and Critical Care EMT—he's the best*

*With Brent Almond, producer, at the Palm Springs Star celebration before his darling daughter Dylan was born*

*With Bette Hawkins (Jimmy's mother)*

*A favorite picture with longtime friend, Arthur Crowley, Esq.*

*With Nate and Beverly Blitzer at a fundraiser for Cancer Research*

*With Dr. David David; Dr. Vera David; Susan Simons and*
*Scott DeShong at the World Unity Award celebration*

*Suzi Wehba and I at the Beverly Hills Hotel attending the shower for my godson, G.T. Suzi is the sweetest Christian I know.*

*Former L.A. Rams star, "Tarzan", Mike Henry with his wife,
Cheryl and I with our Christian brother and friend, Rev. Terry Sweeney*

*With Joyce Rey and Soozie Reynolds Schneider at a fundraiser*

*With Lucy and Dick Heatherton*

*With Meri and Bill Hillier and Mrs. Wink (Sandy) Martindale*

*David Rockefeller, Jr. sharing at the Palm Springs
Walk Of Stars presentation of my Star*

*With Beverly Cohen from the Four Seasons Hotel
What a kick she is!*

176

*With Marci Weiner, celebrity columnist*

*With Rosey Grier and Viola Ives*
*at the World Unity Award celebration*

*With Kate MacMurray, daughter of Fred and*
*June Haver MacMurray and Victoria McMahon*

*Dick Stiles, set designer and Annick DeLorme, former secretary to*
*Merv Griffin with me and my agent and true friend, Fred Wostbrock*

*With Bob Alexander, President of Palm Springs Walk Of Stars*

*A favorite picture of Murray Schwartz,*
*former President of Merv Griffin Enterprises*

—

*With dear friends, Manfred Cieslik and Gerdta Foust*
*Berlin October, 2010*

*My twin nephews, Josh and Shawn*

*Mama's sister, my Aunt Ida*

*Jackie, Carol, Catherine, Chloe, Georgie and Bobby*
*at a family reunion in Florida. I'm between my two brothers.*
*Chloe has done a great job in organizing our reunions.*

*Daddy's sister—my Aunt Marie, Dan and I, Mama's sister, my Aunt Geri*

*With Bobby, Georgie and Chloe at the hospital*
*following Mama's heart surgery*

*Georgia Durante's daughter, Angie*

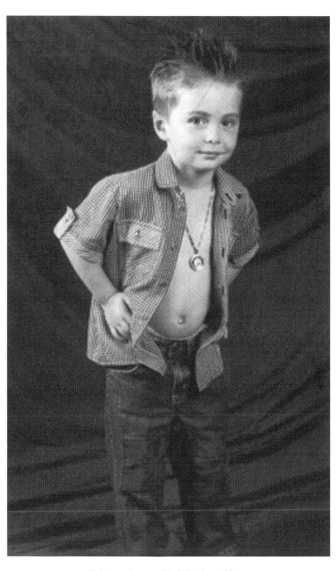

*My godson, G. T. Hamilton*

*Jimmy Hawkin's nephew, Mikey*

*Hunter is my great niece's son*

*My great nephew, Tristan*

*Al and Ceil Kasha's grandson, Dean*

*My favorite picture of Tammy – my personal asst. for the past 25 years*

*My godson, Austin Martini*

*Abigail Martini*
*These are the oldest and youngest of Tammy's five grandchildren*

---

*Analise and Keith, my great niece and nephew when they were younger*

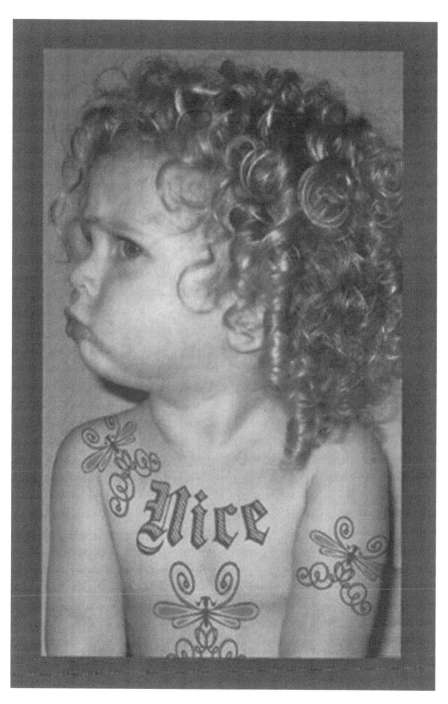

*My great niece, Ava Kibbee, she's such a doll*
*Russell and Monica's daughter*

—

191

*When a man gets up to speak, people listen. When a woman gets up to speak, people look, then, if they like what they see, they listen.*—Pauline Frederick

# CHAPTER SEVEN

# I NEVER DID GET TO SPIN THAT WHEEL

## (BUT I'VE LEARNED TO SPIN THE WHEEL OF LIFE)

Through the years, I've continued to reinvent myself. People say they can't keep track of where I'm headed next. I can't blame them since even I don't know what to expect. One thing I know for sure is that life is an adventure and every experience is valuable.

Learning has always been an obsession for me and I guess that's why *Jeopardy!* is my favorite game show. I love the challenge and even have the *Jeopardy!* theme on my cell phone. Alex Trebek, whom I worked with briefly, has such command of the language and is a real professional.

Being chosen for *Wheel of Fortune* was one of the most exciting times in my life. I must elaborate because not everyone knows the story of those early days and how it all began.

After my divorce from Gordon, I had some major decisions to make. I didn't want to be thought of as just the former Mrs. McLendon. Being known as Susan Stafford once more was essential to me in regaining my integrity.

When Will Smith married for the second time, he stated very clearly that "divorce is not an option". If I had truly believed that, I would have been married only once. I think when most people say "I do," they really believe it will be forever, and I thought so too.

—

After marrying Gordon, I let most of my professional contacts in Hollywood slide into oblivion. Being out of circulation made it necessary to start all over again.

I spent a lot of time on the phone, spreading the word that I was back, asking friends to keep me in mind if anything promising turned up. Networking is important in any business, and it means everything in Hollywood.

Things were looking up as I started getting selected for national commercials. On average, you had to show up for a dozen commercials a week in order to get one call back. I had a good agent, Robert Longnecker, and began representing Eastman Kodak. I also appeared in fifteen Sheraton Hotel commercials and became the Sheraton Girl in Hawaii.

Since dyslexia was an issue, my speech therapist, Dr. Marianne Dunn was invaluable in helping me go over dialogue to pronounce the words correctly. Throughout the years I have turned to her for help and she remains loyal to this day.

When I landed a job working with Bill Stout, an old pro, and Jim Newman, my friend, originally from Kansas City, I was the first woman on *8 Hours Live in America* on KMEX News. Part of my job as the Entertainment Director was to cover new shows in town. I went to Paul Anka's opening and was very impressed with his energy and talent. At the cocktail party before the show, I met Merv Griffin which was a real thrill for me. With Merv was the president of his production company, Murray Schwartz. I thoroughly enjoyed the evening.

I continued my acting career with 20th Century Fox and Universal. When they began looking for a hostess for *Shopper's Bazaar* to work with Edd Byrnes of *77 Sunset Strip* fame, Murray Schwartz thought of me and asked if I wanted to test for the show. He knew that I took my profession very seriously.

I found this side story about Murray fascinating: He was in the historic Entebbe hijacking in 1976. It was an Air France flight with 246 passengers traveling from Ben Gurion Airport to Paris when Arab terrorists boarded during a stopover in Athens. The hijackers, armed with guns and grenades, ordered the plane to divert to Libya for refueling. There, one passenger, a young, pregnant woman, was allowed to leave the plane. When they took off again, they flew south to Entebbe, Uganda, landing in the middle of the night. On the Merv Griffin show, Murray shared that after the terrorists made all the passengers lie on the floor, one brave lady stood up to go to the restroom. It happened to be the mother of Erich Segal who wrote "Love Story". When they pointed their guns at her, ordering her to stay where she was, Mrs. Segal kept walking and said, "So shoot me." Can you imagine the courage that took? Murray realized he would be a real target if the Arabs knew he was Jewish. He swallowed any paper that had his name on it and even chewed his credit cards so the name was not readable. Murray was one of the first 100 hostages released and when he got off the plane, he said he didn't hesitate to kiss the ground. He was just grateful to be alive. To most people, Entebbe is a part of history. To Murray, it's an experience he will never forget as long as he lives.

Back to the show—I was never aware of how many women were tested, but when my turn came, I was totally petrified. Although I had a background in commercials and acting, it was my first time in front of a live studio audience. They tested Edd Byrnes and me for host and hostess at the Television Academy.

We all know that hindsight is a no-brainer. Fortunately for me and for the show, Murray's *foresight* was 20/20. While Murray gave me the opportunity to test; Merv Griffin, Lin Bolen, and NBC would make the final decision. Merv and Murray would prove to be great influences in my life, both of them brilliant in different ways.

The pilot went well, and everyone was very helpful during those two weeks at NBC in Burbank. Renowned director of many Academy Awards shows, Marty Pasetta was brought in to direct and started working with us on run-throughs.

Merv demonstrated how he wanted the show to look and exactly what I was to do. Basically, my job was to introduce the contestants to Edd and turn the letters as they were called out. I know it seems like a simple task, however since it was all new to us, there were a lot of wrinkles to work out—more than you can imagine. We worked together to fine-tune the show's pacing and the overall presentation.

Merv seemed very excited about his new creation. As a child, he and his sister played hangman. For this new game, he combined crossword puzzles with word games and added the shopping feature. Both Merv and Murray felt they had a true hit in the making, and their energy was contagious. Merv flashed his famous smile and was very complimentary, telling me I would be hearing from them. Everyone seemed to feel good about the pilot. We were told NBC would give us an answer within a few months. I continued my acting career and tried not to think about *Shopper's Bazaar*. In truth, the experience never left my mind.

About three months passed and the phone rang. It was Merv Griffin himself telling me I had the job! I don't remember much more about the conversation. I just know I was thrilled, absolutely thrilled! The pilot had been tested by the Academy Directors, and while the executives loved the show, two major changes were made. It was Merv I think, who changed the title to *Wheel of Fortune*.

After I was chosen as hostess, they chose a new host—Chuck Woolery. He was from Kentucky with that wonderful Southern charm. He became a great host and a wonderful friend.

*With Chuck Woolery—original* Wheel of Fortune *host and hostess*

Taping would start in three weeks, and we would shoot five shows a day, three days a week. That's fifteen shows in three days—a tough schedule, but a fun one. Little did I know at the time that I would be a part of this most popular game show for the next seven and a half years.

Regardless of the time that has passed, people are kind enough to remember.

It brought a weekly paycheck and financial security which was so important. And in the male-dominated arena of game shows, it pleased me to say I was the first woman ever nominated for an Emmy on a game show. That was quite a feat in the mid-70s. I'm delighted to be in the company of Betty White who won an Emmy in 1983 as host of the game show, *Just Men*. Every time I've watched her on the delightful *Golden Girls*, I'm amazed at her timing. What a superb actress!

Working on the show also provided the means for me to fulfill a lifelong dream in taking care of my parents. It was as they say, "my turn". Mama and Daddy had made plenty of sacrifices in raising seven children, and I felt honored to make their lives a little easier. When I called to tell them about the job, I asked them to come and live with me in Los Angeles. It was such an exciting time to share with them. They were my best friends, and I needed them to be close.

Chuck Woolery put me at ease from the moment we met on the set. We were like two new kids on the block at NBC. Chuck and I enjoyed a wonderful working relationship for seven years. A large number of viewers thought we were married or at least dating, which was never the case. We had a bond that was not of this world.

I married Dick Ebersol about 2 years after *Wheel* started. At that time, Chuck and his wife, actress Joann Phlug, had a beautiful daughter, Melissa. I often think of Chuck's son, Chad, who was killed during our time on the show. Chad was a sweetheart, and while Chuck took his death hard, his faith sustained him through that difficult time. The fact that we shared the same faith created an even closer fellowship between us. (Ricky Nelson who Chuck adored died the same week in a plane crash.)

Chuck and I had this ability to be open with each other, which is a great asset when you're working together on television every day. We had the same easy camaraderie as Johnny Carson and Ed McMahon or

Regis Philbin and Kelly Ripa. (Early in my career, I co-hosted a show in LA with Regis which was a lot of fun.) I've always found that being spontaneous adds another dimension.

*With Chuck on the original* Wheel of Fortune *set*

Chuck and I never scripted our openings unless it was a special holiday event. We both preferred to "wing it". No fancy dialogue was necessary. I was told the natural chemistry we enjoyed helped make *Wheel of Fortune* a huge hit for NBC Daytime Television.

I think Merv and NBC knew they had a country twosome who brought out the best in each other. *Wheel* was so well received by viewers that we became the number 1 daytime show, receiving thousands of letters each week with requests for autographs and pictures. When I left the show, we had an audience of twelve million.

Chuck was like a big lovable Kentucky teddy bear with such a great laugh—he was like a big brother. Chuck was a fresh, raw talent, not afraid of making mistakes on air which made it most entertaining. He was comfortable in his own skin. We did so many fun things on the show that had never been done before. Shooting on location in major cities brought us to the audience, and meeting the fans across this great country was a hoot. I was told by NBC that this groundbreaking element helped pave the way for future shows. Today, it's nothing out of the ordinary.

I have to admit it was a bit unnerving at times to see how fast those letters had to be turned. Always in high heels (I mean *high*), I had to step quickly while keeping my eye on the edge of the platform. I was fortunate that people have been so kind to me, especially Merv who was one of the best conversationalists I've known.

This was a time when TM (transcendental meditation) was so big. Everyone around Merv had a mantra. I didn't even know what that was at first. One time, Chuck heard my monotone repetition and asked me what in the world I was doing. I told him I was just practicing my mantra. He said, "Oh, no you're not. You're a Christian woman. Stop that right now." He was right.

At first, Murray Schwartz was reluctant to get involved with TM, however he finally agreed to give it a shot. A group from the set had gathered and the Maharishi said he would give each one a special mantra, instructing them to keep it private. He went down the line; and when he got to Murray, he whispered softly into his ear, "Chaling."

I think it was Madalyn Shrier on Merv's staff who was participating; and after the session, Murray asked what her mantra was. She dutifully said it was a secret and she could not reveal it. Murray kept insisting that it was okay for her to tell *him*. Finally, she whispered, "Chaling."

Murray said, "Chaling! That's the same mantra he gave me." Murray walked to the doorway and shouted down the hall, "Anyone want to buy a good secondhand mantra? It's only $200 and hardly used." He always had a quick comeback.

They were great to me on *Wheel*. I had a designated parking space with my name painted in white letters, next to Johnny Carson and Ed McMahon who were the epitome of success. I think the entire nation went to bed with Johnny every night.

Having your name painted on a parking space has a certain status. Just ask any executive or star who's been fired; and before they could get to their car, found the name had been painted over. That's why I believe it's so important to enjoy your job, no matter what you're doing. Our journey here is too short to waste time wishing we were someplace else or even someone else.

—

My dad seemed unimpressed when he came to see *Wheel*. Show business wasn't really his thing. He never made a fuss over celebrities. He said, "They put on their pants one leg at a time, just like I do." His fatherly pride was evident though when I overheard him telling friends to be sure and watch his Susan on television.

As for Mama, walking through the NBC studio was such a thrill. She wanted to meet Johnny Carson and I arranged that with him. She was absolutely delighted, and Johnny was more than gracious to her. What a talent, truly irreplaceable! I will always miss hearing Ed McMahon say, "Heeeeere's Johnny!"

I mentioned my grandfather Joe Pino who was the opening act at the Palace in New York for Jack Benny. William Morris was his agent, and my agent (much later of course) was David Shapira, a super guy, who worked for William Morris.

On very busy days, production assistants would bring me lunch or dinner from the commissary if we were off schedule. This was especially appreciated when it was raining or a hundred and twenty degrees in Burbank in late summer. That's not to say I was into the "star complex"—far from it.

Some days we were running late due to a technical problem. With five shows a day to tape and inevitable delays and interruptions, the schedule was very tight.

I must say it was tiring to be "on" all the time. When people see you in public, they expect you to be as they saw you on television back home in Boston, Kansas City, or Miami—bright, charming, and looking your best. I promise you, I've always admired those who do.

The audience was a major part of our show. They fed our emotions and made us look good. I know everything can be "canned"; and the effect of an audience being in the studio could be electronically reproduced and added later, but what about the contestants?

Imagine standing on a TV stage for the first time in your life and staring at rows of empty seats, trying to look excited without an audience to respond. It would be like getting married with a proxy to fill in. Hey, maybe that's not a bad idea. Just joking!

Seriously, can you imagine how boring it would be if nobody applauded the contestants when they were introduced? If nobody groaned when they couldn't guess the puzzle and missed winning a large sum of money or the wheel stopped just short of a big number? It's the audience that makes people in television and film popular. You folks!

I felt an audience who has taken time to be at the show deserves to be welcomed and acknowledged. That's why before the show, I would often go out to the holding area to visit with the fans. Spending a little time with them seemed to make their involvement in the show a little more special, and let's face it, it made me feel good too. Sometimes people had driven a long distance and waited in the heat for an hour or more. Fans have always been very special to me. Their enthusiasm made all the difference to my heart.

*P.R. shot for* Wheel of Fortune

About twenty minutes before the audience filed inside, I would go out and do my thing.

"Susan, over here!" someone would shout. "Would you stand next to my husband so I can take a picture?"

"Could you come over this way and shake my wife's hand? She'd be so thrilled!"

"Excuse me, is your hair really that color?" *[Sometimes]*

"We've heard that you and Chuck are getting married. Is that true?" *[No, we're just great friends]*

I overheard other remarks as I walked down the line shaking hands.

"You think those are her real teeth?" *[Yes, they are.]*

"I think she's had a boob job." *[No, I haven't.]*

Then they'd turn and face me, smiling and innocent, acting like they'd never said a word. I know Vanna has encountered this as well—it goes with the territory.

Greeting the audience in this way was not in my contract, but I think it made a difference. Our announcer and my friend, Charlie O'Donnell, did such a great job of warming up the audience, and he still does. Sometimes he would let me barge in to greet everyone. I learned a long time ago that it's nice to be important, but it's more important to be nice.

The crew on *Wheel* was the best. Suzi Bagdadi was my hairdresser on the set and remains my friend today. She had a calming influence on all of us and she treated me as if I had the leading role in *Gone With the Wind*. When I left *Wheel*, Suzi left too. She felt a special loyalty to me which meant a lot. Later on, Suzi won an Emmy as Outstanding Hairstylist for *Star Trek: Voyager One* plus nominations for *Star Trek: Deep Space Nine* and *Buffy, the Vampire Slayer*

There was a special tie-in for us many years later. Suzi's daughter, Stephanie and her fiancée, K.J. asked me to perform their wedding. It was a privilege because I had such admiration for everyone involved. The wedding was high atop a canyon overlooking the San Fernando Valley at the home of Connie Selleca and John Tesh. Suzi was Connie's hairdresser for *Hotel* and other roles as well.

Back to the set . . . Nothing was too good for the show. We had great cameramen and sound men and wonderful technicians who worked behind the scenes, operating the gadgetry which lit up the letters as they were called out. Now, they just light up via an electronic letter activator. Everything is faster now, haven't you noticed?

I will never forget Teddy, the Stage Manager, God bless his heart, and Kathy Sanks who wrote all the cue cards. She held them up for Chuck and never once dropped them! No screwups on national television! Our director Jeff Goldstein always wanted the best; and Nancy Jones, our producer, made sure everything went smoothly for the cast. That was her gift and I love her for it. There was a young page named Susan Simons who stood out even then with her cheery disposition and hence has gone on to work as an agent with David Shapira.

As the first woman on a game show to get a microphone, I used the closing of the show as a platform to make statements like "Hey, Chuck, isn't it amazing that we can land a man on the moon but we can't find a cure for cancer? Bye Bye." I had so much more to say, but so little time. One statement can make a world of difference because it forces people to think.

After the first six years of *Wheel*, Jeff Goldstein wanted to move on to other forms of programming and was replaced as director by Dick Carson, Johnny's brother. Dick was very caring and sensitive to people's needs and I really liked that about him.

After Gordon and I brought Rod Roddy to Hollywood to continue with my radio show, I was delighted later on when he enjoyed such great success on *The Price Is Right*. His "Come On Down" was imitated by many. To me, Roddy *was* the show. He was such a fun, original talent! Congratulations to Drew Carey in his new hosting duties!

In about 1980 or '81, I worked at a Jesse Jackson rally where he taught "I Am Somebody." Among the various groups represented were "gifted people" who asked me why they weren't allowed to do the show. I spoke to a friend and now a legend whom we all loved, NBC's president, Brandon Tartikoff, about having them compete on *Wheel*. At the time, he felt the liability insurance and ramps for wheelchairs would have been a huge issue.

I will always remember a story Brandon shared about his parents and the special love they shared. They had been injured in a plane accident and Brandon's dad was thrown outside the wreckage. He risked his own life to crawl back into the plane and pull his wife to safety. It did my heart good to know that the character I saw in Brandon had been passed down from his parents.

As I became accustomed to working at NBC, I started to feel like part of a big family. Across the hall from our studio, Freddie Prinze was shooting *Chico and the Man* with one of the most professional actors, Jack Albertson. Freddie was my friend and came to one of my Bible classes. He was a real sweet kid who got too much too soon and didn't know how to handle it.

Two studios down was *The Tonight Show* with Johnny Carson. Between taping our shows, I would walk through the hallways to see what else was going on. I was by no means the only one curious enough to peek inside a studio door to see the new set or watch a rehearsal. Those of us who worked regularly at NBC in Burbank did it every day.

There was a long corridor which connected all the stages, and it was used to move scenery from the carpenter shop to the stages. Producers, writers, artists, office staff, even the studio pages all took a lunchtime stroll, eyeballing the action.

No one seemed to mind, providing the rules weren't broken. No talking or making noise if a rehearsal was going on, no entering a studio if the red light was blinking, and no knocking on dressing room doors if there was a Do Not Disturb sign in place.

I remember it was a Tuesday, and it had been a difficult day. It was pouring rain outside, Chuck had a mild case of the flu, the lighting system had broken down, and the audience had become restless. When the third taping of the day was over, I retired to my dressing room, needing a little solitude.

I put the Do Not Disturb sign out, propped myself up with some pillows on the couch, and put my feet up, sipping a cup of hot tea. I was just starting to relax when someone knocked insistently on the door. "Gee, can't I even have a few minutes of quiet?" I mumbled to myself.

I put the cup of tea on the floor and called out, "Come in!" They tried, but I had locked the door. Again they knocked, louder and more insistently. "Give me a minute!" I shouted out, not in the best of moods.

I opened the door quickly, wondering what could be so important. Standing there in a bright blue dressing gown with a turban towel on her head was Lucille Ball.

"Sorry to disturb you," she said in that famous gravelly voice. "I'm about to shoot some scenes for a *Bob Hope Special* across the hall, and I made a promise to myself this morning that I'd make the time to come and say hello."

"Well, hello," I said, suddenly feeling like my feet were glued to the floor.

Ms. Ball continued, "I watch you a lot and think you're good, damn good."

"Well, thank you," I managed, at a loss for words. I had grown up watching *I Love Lucy*, and here she was at my dressing room door.

---

"Now, I want you to keep trying your best. Years ago, before you were born, I started out as an extra, and I made every effort to be the best extra in town. There were a lot of extras in those days and the competition was pretty stiff. But you're lucky, there's just you. Only you! Just don't get complacent. Every day, try to be the best. You promise me you'll do that?"

"Yes, of course," I answered.

"Good," she said. We looked at each other for a moment, not speaking. Then she held out her hand and shook mine warmly.

"My name is Lucille Ball [as if I didn't know], and I want you to keep in touch with me. Okay with you?"

"Yes . . . yes . . . of course I will."

She quickly wrote her number on a piece of paper from her pocket and handed it to me. "Gary and I are having a New Year's Eve party over at the house, and I want you to come. Just give me a call."

"Yes, yes, I'd like that. Thank you."

"Keep up the good work. Okay, kid?" She turned and was gone, leaving me standing in the doorway with my mouth hanging open.

"I can't believe it. That was Lucille Ball!" I said to myself, closing the door in slow motion.

Then I realized I'd never even asked her in, and she had just invited me to a party at her home. This was an unbelievable thrill and a memory I will *always* treasure!

When I called her later for details about the party, Lucy was so gracious. I dressed carefully for this special evening. When I arrived, Lucy and her husband Gary welcomed me like an old friend. I was introduced to Bob Hope and his wife Dolores and Buddy Rogers and his wife Beverly (Buddy was such a dashing man, best known for his silent movie, *Wings* and the fact that he was married to America's Sweetheart, Mary Pickford for over forty years until she died in 1979).

It was an unforgettable evening. Lucy was such a kick and that was the beginning of a special friendship. It was such a pleasure to look at the memorabilia and pictures which were displayed so beautifully. What a wonderful talent! Lucy gave us all so much laughter and delight.

It turned out that Lucy and I had the same milk man and we used to send notes back and forth to each other via our private delivery service. When Lucy's mother died, I sent a sympathy note and Lucy said, "Now, that's what I call saving a dime!" She had told me to save my money and it turned out to be a nice way to show her I appreciated her advice.

Back to my little corner of the world—when we broke for dinner, if I had time, I would walk down to the greenroom where the guests of *The Tonight Show* were waiting to go on stage to talk to Johnny Carson. That was always fun!

Fred De Cordova, the executive producer who exuded charm; and Peter LaSally, his producing partner always made me feel welcome. I was also able to spend time with Danny Ford, John "Pappy" Ford's grandson, who had just started working for Johnny. I hadn't seen Danny for a while, and it was pleasing to see that he is a real chip off the old block. After all, it was John Ford who gave me the name Stafford as a complement to his name.

One day, we found ourselves waiting on the set for Chuck who was *never* late. The production assistant called his home several times, without getting an answer. Always the consummate professional, Chuck made a habit of arriving at the set early and was always ready to host the show. Since no one had heard from him, we had no choice but to go on with the taping. When the whole crew is waiting, time is money.

But who could host it? Maybe they would trust me and I could finally spin the wheel. I mean I had watched Chuck a thousand times. I could do it, but someone else would have to turn the letters. How difficult would that be? While I was contemplating this, our producer Nancy Jones enlisted Alex Trebek who was shooting *High Rollers* right down the hall, and he began hosting the first of the five shows that day.

Back to Chuck, I couldn't get him off my mind, and I was alarmed because this wasn't like him. When we took a break, I was able to reach actor Cesare Danova; and he called our friends Pat and Shirley Boone who lived nearby, asking them to check and see if Chuck was okay.

Shirley told me how it all unfolded as she and Pat hurried to Chuck's home. His housekeeper let them in, however she didn't seem to know where Chuck was. They looked all through the house and couldn't find him. His car was there so they were extremely concerned.

Shirley had been at Chuck's home a couple of days before, and he had shown her a large playhouse in the backyard which had been built for his daughter, Melissa. They went out the back door and didn't see anyone. When they looked in the window of the playhouse, they saw Chuck lying on the floor. The door was locked, so Pat broke the window and was able to get in. Shirley ran to call the paramedics while Pat tended to Chuck. When the ambulance came, he was taken to the hospital and the doctors revived him. We all thank God that Pat and Shirley were able to find him so quickly and knew what to do.

Chuck has never been a drinker or user of anything, but he was going through a difficult time with his marriage as I was with mine. Chuck had just learned that his wife Joann Phlug was seeing my husband, Dick Ebersol, and it all but destroyed him. Everyone else seemed to know except Chuck. Ashamed as I was, the blame all fell on me. I can't change that; however, I'm very sorry it happened. Later on at NBC, I heard someone say that Chuck had almost "bought the farm". Can you imagine? That's what they called it. I hadn't heard the expression before.

Chuck missed only two days; and when he came back to the set, everyone did their best to respect his privacy. It was a sensitive area, and it only showed itself once in the most beautiful manner. Chuck insisted that Joann and Dick and I get together with him to talk and pray. I really admired his integrity in confronting the situation, and it did bring some healing.

We had enjoyed seven years of phenomenal success with *Wheel*, and it was time for contract renewal once again. Chuck's agent, Danny Moss, called Merv, saying Chuck wanted to renegotiate. While Merv was willing to go a little higher, he wouldn't meet the amount Chuck requested which was parity with Richard Dawson on *Family Feud*. Chuck sincerely felt that since we had the number 1 show on daytime television, his request was not out of line. Merv wouldn't budge, and there was no more room for discussion. As I said on *E! True Hollywood Story*, although I agreed with Chuck, I also saw Merv's side. Merv owned the show and he had the final word.

Chuck made his decision to leave, and instead of the time and extra expense it would take to test for a new host, Merv and NBC recruited Pat Sajak for the job. Pat was already under contract to NBC as the local weatherman as I understood the story. Viewers often ask how someone gets hired, and, at times, it is simply a matter of economics. Television is operated much like any other business.

For me, the change was major. Chuck and I had been a real team for seven years. We had a certain rhythm which is not easily obtained. When Chuck left, there was a piece of me that went with him, and who could expect anything less?

---

*With Chuck on our last show together*

*Memo from Pat Sajak*          *With Pat on the set*

*[Susan - What a terrific way to start the
day—just walk in and get bombarded
by compliments. Thank you Pat]*

I tried my best to help with the transition for the sake of the show.
Pat worked hard, and before long, we were dancing together quite well.
The only problem was that my enthusiasm as the hostess had already been
changing. While I initially felt like Cinderella, now it seemed like the

bubbles were popping, one by one. I loathed being thought of as Susan Stafford, the "letter turner". I always felt reduced somehow. It's not that I wasn't grateful for the job. But something was going on inside—it was like an intense itch that I couldn't reach.

Everyone thought I had a dream job. Although in many ways that was true, it had lost its charm. I wasn't sure what I wanted to do; I just knew I wasn't happy. Many days after the last taping, I would wave a cheerful good-bye to everyone. Then without stopping to remove my studio makeup or change my stage dress, I would put the top down on my convertible and

*Pat Sajak and I with* Wheel of Fortune *creator, Merv Griffin*

go for a drive—just drive—anywhere, it didn't matter, Mulholland or to the beach. Each time, I would ask myself the same question, "What did you really accomplish today?" The answer wasn't very gratifying.

Sure, I'd turned the letters on cue and introduced some contestants with fixed nervous smiles to Pat. I had acquired some degree of financial security and was able to help out some friends who were in dire need. I was supporting Mama and Daddy and they were helping me as well. They kept the house in order and cooked my dinner when I was tired after a long day at the studio. I loved having them there. It sounds like I had a lot going for me, and I did, but there was also a void in my life. I felt a need to do something more, something that would really count.

———

Through the encouragement of friends, on our hiatus from *Wheel*, I took a trip to India with a small group headed by Father Herbert De Souza. While I had never been so dirty or so hungry, I hadn't been this happy in a very long time. My heart was stirred as I became aware of the many needs. It was such a sobering experience to work alongside Mother Teresa's nuns, caring for the "untouchables" with Hansen's disease (leprosy). It is the oldest disease in history. This experience, which I will share in detail later, fed my soul as nothing else had. All I knew for sure is that I would never be the same again.

After all I had seen, I could no longer be content mindlessly shopping for the latest designs and attending endless black-tie fundraisers. Donating money may seem noble (and it is), however most philanthropists live in a safe area, untouched by true human suffering. Something happened to me in India. I discovered a happier Susan—a better, deeper Susan.

I found it extremely difficult to go back and take superficial matters in America seriously. For socialites in Beverly Hills, a big disaster is seeing an imperfect nail after leaving the manicurist. I understand that too, however when people in India often wonder where their next meal is coming from, the contrast is quite drastic.

*With Buddy Hackett*

Helping others is for me, the secret of life; and yet, I have received so much in return. While working with leprosy patients, I asked a translator to help me converse with the people. He told me they were praising God for our being there. Mark Twain said that "Kindness is a language the deaf can hear and the blind can see." Buddy Hackett had the phrase printed on T-shirts and jackets. I experienced this for myself so clearly and know how essential kindness is for us all.

My friend and producer, Nancy Jones started calling me "Florence Nightingale" when I shared my concerns. Back on the set, I kept recalling vivid images of dear people I had met in the slums of India which they sardonically called "Hollywood". Father Herb and the nuns I met performed their selfless work on a daily basis. Even though I'm not Catholic, I sure enjoyed working with them. While this may be hard to believe, I've even considered becoming a nun.

When I began to talk to close friends about actually leaving *Wheel*, they thought I was nuts. Was I? Could all these people be wrong? Why did I feel so compelled to leave?

"India may have been a religious experience," they said, "but you can't give up all you have just to be a Good Samaritan." Merv often called me Mother Cabrini.

To even think of leaving a job that paid this well with the success I had achieved seemed *pure madness*. Especially with the talk about syndicating the show and going nighttime. That meant more press, more money, and naturally, more fame. Wasn't that the whole goal in show business?

On the other hand, it also meant increasing the time I would turn letters and continue to feel diminished. As I began my fourth year on the show, I talked to Father Bluette (the priest for Frank Sinatra and the renowned lawyer Greg Bautzer) about my dilemma, and he advised me

*With Pat Sajak on location, while trying to make my final decision to leave* Wheel of Fortune

to stay with the show. He said, "You're already doing something very special, Susan. You're cheering countless people up each day as they watch you from the privacy of their homes or from a hospital bed and you make them smile. Now that's more than I can do from the pulpit once a week, and they see *you* five days a week. Please think carefully before you do anything rash."

I did feel a quiet dignity in spreading love to so many through the television screen. I have many causes and sometimes wish I had a better way to express these opinions. But now the itch to move on had increased and it was getting stronger with each day. I was all too aware that my eyes had lost their twinkle. In the silence at night, my soul cried out to do more with my life and to have the strength to do it.

I tried to deal with this in a constructive manner, however it was becoming very difficult. I shared my heart with my mentor Ruth Carter Stapleton, President Jimmy Carter's sister. Ruth's mother, Ms. Lillian, had gone to India thirty-five years earlier, so Ruth understood my longing. While Ms. Lillian could have stayed in her comfortable home, she was driven to help people who were dealing with such poverty. The deep feelings Ruth's mother felt long ago, were now so clear to me.

Ruth shared with me about Dr. John Stehlin who was doing such wonderful work in cancer research at St. Joseph's Hospital in Houston, Texas. I remembered the name, having seen him talking with David Hartman on *Good Morning America*. I was truly fascinated with his research work using white rats to gain information about cancer, and I was also fascinated with him.

A short time later, my longtime friend, whom I'd met at John Ford's house, the Classic actress Joanne Dru, had cancer and was being treated by Dr. Stehlin. I drove to Joanne's home to see how she was doing, and we celebrated New Year's Eve quietly with her two little dogs and a glass of champagne.

During our time together, I shared my desire to do more with my life than "turn letters". I asked Joanne to mention to Dr. Stehlin that I would like to work at his clinic in Houston which was considered by some, one of the foremost medical centers in the world. I was hoping he would grant me a formal interview.

Within three days, Joanne called and said Dr. Stehlin was very interested in meeting with me. Daddy always said, "Don't think with your heart." I later found out I needed to use my head *and* my heart, and then pray for God's direction.

When we met, we discovered a mutual compassion for people who had lost hope. Dr. Stehlin was one who did not give up easily, which I admired. We talked about the human side of cancer and the emotional and spiritual support which is so essential for recovery.

We discussed the possibility of my working at the hospital. Dr. Stehlin said there was an important position available; however, it would be without salary. He offered me a chance to work "in the trenches" as an intern in Pastoral Care Education. My *heart* said yes immediately, however I told the doctor I would let him know. I was in awe of him as a man and also with his skill as a doctor working with terminal patients. I really needed to think this through.

What a jump this would be from *Wheel of Fortune*! Maybe I *was* crazy like my friends thought. With all the compliments that had come my way, somehow I didn't believe it for myself. At the beginning of my career, it was all so exciting, but each time someone introduced me as a "letter turner", I felt invisible inside. Was I just trying to escape? How would I know unless I actually took this chance?

Deep down, I needed to know that my life counted, that there was a reason for my being here. The general public tends to think celebrities are happy, rich, and have no real problems. The truth is, there is more insecurity, more sadness, more lack of self-esteem in show business than in almost any other occupation. People in the limelight tend to die younger due to the high stress factor of always having to perform and present a good front. Each performance is expected to outshine the last, and celebrities learn early on that the "the show must go on" regardless of how you're feeling or what personal catastrophe has just taken place.

I guess I've always been a little wary of people's motives toward me, as a lot of us are. We all wonder if people like us because of our celebrity status or because we may be married to important people. Sometimes they want us to attract donors for a charity event or to elevate their status or any number of other reasons.

In preparing to leave the show, I found out who stayed with me and who had just been along for the ride. I'm grateful now because I always wondered; *do they like me for myself?* And I found out they really like me! Apparently Sally Field learned that as well.

I started confronting my fears with a clear, loud voice. I said, "There has to be more than this, Susan. You *must* move on!"

Doing the show was more work after Chuck left. Not because of Pat Sajak—he was very polite and good to me—it's just that something essential had died.

---

In looking back, after the first six years, I realized I no longer cared as much. That wasn't like me. I had always cheered the contestants on, wanting them all to win. The downward spiral continued, and three months before I actually left, I knew I would be moving on. I prayed constantly, asking for direction. You don't have to be Albert Einstein to know when a piece of you is missing.

*On the* Wheel of Fortune *set*

I was given a lot of attention as one of the highest-paid game show ladies; however, the recognition was only good for so long. I learned to be all things to all people to such an extent that I pushed the "real me" down. It's like when a wastepaper basket is already full and we keep stuffing the paper down instead of emptying it and starting fresh. That's a good example of what I was doing. I needed a fresh start.

So on September 2, 1982, seven years and seven months from the day I started working on *Wheel*, I asked for a meeting with my friend and boss Murray Schwartz. Merv, as I recall, was in France. I was very excited with the anticipation of being of service with the patients in Houston—I couldn't wait to make the change. I had to do it *now*! I always felt like my trip to India sparked this thinking. Maybe it stemmed from living with the doctor in Rolla during those formative years as I went along on the house calls and saw how great it was to serve others.

"Murray, I can't wait to tell you! It's like a dream come true. The good news is I'm moving to Houston to work with Dr. John Stehlin at his cancer clinic. The bad news is . . . I'm leaving the show. My contract will be up and there will be countless gals wanting the position."

Murray looked at me for a long moment, not believing what he had just heard. "You're going to Houston to take care of cancer patients, people who are dying? Susan, you can't be serious. Even for you, this is a stretch."

"I'm very serious, Murray. I can't expect you or *anyone* for that matter to understand. It's like a special 'calling from God,'" I replied.

Murray reached across his desk and took my hand. "Susan, stay with us, and we'll make sure you have enough time to work with cancer patients. You can answer this 'calling' at St. Joseph's Hospital right here in Burbank across from NBC. I can see this is important to you, but there's no reason to leave your job to make your dream come true. Everyone loves you here, and this is not the time to leave when we're getting ready to go nighttime. We're talking major money! I can't let you pass this up. It would be a very foolish decision!"

Although I appreciated Murray's sincerity and his concern, by now, my decision was firm. "It has nothing do with money, Murray," I explained. "After what I experienced in India, I have to go where I can serve, and it's not something that can be compromised."

Murray knew I was very involved in what some people called "religion" after many years of dancing around the edge. I had become what I thought to be a true Christian, through the ministry of Pastor Jack Hayford at Church on the Way. (It's actually a process that takes a lifetime.) I had been spending more of my free time in Christian fellowship and had even started a Bible class in my home for The Vineyard led by Rev. Kenn Gullikson who performed the wedding ceremony when I married Dick Ebersol.

"You're quite sure about this?" Murray asked. "I think you're making a *huge* mistake."

"I've never been more sure about anything, Murray."

As we continued to talk, Murray reluctantly conceded. "I'll call our business affairs office and tell them. I can't believe you're actually leaving, however if this is what you really want, I'll make the arrangements." Murray walked over to my chair as I stood up, and we hugged each other. As president of Merv Griffin Productions, he had taken Merv to the top. While Murray had been wonderful to me, I knew it was time to move on.

A few days later, Murray again pleaded with me to reconsider. He had delayed calling Business Affairs, hoping I would come to my senses. Murray reiterated what it meant to go nighttime with the show. My contract was about to be renewed, and we already had a well-established audience who would love to watch in the evening. While I understood

—

the significance, the money and fame had simply lost their glow. It's a great show, and I knew that whoever took my place would do well.

Even though I offered to fly back and forth until they found a replacement, Murray and Merv didn't want that. I agreed to stay until they found a new hostess. I suggested Altovise Davis, Sammy Davis Jr.'s wife or Janet Jones, Wayne Gretzky's wife. A couple of weeks later, Murray introduced me to a darling girl named Vanna White. As we all know, Vanna has done a great job with the show, and I'm sure she is *one* person who's glad I made the decision to leave *Wheel*.

*Here I am with Vanna*

(During his last months, I visited my dear friend, Fred Travalena, my favorite comedian/impressionist, in the hospital. I'm so so proud of him for fighting this health challenge so hard and standing on the Word of God. He and his wife, Lois truly relied on the strength of the Lord during a most difficult time.)

As we were talking, a friend of Fred's, a man I had not seen since 1982 walked into the room ... it was my original manager, Milton Suchin. How wonderful it was to see each other after all these years. As we reminisced, he shared something I hadn't heard before. Milton said that after I told the top guns at Merv Griffin Productions that I was leaving, they contacted him, thinking this had to be the coolest move they had seen to get more money. They asked how much it would take for me to stay. Milton said he had a hard time believing it himself, but there was no hidden agenda. When he assured them money was not the issue, they were astonished. In show business, ploys like this are common to get what you want. This was no ploy, it truly was a "calling".

The success of the show has not diminished; it has continued to exceed all expectations. And I learned a most important lesson—the success of my life can *never* be measured in money. At one time, that was the goal, however in answering to a higher authority, I discovered benefits that can't be compared on a monetary basis.

When Vanna's boyfriend died in an airplane crash in 1986, they called me in as her replacement to give her a little time to deal with losing John.

Returning to the set brought back a lot of memories. One thing that was different however was the wardrobe. I had always worn such beautiful clothing, including the stunning Giorgio gowns, but now the dresses they chose for me were a bit dowdy. I guess they felt it best to keep me in low profile since it was only for a week. I understood, however when I look back on that time, I find it a bit humorous.

Years later, Vanna's attorneys contacted me when they were involved with a lawsuit over the use of her likeness or image on the *Wheel of Fortune* board game. As I recall, when they used my face on the first board game, I was paid $500. I told them I would testify on her behalf if necessary. Even though it didn't come to that, I would have been happy to help.

Having the opportunity on *Wheel* was a dream come true and it's only natural to miss the money. I will always thank Murray Schwartz for even considering me for the hostess position, Lin Bolen for the screen test and Merv Griffin for the opportunity. I've always felt that women are capable of doing more on television than just standing there, pointing to items and looking pretty. Being the first woman to get a microphone was a real accomplishment; and for that, I am most grateful.

Looking back at my seven years and seven months at NBC, I think of the magical memories. Great game show legends such as Bill Cullen, Bob Eubanks, Wink Martindale and Peter Marshall became personal friends. Working with Merv Griffin was wonderful, and seeing Johnny Carson and Ed McMahon so frequently was a real plus. I met the absolute greats—Lucille Ball, Bob Hope, Buddy Rogers, Frank Sinatra, Dean Martin, John Wayne, Sammy Davis Jr., Milton Berle, Rowan and Martin, John Belushi, Jackie Gleason, Jimmy Stewart, Kirk Douglas, Elizabeth Taylor, Richard Burton, Gilda Radner, Burt Reynolds, Dinah Shore, Tom Jones, Phyllis Diller, Danny Thomas, and countless others.

I was there to see two bright new comics get their start—Leno and Letterman. I recall the wild set of NBC's *Midnight Special*, featuring the crazed antics of a true original, Wolfman Jack. Each week, I was able to meet rock royalty as well as new kids like Elton John, KISS, Linda Ronstadt, Helen Reddy, Donna Summer, the Jackson Five, Billy Davis Jr., and Marilyn McCoo—those are exciting moments to recall.

When I received the first Emmy nomination as a woman on a game show, it proved that my peers were watching. At award shows, people often say what an honor it is to be nominated. When I had the privilege of experiencing it for myself, I can tell you they're right. It truly is an honor.

—

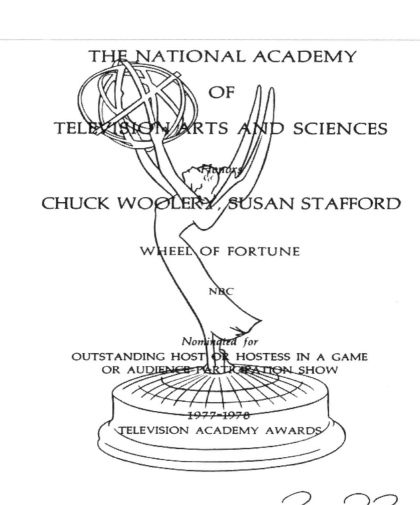

THE NATIONAL ACADEMY

OF

TELEVISION ARTS AND SCIENCES

*Honors*

CHUCK WOOLERY, SUSAN STAFFORD

WHEEL OF FORTUNE

NBC

*Nominated for*

OUTSTANDING HOST OR HOSTESS IN A GAME
OR AUDIENCE PARTICIPATION SHOW

1977-1978
TELEVISION ACADEMY AWARDS

President

Chairman of the Board

I have always felt a woman can do a good job of hosting a game show. Men don't have a corner on talk and fun and exchanging humor.

Marilyn Beck printed this article in her syndicated column, dated September 15, 1982:

## DOING FOR OTHERS

*Susan Stafford has left her post as co-host of NBC's* Wheel of Fortune *to minister to cancer patients at Houston's John Stehlin Cancer Foundation. Susan, who has been with the game show since its debut in January, 1975, will do public relations work studies at the facility that is operated in conjunction with Houston's St. Joseph's Hospital. "It's a decision that's been coming for a long time," says Susan. "The Ministry is where my heart is. It's important that people do not die alone and I believe the John Stehlin Foundation preaches hope in that regard."*

A new season in my life had begun and this one was a deliberate choice. While it was not a sudden decision by any means, it *was* a dramatic change. I believe many people come to a time in their lives when they feel a need to grow and become more than they have ever been before. While most of us never get past the talking stage, we're all familiar with those good intentions: "I want to take a class at the university;" "I need to end this relationship" or "I would really like to move to another state or country." The truth is, few of us actually have the fortitude to act, to follow through with our dream for a new and different future.

I often shared my heart with my precious friend, actress June Haver MacMurray (to me she was a saint). Before continuing as an actress, June spent one year as a nun at a convent in Leavenworth, Kansas, so she understood more about the longing I felt than some. While we were on a trip to Israel with the Media Fellowship group, June extended a special kindness to me. At

*With June Haver MacMurray*

the time, I was committed to attending a twelve step program every day for 90 days. I was pleased to find a location in Jerusalem which was the only meeting in English and told June I was going that evening. Since I didn't know the area or the people, she insisted on going along. As I looked at the listing however, it indicated this was a "closed meeting" which meant that everyone attending had to be an alcoholic. June came up with a great solution and said, "I have no problem playing that role for an evening." We hailed a cab and off we went. When it came time to introduce ourselves to the group, my dear friend said, "My name is June and I'm an alcoholic." She went on to tell a sad story about how she realized her life was falling apart in every area and knew she desperately needed help to stay sober. Now don't get me wrong. I take the twelve step program very seriously, however in this instance while in a foreign country and a stranger to the group, it meant everything to have June with me.

It has been my joy to visit Mother Superior Dolores Hart (yes, she co-starred with Elvis) at the Abbey of Regina Laudis in Bethlehem, Connecticut. Mother Placid has been so dear to me there. These nuns are uniquely alive, alert, and informed. The special times of prayer and reflection surrounded by peace were a real gift to my heart and soul.

My days on *Wheel of Fortune* will always shine brightly. And in the process of sorting it all out, I have found the true security I longed for, one that has no price tag and can never be taken from me. I so wanted to go on with my life, and I knew I wasn't really hurting the show by leaving. Chuck and I enjoyed a great following with the number one

*My final day on* Wheel Of Fortune *with Pat Sajak*

daytime show, and now the audience had taken to Pat. Merv had a winner with *Wheel of Fortune*. Chuck and I had been a real team; and in retrospect, I think it worked out better for Pat as the new host to have a new partner. Everyone loves Vanna, and she has done a great job.

I'm proud of my association with *Wheel* and the show was certainly good to me. It was Merv's creation and is one of the longest running game shows in television history. (Congratulations to Pat and Vanna on completing over 5,000 shows! After the years I spent on *Wheel*, I know what an accomplishment that is.)

Merv was always extremely nice to me. I remember when he asked me to join him at a high-caliber horse auction in Arizona. The horses had superior bloodlines—potential Kentucky Derby winners. I knew a bit about horses from my days with G.K. and the horses we raised. The conformation on these beautiful creatures was the best I had ever seen. The opening bid started at $100,000. Looking around at the action, I nonchalantly adjusted my hat, and the auctioneer said, "Yes! That's $125,000 from the lady in the lovely silver hat." I looked up to see him pointing at *me* and almost fell off the bench. I sat like a statue from then on, literally willing someone to bid higher. I don't think I took another breath until I heard the next bid. Merv couldn't stop laughing when he saw my reaction.

Merv had a wonderful home in Carmel, one of the most gorgeous areas in California where I visited quite often. During one of my stays, we got word that a wildfire was heading across the canyon and were concerned that his home may be threatened. Merv didn't hesitate for a moment. He started taking pictures off the wall and asked me to help as he gathered the sterling silver and china. We placed them in the shallow end of the pool. What a solution! Merv was always quick on his feet and very creative. That worked extremely well for him in the world of game shows and in other business ventures as well.

Merv was a very powerful man, and it's not surprising that he wasn't pleased with my decision to leave *Wheel of Fortune* just as it was going nighttime. As it played out in the process of time, the choice I made worked well for everyone. I continued to see Merv from time to time at special events and enjoyed that familiar smile which could always light up the room.

I remember asking Merv many years ago if he had thought about the epitaph he would like for his tombstone. After a moment's pause, he smiled and said, "I won't be right back." That's Merv—he never missed a beat. The last time I saw him was a couple of years ago at an event where

Lorna Luft, Judy Garland's daughter was singing. Merv was escorting Nancy Reagan. They were such close friends and I admired how tender he was with her during those long years when President Reagan was so bravely dealing with Alzheimer's.

Merv never lost his sense of humor. When he was hospitalized at Cedar's Sinai in Los Angeles for a recurrence of prostate cancer, this was his statement to the press, "I was ready for a vacation; however, this wasn't the destination I had in mind."

None of us were ready to say good-bye when Merv passed. He had always been such a vibrant presence in any gathering. His life was entertainment, and he did it so very well.

As he shared on a clip on *Larry King Live* when asked why he left his successful talk show, Merv said, "I just didn't want to do it anymore." He went on to create other areas of interest. I certainly understand since that was the same conclusion I came to in leaving *Wheel of Fortune*.

Changes come in many forms and when I met Dick Ebersol during my second year on the show, it definitely brought a change to my life and to his as well.

*When I dwell for any length of time on my own shortcomings, they gradually seem mild, harmless, rather engaging little things, not at all like the glaring defects in other people's character.*—Margaret Halsey

# CHAPTER EIGHT

# THE CIRCUS OF CHRISTIANITY

Everything in my life quickly changed and sparked a whirlwind of events. When I met Dick Ebersol, NBC's "Wonder Boy", he was the youngest network vice president. I had been going through a period of deep introspection, wondering where my life was headed.

Dick displayed the excitement of a man with high goals and a great career ahead of him. A genius on the order of Gordon McLendon, Dick was a challenge to my mind. I have always loved to learn; and he captured my attention.

At that time, Dick was partially responsible, along with Lorne Michaels, for the early success of *Saturday Night Live,* one of the most bizarre, creative shows of this era. It was *hot, hot, hot,* and still is. Lorne has continued to do great work ever since.

Dick was young and smart, from a well-respected family in Connecticut. Just after graduating from Yale, Dick got his start in sports with Roone Arledge who treated him like a son. Roone Arledge was a sports broadcasting pioneer and Dick learned from the best. (In recent years, as chairman of sports for NBC, Dick negotiated multiyear contracts to produce the Olympics. I'm so happy for this accomplishment, knowing his passion for the Olympics, even as a young boy.) Often a man with that much drive is very shrewd and that he was.

The little I knew about sports I learned from my former fiancé Don Klosterman, general manager of the Los Angeles Rams and the Kansas City Chiefs. He came from a wonderful Irish family and was the twelfth of fifteen. Don never met a stranger and was loved by everyone. When his mother, Wendy passed away, the Irish wake at my home went on for three days. So many people came to celebrate her life, a couple of the family members even slept in the bathtub because I only had so many beds and couches.

Don had such a great personality and sense of humor. He played college football as a quarterback at Loyola University and then for a pro team in Canada. He was an avid skier and while on the slopes between seasons, he tried to avoid a skier in his path and ran into a tree, damaging his spinal cord. When the Dr. told Don he would never walk again, he picked up a flower vase as the Dr. left, hitting him in the back of the head and said, "At least I can still throw."

Never letting anyone's opinion put limitations on what he could achieve; Don wasn't one to feel sorry for himself. Although it was a struggle, he learned to walk again and inspired us all. Even though he was left with a limp, you could almost see the courage flowing from his pores. When owner, Georgia Frontiere moved the Los Angeles Rams to St. Louis, Don picked himself up and got a job at the Hollywood Park racetrack. He saw everything as a challenge and reveled in overcoming obstacles.

It's always interesting to contemplate how life would be if I had taken one fork in the road instead of another. Back to the path I took . . . .

Brandon Tartikoff, then president of NBC, brought Dick Ebersol along one day as he visited the *Wheel of Fortune* set. When we were introduced, I remember Dick was wearing an expensive camel blazer, nicely pressed slacks, and loafers without socks. The dressy casual style was refreshing and peaked my curiosity about this man with the infectious enthusiasm. Dick invited me to go swimming at Malibu the next day. The beach is my favorite place to relax; and we had a leisurely day of sun and bodysurfing, getting to know each other, or at least, trying to.

I liked Dick's style, and it all seemed to fit—two young, available personalities with careers on the rise. Two days later, Dick and I were scheduled to fly to New York. He was going for the Friday and Saturday

*Dick Ebersol and I*

taping of *Saturday Night Live* and I was representing *Wheel of Fortune* with the NBC affiliates. Since we were just getting to know each other, traveling together made the trip more enjoyable.

On the flight back to California, somewhere over Omaha, Dick proposed to me. Even though we had known each other only ten days, this fascinating adventure seemed made-to-order. Dick was handsome, successful and truly wanted to get married. It was easy to convince myself that he was "the one". We started planning the wedding right away and found ourselves exchanging vows only eighteen days after we met. Close friends who knew my impulsive nature were not shocked since my life usually had a drama all its own.

As a "born-again fanatic", I was determined to have this marriage "God's way", not trusting myself to stay pure during a long engagement. At times, I had put the Lord on the shelf, asking Him to look the other way while I indulged in whatever temptation presented itself. My faith had been strengthened after numerous slips, and I wanted so much to please God.

Due to Dick's charismatic personality and my idealism, we wrote our own little scripts and proceeded to play out our parts. We were married at producer, Burt Sugarman's house in Malibu. Burt had purchased it from Claudine Longet and Andy Williams.

Burt was Dick's best man, and Carol Wayne (the sexy blond who often appeared on *The Tonight Show* with Johnny Carson) was Burt's wife. While Carol was not a friend of mine, in wanting to please Dick, I asked her to be my maid of honor.

*Dick and I exchanging vows,*
*Rev. Kenn Gullikson officiating*

Among the guests were John Belushi; Chevy Chase and his wife at the time, Jackie; Sammy Cahn and his wife. Sammy was an Academy Award winner who wrote the lyrics to songs like "Three Coins in the Fountain" and "High Hopes". Also attending were special friends, Jimmy Hawkins (from *It's A Wonderful Life*); Mike Henry (*Tarzan*); Bullets Durgham (Sinatra's manager) and his wife, Marian Montgomery. The ceremony was at the edge of the waves at sunset, such an idyllic setting.

*Daddy and I, Rev. Kenn Gullikson and Dick*

I couldn't help noticing John Belushi putting the moves on the minister's wife. I was so proud of how Joanie Gullikson handled it gracefully without embarrassing John or herself.

There were several funny moments—hysterical is more like it as you might imagine with that guest list. One of the best was when Sammy Cahn pointed to the two crosses I had placed in the water and said, "I always wondered where Abbott and Costello were buried."

Following the wedding, Dick and I stayed at Burt's house. This was our wedding night, the one we had anxiously awaited. The stars were shining bright, waves were crashing on the beach, and we were alone with soft music playing in the background. I can often picture how my life has played out like a movie script.

In this scene however, the wardrobe lady would have been exasperated. Instead of wearing the gorgeous negligee laid out for me, I climbed into flannel pajamas, adding knee socks and my thick, comfortable robe. I had an unbelievable cold and this was no movie set where the show must go on. Between sneezes, I wasn't up to anything. I was too chilled to even think of sitting on the balcony to enjoy the view with Dick. He had agreed to wait until our wedding night (18 days) and now my husband had to settle for watching me pile on more covers to get warm. The setting was the only romantic part of this scenario.

We had the place all to ourselves, no servants and, as it turned out, no food. In all the busy preparations for the wedding, it never crossed my mind to check the pantry.

The next morning, I was still bundled up as we went to the kitchen to have our first morning cup of coffee together. Dick started looking for something to eat. He looked in the fridge—nothing! Then in all the kitchen cabinets—empty! Finally, he looked in the bread bin and found *one* slice of bread, the *only* morsel of food in the house. Dick popped it in the toaster and we waited.

We looked at each other lovingly and smiled. At last the toaster dinged and out popped a nicely browned slice of toast. Before I could say diddly-squat, Dick had buttered the single slice and eaten it! All of it! No thought of cutting the one and only piece of toast in half. No sirree. Dick found it, he toasted it, and he ate it! That action left me speechless.

While that may seem minor, what *wasn't* minor was the blow that came the next day!

Before we were married, my parents were living with me in my home on San Ysidro in Beverly Hills. In fact, I bought the house sight unseen, via a good friend, Dr. Marianne Dunn. I was out of the country and my lawyer and friend, Ed O'Sullivan said it was a good window of time to invest some money.

Mama and Daddy were my best friends and having them with me meant everything. Dick had agreed wholeheartedly that they could live with us after the wedding. He actually seemed enthused about the togetherness of family and said, "I think it will be a good arrangement for all of us."

The day after our wedding, however, Dick said that after thinking more about the situation, he had changed his mind. He told me if he wanted to walk nude through the house, he couldn't do that while they were there. To him, it was like, "Oh, by the way"—just a simple matter. To me, it was a deal breaker! If I had brought a couple of children into our marriage, would he have sent them away as well?

It's always easy to look back and see the whole picture. We were both immature and not willing to budge. I guess it's reasonable to think that newlyweds deserve some time alone, however my mind was made up and so was Dick's. I felt betrayed and couldn't carry on a civil conversation with him. We were both very immature and hardheaded and knew next to nothing about each other. We just happened to be at opposite poles and there we stayed.

At the time, it had all seemed so romantic as we got caught up in our rush to get married. In not taking time to discuss even tiny issues, we gave even less thought to the monumental ones.

The truth is that Dick was in the place I was the first time I got married. He wanted a home and a life partner, just as I did with G.K., however our lifestyles and stubbornness didn't warrant that type of life.

228

Although we stayed legally married for five years, it became a total nightmare and was unfair to both of us.

I was having difficulty finding a balance in my faith and in my personal life even before I met Dick. Part of the problem from the beginning was being caught up in the "Christian trap". I was very shortsighted—thinking only of the celibacy issue. We hadn't included God in this decision—we just went blithely on our merry way without realizing there was no basis for a relationship. It didn't take long. I knew we had made a big mistake, and I really needed to talk to someone.

My friend Bill Greene, president of Carter County Bank in Tennessee, said that whomever I spoke with last determined what I believed. There were times when I was way out in left field and needed help making decisions which would greatly affect the rest of my life.

I went to some trusted friends and poured out my heart. I was in major distress and didn't know what to do. I shared that although Dick and I had gone through the ceremony, because of my misgivings, we had not yet sealed it (my excuse for being too angry to go to bed with my husband). After listening to the whole story, they prayed for me and said this commitment had been made before God and was one I needed to live out. This was *not* what I wanted to hear. All marriages have their struggles and knowing how impulsive I was,  I'm sure they thought if I just gave it a chance instead of trying to run, we could find a way to make it work. That was the last thing I wanted to hear—I just wanted *out!*

Much to my distress, my parents went back to Missouri that very week. They really wanted us to make a go of our marriage, and not wanting to interfere, they left quietly. While that increased my admiration for them, it also fueled my resentment toward Dick. I felt betrayed; and from that moment on, I had no desire to even *try* to make the marriage work, regardless of anything Dick had to say. I locked him out of my heart and threw away the key.

If someone came to me with that same cry, after living through all the misery, it would be a hard call. The truth is, I was reluctant to accept the fact that I had been that trusting. So much pain could have been avoided had I left then or, better yet, not been in such a rush in the first place. If Jay Leno had interviewed me at the time, his question would have been very appropriate—**"What were you thinking?"**

On the flight from New York, we had pictured a wonderful future together—happily ever after with the white picket fence. Both of us looked like Vogue models and lived in the entertainment world of make-believe. In that atmosphere where the *outer person* is constantly stroked, our souls had yet to mature and deepen. While Dick did try and wanted to make it work, I agreed to stay, but it was no picnic for either of us. Oh, we finally slept together as husband and wife, but our marriage was a far cry from what either of us expected. Our whole time together was a travesty for both of us and on any possibility of pleasing the God we only thought we knew.

My career was going strong on *Wheel of Fortune*, and from time to time, we shot on location in Florida or Chicago. Dick's responsibilities were increasing with NBC, and *Saturday Night Live* was a hit. He was under a lot of pressure and had to spend more time in New York. While being on *Wheel* required that I live in Los Angeles, my refusal to quit my job and move to New York increased the disharmony between us. The show's creativity began crossing lines with censors, and Dick was facing a major challenge. Brandon Tartikoff was Dick's ally in this regard, and they presented a united front when tensions ran high. This wild and crazy bunch constantly tested the limits of what can be shown or said on television.

One time I went to New York with Dick and sat in the audience to watch *Saturday Night Live*. The camera showed a close-up of me with the caption underneath "Is she still a virgin?" Everyone thought that was hilarious, and even though I have a good sense of humor, I felt very uncomfortable. We both paid for that one.

A relationship that escalated too quickly because of my commitment to celibacy, ironically turned into infidelity on both of our parts. Dick soon learned the only way for him to have sex was to find someone else because I certainly wasn't going to cooperate. I'm sure he felt deceived and I just wanted *out*. Male companionship was readily available and after a few drinks to numb my conscience, any inhibitions I had left, went out the window.

We had a beautiful house in Mandeville Canyon; and even though we were both successful, no amount of money brings the satisfaction we all seem to think it will. That has been proven time and time again in countless Hollywood marriages.

Many high-profile people were invited to our dinner table like Rock Hudson and David Rockefeller Jr. When my dear friend and mentor, Ruth Carter Stapleton (President Carter's sister) and their mother, Ms. Lillian, were visiting California, I gave a little dinner party. Ms. Lillian was a real character and that day she was wearing a pin with this message—"Please don't hug me, I have broken ribs". People were extremely considerate as they approached her. Truth be known, she simply didn't like people squeezing her and this was an easy way to handle it.

Ruth lived in North Carolina, and I wanted to introduce her to some friends during her visit to L.A. Dick stayed in his room the entire time, watching tapes of some games he had missed. He didn't care to visit with anyone, and now, I understand it better. I seem to prefer my own company as well. Dick was far ahead of me at the time. At least he knew himself.

We were often at odds with one another, and when someone is rude, it makes me angry. I realize now that all Dick wanted was a wife, a real marriage, and a friend.

Former Gov. Edmund G. "Pat" Brown and his wife, Bernice, were some of my favorite guests. Pat and I had met on a plane a few years before when he was governor of California. I was returning from a trip to New Orleans on location, flying first class. When the governor got on board, he looked around the cabin, sat down beside me, and asked, "Is this the last seat on the plane?"

Glancing at him, I said, "I think I'm sitting next to a Democrat."

The governor threw back his head and laughed. He said, "That's okay. I'll still sit with you."

I held out my hand and said, "Hello, Governor, I'm Susan Stafford."

That began a warm and easy friendship which we thoroughly enjoyed until his passing over twenty years later. I knew that he truly cared about the people of California, and even though we differed on some political issues, we had a deep respect

*Interviewing Gov. Pat Brown on my CBN show* Alive

for each other. He instilled in his family a wonderful sense of democracy and service.

I will always treasure the wonderful words Gov. Pat shared in a letter a few years later. *"I'm impressed with your intelligence and knowledge of human beings and human affairs. You are warm, generous and effective in dealing with all kinds of people. You have vision and are dedicated to the people and work in your life. I can frankly say that I've never met a person I have respected or admired more."*

His words were so generous and really touched my heart. Through Gov. Pat and his wife Bernice, I met the rest of the family.

During his term as Governor, Jerry Brown was invited to one of my parties and was accompanied by his bodyguards. They came in first to check the house and the guest list. I couldn't imagine anyone wanting to hurt Jerry. I always admired his sister Kathleen who took a stand as State Treasurer, never hesitating to stick her neck out on tough issues. I always considered the Brown dynasty to be friends of the people, but what would I know? I'm only a Republican. I felt like the only one in L.A. until I met Kathleen's husband, Gordon Van Sauter, who is admired by many and also a life long Republican. California is facing some tough issues and Jerry Brown has proven to be a great Attorney General.

After nearly five years of a very combative marriage in which we spent little time together with two high-profile careers, Dick and I agreed to make one final effort by going to therapy. We went to separate therapists; and I have this secret notion that one day, our respective therapists met for lunch in Beverly Hills and laughed themselves silly over our problems. Unethical though that would be, I wouldn't have blamed them. It was all pretty sad, however many screenplays are written about stories like this. Who knows, maybe they both gave up therapy and became screenwriters.

We could have had it all, just like Bogie and Bacall if we had only known ourselves better. It seemed like such a waste at the time. I realize now that no experience is a total waste if you can learn from it. Going through this process of sharing, causes me to experience the emotions of those days once again. Even now, I have a choice—I can remain stuck in the mire that pulled me down, or I can focus on the lessons and continue to grow. One thing I've learned the hard way is that whatever we focus on becomes magnified.

We were both spoiled and hardheaded, a perfect example of how *not* to begin a marriage. While Dick was making a bigger name for himself, and I was enjoying the limelight as well, our marriage never really had a chance. For a time, we tried what a friend calls "putting frosting on the burnt cake". You can cover it up and make it look presentable, but underneath it is unpalatable. That kind of façade can only last for so long and in this case, even the frosting couldn't hold up.

It wasn't all negative. Dick was a staunch Yankees fan—I mean a fanatic. The funniest thing that ever happened in our marriage was when the Yankees won the pennant; Dick returned home and immediately cut the pant legs off his good suit. In his excitement, he wore that suit to work to celebrate the victory. I thought that was a kick! Yankee fans understand his enthusiasm.

One other thing that amused me was how Dick would hum when he ate mashed potatoes and peas mixed together. It was one of his favorites. Don't know why, but that always amused me.

Family has always been important, and the best part of marrying Dick was getting to know and love his parents, Peggy and Charles Ebersol. They were the most wonderful people I will ever meet and I always adored them, before and after the divorce. Peggy told me a long time ago that I had diary material for a book. She planted the seed and was always a dear friend. I truly miss the love they gave me. Dick's brother, Peter and his wife, Carol, were a special joy to me, the kind of people most of us would *like* to be. They still are. I wanted to show a picture of Peter and Carol and their family, but if there was anything negative about Dick in the book, Peter was reluctant to have it included. That's what I call brotherly love! True loyalty that I admire.

During our time together, Dick and I entertained many people related to his work. As I think back, I can still see a smiling O. J. Simpson and his wife, the beautiful Nicole, at one of our parties. It pains me to think of her even now. It was apparent that she, too, was just searching for happiness.

I realize that our problems did not compare with what others have experienced. And if (that big word *if*) we had both been more mature, we might have been able to weather the storms.

One special friend was the great talent from *Saturday Night Live*, John Belushi. With John, there was no formal entertaining. John loved to make people laugh, and nothing he did stood on ceremony. To Dick's credit, he not only showed concern for John, he flew him to California to stay with us for a while. Dick was worried about Belushi and sincerely tried to help.

It's no secret that drugs were freely shared among some of the cast members of *Saturday Night Live*. Belushi always slept late; and one day after he left for who knows where, I went in to make his bed and tidy up the room. When I opened the door, I didn't know where to start. There were literally hundreds of beer cans strewn around the room with some flattened under the mattress. Beneath the beer cans and in various piles were countless marijuana butts. Parents often joke about using a shovel to clean a teenager's room; if you magnify that, you'll have an idea of what I found.

Belushi was one who always kept us entertained. One night, a small group had gathered; and by 3:00 AM, everyone else had gone home, and John and I were still talking. Dick looked sleepily at the two of us and said he had to get up early and was calling it a night.

John and I continued our philosophical conversation as we solved the problems of the world. About 4:00 AM, he suggested we go to an all-night deli and get some breakfast. That sounded good to me. We wrote Dick a funny note in case he woke up, saying that we had run off together.

When we arrived at Nate 'n Al's, John ordered a full breakfast of ham, eggs, hash browns, pancakes—the works! He was talking away, very animated as usual, when suddenly his head dropped full face into the middle of the eggs. Naturally I expected the worst. I just knew he was dead.

Tomorrow's headlines flashed through my mind—*While Out For a Night on the Town with NBC's* Wheel of Fortune *Hostess, Susan Stafford, (wife of* Saturday Night Live *Producer, Dick Ebersol), John Belushi Suffocated in a Plate of Eggs.*

When he didn't move, I shook him gently at first, "John, are you okay? PLEASE be okay!" I couldn't believe this was happening! I quickly yelled for the waitress to call 911 and felt his wrist for a pulse.

Just then, John lifted his head, looked at me through the egg yolk dripping from his eyebrow and said, "GOTCHA!" I didn't know whether to slap him or hug him. It was panic and relief all at once—I was just grateful he was alive.

You never knew what to expect from the whole gang at *Saturday Night Live*. So many of them lived in the fast lane. In the midst of all that was happening with us personally, Dick adored Belushi and really did try to help him overcome his drug problem. What a talent he was in the world of comedy and what a tragedy to lose him so young! We don't really know what brought him to that place. Who are we to judge? Except for the grace of God, it could have been any one of us.

After Dick and I both found other interests, we realized there was no future together. Instead of continuing to cut off the dog's tail an inch at a time, we got the divorce which had been a long time in coming.

When Dick met Susan Saint James, they hit it off. Susan co-starred with Rock Hudson in the wonderful television series *McMillan and Wife*. She is a very talented actress, and I truly admire her work. The show was produced by my friend, Leonard Stern who also produced *Get Smart*. Leonard was always helpful in encouraging me during my acting days, so there were several connections here.

When Susan Saint James and Dick decided to marry, they faced a major obstacle with the Catholic church due to strict rulings regarding divorce. There was only *one* way—if Dick's marriage to me could be annulled. The Archdiocese in Hartford, Connecticut, contacted me, asking if I would comply with this request. Annul means to make void as if it had never happened, no longer legally binding—that seemed perfectly acceptable to me. I asked for the counsel of my friend, Fr. Terry Sweeney, Jesuit priest and a producer at Paulist Productions. He had been aware of our situation throughout the marriage and agreed without hesitation.

Even though it hasn't worked for me, I do believe in marriage. Knowing how important my own faith is, I wanted to do whatever would help give Dick and Susan a good start.

The only time I give it a second thought is when someone asks how many times I've been married. We always seem to be explaining ourselves and so many answers have to be qualified in some way. I don't think life is supposed to be this complicated.

When Rock Hudson made his journey, I saw Dick and Susan at Rock's home the evening of his memorial. We were different people by then and had all grown so much, it seemed like a whole different lifetime. When I saw Dick with his son, Charlie at the funeral of our precious friend, Brandon Tartikoff, Charlie seemed like an exceptional young man.

A few years ago, the story was broadcast nationwide when Dick and two of his sons, Charlie and Teddy, were in a small plane in Colorado that crashed upon takeoff. Shirley Boone called me when she heard the news and we started praying. Charlie, a college student at the time, heroically saved his dad's life by quickly getting him out of the plane to safety. Charlie tried so hard to find his brother Teddy, but his body was sadly not found until days later, such a devastating time for the family.

My heart went out to Dick during this unbelievable tragedy. It was quite a shock during those days to realize how much Dick meant to me. I wanted to go and be with him so he would know how much I truly cared, however this was *not* the time nor the place. I finally felt love for Dick in the way it was meant to be—unselfish and pure. The wall I had built around myself to keep him out had finally crumbled. I had to realize that there is no life in the land of "if only". Our time on earth is simply too short to waste valuable moments dwelling on the past. My prayers continue for Dick and Susan and their boys.

This saga almost ended "and they lived happily ever after". Although it would be nice to live up in the clouds, I was reminded again of a major reason we didn't stay together. When I saw Dick at the memorial service for our dear friend, Johnny Grant, I greeted him warmly, from my heart. During our brief exchange, however, it became more than clear to me once again—it was the same old, same old. The decision we made to go our separate ways was definitely the right one.

Turning to leave, I realized how grateful I was to just be with God. Trying to keep up a façade while lying to yourself is not the way to live.

In the process, I've found that caring for people who really need you is more than satisfying to the soul.

Congratulations to Dick who was recently inducted into the National Association of Broadcasters Hall of Fame. When people mention it to me, I tell them no one deserves it more.

*I don't want to get to the end of my life and find I have just lived the length of it. I want to live the width of it as well.*—Diane Ackerman

# CHAPTER NINE

# THE BIG "C": FRIEND OR FOE?

Cancer is one of the most dreaded words anyone can hear. That diagnosis marks a turning point when nothing is ever the same again. People wish they had taken better care of themselves, and it causes friends and family members to pay better attention to their own health. It's also a great reminder that we are on this earth for a limited time and that influences many of the choices we make.

When I arrived at St. Joseph's Hospital in Houston, even though I didn't talk about my background, every so often, someone would catch on and say, "*Now* I know why you look so familiar." I wasn't there to talk about myself. I had gone there to serve "in the trenches" as Dr. Stehlin called it,—a very apt description.

*Chaplain Intern team (That's me in the second row on the left)*

As a chaplain intern, I was up no later than 5:00 AM to start the day, and I had been busy with patients all morning. Looking at my list, I found the next room number. Knocking on the open door, I walked in and started to introduce myself.

Without even looking up, the man waved his hand, motioning for me to leave. "Just come back later, I'm watching my favorite show right now."

One quick glance and I saw it was *Wheel of Fortune*. He said, "They have a new replacement on for Susan Stafford, and I want to see how she's doing."

Quietly turning around, I realized how much my life had changed. Dressed in the plain uniform issued to chaplain interns, regulations prohibited wearing makeup. Imagine! Just a few months ago on *Wheel*, I was wearing designer gowns and had my own makeup lady and hair stylist. Was I prepared for this?

Later on, I returned to the patient's room, and as we talked, he started looking me up and down, motioning for me to come closer. As I started to ask what he needed, I saw the sheet rise up in the middle of the bed. I realized that certain expectations aren't limited to Hollywood. Excusing myself, I said, "My supervisor is waiting for me," and left quickly.

Although I knew in my heart that leaving the show was the right decision, that doesn't mean it was an easy one. That year proved to be one of the most difficult for me emotionally as I dealt with death on a daily basis, but it was also one of the most fulfilling. This forced me to want to grow even more.

The head chaplain warned us about getting emotionally involved with our patients. He said we could be much more effective by maintaining a professional attitude. I assure you, that is much easier said than done when you really care.

Most people don't like to talk about death. Remembering this is someone's mother or brother or father or sister made me realize the importance of being there for them. If they were unable to talk, I could help anticipate the need and make them comfortable. If they asked for prayer, I was there to help them express a request. If they needed a pain shot, I could help expedite it and if they just wanted to talk, I was there to listen. There were times I was so exhausted, I wanted the shot myself.

As a chaplain intern in a Catholic hospital, the nuns and priests assigned me to all the Protestant patients on the terminal floor. One of the highest privileges I had was when someone would say, "My mother is being operated on tomorrow. Can you be there in surgery to pray over her? I can't tell you how much better I would feel."

If surgery were scheduled, I was there by 5:30 AM to pray with the patient or I sat and waited with the family. Other times, I scrubbed up to be in the operating room. I felt so privileged to be there to serve and to learn.

Seeing how magnificently our bodies are made is awesome. All the computers and space shuttles ever designed are not as fascinating as the human body. As I watched Dr. Stehlin operate, I was amazed at his skill and endurance, working sometimes for seven to eight hours without a break. Considered a hero for his groundbreaking research with white rats, Dr. Stehlin reminded us that *he* was not responsible for the process of healing. That was put into place long ago by the One who created us.

If leaving *Wheel of Fortune* was a test of my faith, there were more tests to come and this was just the beginning. As Chaplain interns, we were taught to use our powers of observation in writing reports on each patient assigned to us. Were the curtains open? Was the patient receiving cards? How much family contact did they have? Were they watching TV or interacting with their roommate? Were the ladies applying makeup, and were the men shaving? I learned that if a patient is depressed, the blinds are often closed and the TV is off. If someone comes to visit, they pretend to be asleep. They often prefer to lie in the dark feeling sorry for themselves.

According to Elizabeth Kubler Ross, there are five stages of death and dying:

1. Denial
2. Anger
3. Bargaining
4. Depression
5. Acceptance

This also applies to divorce and a lot of other issues as well.

For each patient assigned to us, we had to write a report twice a week and make notes on their chart about the visit each day. We also had to know who was scheduled for surgery and who was considered terminal. In addition, we worked with the families who often needed more help than the patients. Even though it was an exhausting year, I wouldn't trade those experiences for anything.

I had one lady who always had her blinds open, her makeup on, and a Bible open on her bed. I wrote a glowing report on her. My supervisor, Father Duffy called me in to talk. He asked me some very pertinent questions about my observations. While she looked like the textbook case of someone recovering nicely, he said this was one of her many visits to the hospital. She knew she had to play a certain role to win a lawsuit with her insurance company. As I learned to look below the surface, it became a real eye opener.

One day in class, Father Duffy showed us a film about a lady living in Manhattan. She was seated in a chair wearing a hostess robe. Her husband was a psychologist, and she had gathered her family together to tell them she had cancer. She was quiet for a moment as she looked at each of them.

She said softly, "I don't want to die a slow death with cancer. I need to know how you feel about euthanasia."

Father Duffy stopped the tape, asking us to note what we had seen so far. The following week, he played the rest of the tape. When the lady got her family's feedback, only two disagreed with her. She said she didn't want anyone to feel guilty about the decision to take her life.

As the end of the tape disclosed, a month after the talk with her family, the lady laid out the dress she wanted to be buried in, took her pills, and left a note for her family. She took her life on a Sunday morning just as she had planned. Now here's the rub—maybe you've already guessed it. They later discovered she *never* had cancer! She simply didn't want to live anymore and this was her way of handling it.

That story really hit me hard. I learned that some people have a desperate desire to end it all, while others will fight to live until their dying breath. We were taught not just to hear the *words* a person says, but to *listen* for the deeper meaning. When we related to the person according to their real feelings, we were able to help them in their journey more fully.

No one should have to die alone, and I felt extremely honored to share in those very private times. Everyone is different. While I can't tell someone how to think when I'm not in their shoes, I *can* be there to love them and to hear their heart. That's what pastoral care is all about.

The year in Houston was one of the hardest times in my life for another reason. It seemed like almost everyone I prayed for died and it began to seriously test my faith.

I remember when Buzzy was dying and he was trying so hard to hold on for his wife, Brenda. On Christmas Eve, I took her to the convent for a special service with the nuns. I thought, *if Buzzy can just get through Christmas . . .* You know how we always wish for that. Why not say, "If he were to die tonight, he won't have to suffer through Christmas." The truth is, it's very difficult to let our loved ones go.

I said, "Buzzy, you might make it through until Christmas and you might not. Outside of your health, what would you really want for Christmas?"

He hesitated . . . "I'd like to have one last cigarette."

I told him I would go get him one.

He perked up, "You will?"

I said, "Buzzy, you haven't had one since you've been here and if that's what you really want, I don't think one cigarette will hurt you now."

It can be very difficult for people to leave their loved ones. Sometimes, we had to ask daughters to leave the room so their mother could let go and die. She may have been ready, but tried to hang on longer for them.

Giving a loved one permission to die in peace is a real gift. Being in the most comfortable atmosphere possible is also a key factor. When there was nothing more he could do medically, I saw Dr. Stehlin send people home to spend their final days with loved ones. His patients always came first, and I admired him for that.

When people have cancer, they are often more sensitive than usual. One of my patients had breast cancer; and as they were preparing her for surgery, she told her husband how sorry she was. She was already feeling "less of a woman" and didn't want it to change things between them. Her husband took her hand and said, "Don't worry sweetheart. I've always been a leg man anyway."

Most people don't like to talk about death even though it is inevitable. Being at someone's bedside and helping them make that transition is one of the most fulfilling things I have ever done. When a person's heart is heavy, there is often a need to share about what has gone wrong in life. Holding secrets inside can be quite a burden and talking it through with someone who will listen is very healing to the soul.

I learned the importance of allowing a person to share their deepest concerns at such a tender time and find it an honor to be trusted in this way.

—

My favorite patient was Linda who was about thirty-three. She was Baptist and had been assigned to my care. Her husband and family knew her time was short and didn't want to leave her side. Wanting to give Linda's family a touch of home, I used a recipe Jack Palance had given me and fixed Hungarian-stuffed cabbage for them. Little things make such a difference, especially when someone is hurting. Their appreciation was so great, you would have thought it was a gourmet meal. Even though Linda was still with us, they were already missing her.

One day, Linda stopped taking her pain medication. She told me that when she approached her Lord, she wanted to be alert. She had cancer of the throat and whispered in a barely audible voice, "Susan, come here." With a glow on her face, she said, "I'm getting ready . . ."

I leaned closer and asked, "You're what, honey? What did you say?"

She whispered plainly this time, "I'm so excited, Susan. I'm getting ready to meet the Lord." Then she continued, "I wish you could go with me." Such a precious moment passed between us as I assured her, "I'll be there with you one day, I promise."

Linda died that very night in total peace. Let's face it, everyone wants to go to heaven, we just don't want to die to get there.

I had been in Houston for several months, and even though I was so very busy, I missed my friends in California. It meant everything when a few of them came to visit like Pastor Bob Rieth, Rev. Terry Sweeney, and Barbara Valentine. Barbara was in Houston shooting a show with the women astronauts.

They all went on hospital visits with me. We buried a six-year-old boy during Barbara's stay, and she took it very hard because her son, Todd, was young, and she could really identify with that family. Saying good-bye to any patient was difficult but especially so when it was a child who hadn't even experienced life yet.

Father Duffy saw that I was getting depressed by the cruel inevitability of cancer and moved me to the maternity

*Rev. Terry Sweeney and I talking with Dr. John Stehlin and his sister*

ward. My first patient was a woman giving birth to twins. I was so excited and we both gave praise to God.

Then one of the twins died.

Oh no! They were so tiny, so frail, but I reassured the lady the second twin would survive. God would see to it. He just *had* to allow that baby to survive. Two days later, the second twin died.

*Ruth Carter Stapleton,*
*my mentor and friend*

My faith was at an all time low. I called my mentor, Ruth Carter Stapleton, and she came to be with me, giving her unconditional love as always. Seeing them die was getting too painful as I suffered along with my patients. Having Ruth there was great medicine because she always knew how to encourage me. Our times together were so memorable.

I recall being at a dinner party when everyone was asked to share who we most admired. Many gave the names of famous stars. I chose Golda Meir. When it was Ruth's turn, we all waited with great interest. The person she chose was her sister-in-law, Rosalynn Carter. Ruth said she had always respected Rosalynn for her character and her wisdom.

Ruth never ceased to amaze me. She had a strength that I admired and wanted more for myself.

One of the funniest stories about Ruth occurred when she had to get a passport picture taken quickly because she had to leave on a trip. Her husband kept pushing and pushing, trying to hurry her up and she couldn't move any faster. Although Ruth was not ready, she finally threw a scarf over her head and dashed out to the car. She actually had her passport picture taken with her hair still in curlers. I found that hilarious. It told me a lot about her personal sense of security.

Ruth spent several days with me in Houston, visiting my patients, praying with some, laughing with others, giving encouragement to each one. She was a real trooper. Little did we know that Ruth herself would get cancer.

In August of 1984, I called to tell her I had a chance to go to the Vatican and stay inside those historic walls. Ruth had pancreatic cancer and the doctors told her the time could be short. I was excited about the trip, but afraid to leave Ruth. In her pleasing southern drawl, she said, "Susan, you go ahead and enjoy yourself, because whether I see you when you return or I see you later on, we *will* see each other again."

That was my last conversation with Ruth. I was in my room at the Vatican when the phone rang and my friend, Mark George called to tell me Ruth had passed on. The sense of loss I felt was so enormous. Her passing was the hardest blow I had experienced up to that point. I asked Cardinal Schotte if they could ring the bells in her honor and the Pope gave his permission. Hearing those chapel bells was very comforting.

I was so angry with God for taking her, and it took some time for the anguish to diminish. Ruth taught me so much, and in many ways, she is still with me. I'm so thankful that her spirit will never die, and as Ruth said, I *will* see her again.

Thinking back on my time in Houston, I realize that Dr. Stehlin was my vehicle in making the decision. I was drawn by his charm almost as much as by my desire to serve. Even if I had not gone to Houston, the time had come to leave *Wheel*, and it would have involved some type of service. There was so much I had to learn by going through that process. Since then I have lost so many people close to me and believe that life is a circle. God sends us to earth as babies, and He wants us to return to Him when we die.

As the chapters of my life continue to unfold, there have been new faces and unbelievable experiences; however, the force behind it all has been God himself. He has nourished my soul as I embarked on each new adventure, through the leprosy work, the cancer and AIDS patients and the drive to continue my education.

Each step has been part of His master plan for which I am most grateful. Jeremiah 29:11 states, "I know the plans I have for you, says the Lord, they are plans for good and not for evil, to give you a future and a hope."

Sometimes I get a little shaky, being human and all. I've had the opportunity to see all spectrums of life, and I always want to be the best Susan I can be.

I like the title of John Ortberg's book: "If You Want to Walk on Water, You've Got to Get Out of the Boat". Life is a precious journey, and playing it safe is not always the answer. I've found that unless you're willing to take some risks, you never know which doors may open for you. What's behind Door Number Two may just change your life.

—

*You must be the change you wish to see in the world.*—Mahatma Gandhi

# CHAPTER TEN

# INDIA CAPTURED MY HEART

I have always enjoyed the interaction at small dinner parties where you can really get to know people. One summer evening, I had invited Rabbi Magnum, Gov. Pat Brown and Bernice, Pastor Bob Rieth, and a Jesuit priest from Loyola, Rev. Terry Sweeney. He asked if it was all right to bring a Catholic priest from India with him and I assured him that would be fine.

When Rev. Terry introduced his friend, Father Herbert DeSouza, the first thing I noticed was his quiet dignity. His accent was charming and in his eyes, I could sense a depth of character.

As I was completing dinner preparations, Fr. De Souza came into the kitchen and offered to help.

"It's very kind of you to include me," he said as he began to help chop vegetables for the salad.

"I'm pleased you can be with us," I said. "I understand you're visiting from India."

"That's true. I'm trying to raise some funding for a small film school and medical institute we are starting in Ahmedabad."

I said, "My dad would like to be in on this conversation. He always felt we should take care of America first."

Fr. De Souza said, "Susan, my dear, it is one world."

"Are you making any progress?" I asked, chopping a few green onions.

"A little. But raising money is difficult in the best of times, especially when the need for those funds is such a great distance."

"Father, would it be presumptuous if I asked what you have in mind?"

"No, not at all. So many things," sighed Father De Souza. "It is principally for our leprosarium. We have many people to treat and so little money to buy the drugs and medical supplies plus teaching them proper hygiene."

"Father, I wish I could help," I said, "but I doubt that a couple of hundred dollars would make a difference."

I added the vegetables to the lettuce, quickly tossed the salad and carried it into the dining room. Father De Souza followed, bringing the stack of plates. As he set them on the placemats, he said, "Miss Stafford, though two hundred dollars would certainly help, there is something else you could do which is worth far more."

"What would that be?" I asked.

He touched my arm and I turned to face him. His dark brown eyes seemed to look deep into my soul, and somehow I knew it was important to listen to what he had to say.

"Come to India. See what we need firsthand and tell the people when you return to America."

"I'm honored you think I could be of help."

"So you'll come?" he asked.

"Well, I'm not sure. Maybe I could get away during my hiatus from *Wheel of Fortune*," I replied as the other guests found their places at the table.

Father De Souza smiled and asked, "When is your hiatus?"

"I don't know the dates yet. It will be sometime during the fall."

Father De Souza was gentle, yet persistent. He smiled at me again. "Would that be October or November? Because January is actually the best time."

"I'm not sure, but when I find out, I'll try to let you know."

I realized that all of my dinner guests were looking at us, caught up in our conversation. One of them said, "He will never let you alone until you agree to go."

"All right, I promise to let you know."

It was time to eat, and everyone joined hands as Pastor Bob Rieth asked the blessing.

It took nearly four years of the father's persistence before I boarded the plane bound for India, during a short winter hiatus on *Wheel of Fortune*.

Ahmedabad, sometimes called Gandhi City, is one of the great holy places in India where millions of Hindus make their journey to bathe in the Ganges to cleanse their spirits.

I was totally unprepared for the extremes of poverty and malnutrition I saw, including their use of the roads for defecation. Most Westerners who live lives of absolute luxury in comparison can't comprehend this type of life. Sure, I'd seen pictures of India in *National Geographic* or on a *PBS documentary*, but *nothing* could have prepared me for all the sights, sounds, and especially the smells we continued to encounter.

As long as I live, I will never forget driving into Ahmedabad for the first time in 1982. The sight of so many people living out in the open, cooking on small sandalwood fires, trying to get enough food to nourish their children was a severe culture shock. Even though they had so little, these beautiful human beings were very gracious and they touched my heart. That first trip to India challenged me in a way that would eventually change the course of my life.

Joyce Rey, formerly married to Alejandro Rey; Billie Jean Campbell, formerly married to Glen Campbell; and Rev. Terry Sweeney, formerly married to the Vatican, came with me on the trip. The experience had its impact on all of us. This was long before *Slumdog Millionaire* brought so much attention to India.

Billie Jean would return to India nine times; and Father Terry, after much research on marriage in the priesthood and countless letters to the Vatican, fell in love with a beautiful gal named Pamela many years later and they were married. They wrote a wonderful book together entitled "What God Hath Joined". They are very dear friends for whom I have the utmost respect.

As we sat in the back of a dilapidated taxi, bouncing over roads filled with potholes, all of our senses were heightened. Although I've traveled in many countries, I had never experienced anything like this before. The intense smoke and pungent odor of food cooking, mixed with the stench of open sewage in the street. The smell was overpowering. It wasn't possible to hold your breath long enough to escape it.

Masses of impoverished humanity filled the streets to capacity, crowding around the cab every time we stopped, either begging for money or trying to get a look at these wide-eyed Americans. We clutched each other's hands tightly, not knowing what to expect next. Before we arrived, Father De Souza had made us promise not to give a penny to a beggar, not even one. Now I understood why. There was no end to the press of the crowd.

The Father cautioned me about opening my mouth wide since the gold crowns on my teeth could be visible. I had always considered myself "street smart", however my previous overseas travel with Gordon was always first class. I had no idea how different things could be in Third World countries. Did I listen to everything Father DeSouza said? Not at first, however I learned to heed his instructions carefully.

While I think of myself as being sensitive to others, I had a lot to learn. It was very hot and with no air conditioning available, I brought along a plastic spray mister which I had filled with water. I was casually spraying the mist on my face when I looked around to see the shocked faces of the Indian people. I was just trying to keep cool, not realizing they didn't even have water to *drink*. I was so embarrassed and took great care not to make that mistake again.

The convent where we stayed was run by a few of Mother Teresa's nuns. They greeted us with such kindness, showing us to our rooms which were sparse. There was one small bed and chair on dirt or concrete floors and no room service in sight. After evening prayers, all was quiet until 5:00 AM when we would be awakened by the nuns singing their prayers.

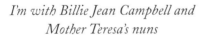

*I'm with Billie Jean Campbell and Mother Teresa's nuns*

*Sweet picture of Billie Jean taken with Mother Teresa*

As I lay on the little wooden bed that night, there was no way I could sleep. I was overtired from the long flight, and the contrast of being in this strange country caused me to reflect on life back home. So many thoughts were brewing inside, and turning letters on a game show half a world away seemed so insignificant. Would the part of me that wanted to stay and help, override the other part which wanted to go home?

The next morning, I noticed a beautiful field of flowers across the way. When I commented on it, one of the nuns said, "Those are poppies. They are used for special celebrations." Now this was a custom I found very intriguing. In many countries, beer or wine is customary with meals, but opium was a real surprise.

When Father De Souza took us into the leprosarium, it was one of the most difficult moments I've ever had to face. To see the men and women up close, many without noses, ears or fingers, others lurching around on gnarled stumps was almost too much to bear. And everywhere I looked, there were flies. Thousands upon thousands of flies were crawling over open, oozing wounds and flaking skin. Father De Souza gently took me by the arm, guiding me through the devastating sights, stopping to give gentle words of compassion to the afflicted.

When we came to the children's area, it was heartbreaking to look into their eyes, having just seen what the future held for them. At first glance, they looked almost untouched except for their pale discolored skin. That was the first indication of the onset of the disease. Father De Souza explained that drug therapy was available; and while it could only arrest the disease in adults, everyone concerned with leprosy believed that with children, a total cure was possible if you caught it in time. No wonder he had been so insistent that we come and see for ourselves.

Drugs cost money, and he was hoping fundraisers could be held through our contacts in the entertainment industry. He *never* let go of the dream of getting help for his people.

In the following days, Father De Souza encouraged me to help with the dry lepers as opposed to the wet (infectious type). I gave out medication and assisted the nuns with endless scrubbing and disinfecting. He wanted me to take a closer look at the problem, to understand how important it was for the work to continue.

As a human being who cares deeply, I could not possibly just go home to America and ignore the utter devastation which affects so many lives. Even though I didn't

*A dear man suffering from leprosy.*
*He was blind and crippled.*

understand the language, their eyes revealed little hope for the future. I wanted to find a way to get the message out. Money and medicine were needed, along with people whose skills could help make the lives of these dear ones more manageable. So much to do and so little time.

When I first told my mother I was going to India to help in the leper colony, she was understandably concerned about my safety. There was no way I could explain all I was seeing and feeling. My heart was so deeply touched by this experience. If I were to call and tell Mama and Daddy I was thinking about staying, what would their reaction be? While trusting them to sell my home was not a problem, they lived with me and any decision I made would affect them as well. So much was running through my mind. Even though I didn't want to hurt Mama, saying good-bye to these pleading eyes was going to be difficult. Wisdom told me to take time to think it through and I listened to that inner voice.

When I went to India, I wasn't aware of the rules. Every country has them, however most Western visitors are oblivious to their existence. Since we don't understand their customs, we can unknowingly seem disrespectful. Because of this, Americans are not always the best ambassadors.

They have strict rules regarding clothing. Western women shouldn't wear the skimpy fashions we are accustomed to in America. In fact, no part of the leg could be showing, and it's certainly not okay for Western men to go without shirts in the streets, no matter how hot it may be. In India, alcohol is banned. And if you run over one of their sacred cows, you will never see the light of day again.

*Getting to know those in India with leprosy and their children*

It's also important to know about the caste system, one of the most rigid social orders in the world. For instance, Brahmans are from an upper caste, the exact opposite of being an "untouchable". "Untouchables" are expected to perform menial tasks, such as sweeping the streets and collecting human excrement and cow dung off the sidewalk. They are required to wear a bell around their neck to warn Brahman and other high caste people in India that they are walking in their direction, so they won't have to look at them. From a Brahman's point of view, if they even *look* at the unclean, they will become unclean also and that has to be avoided at all costs.

I learned that the only center for leprosy patients in the continental United States was in Carville, Louisiana, from 1894 to 1999. In 1873, Father Damien began a center on Molokai in Hawaii. After sixteen years of working with the patients, he contracted the disease himself and died at the age of forty-nine.

Our last day in India, was National Festival Day in which flying kites is traditional. Billie Jean Campbell and Joyce Rey and I decided that those with Hansen's disease, so sadly isolated, should take part in the celebration. We went into town and purchased forty-eight kites, one for each patient to fly. We couldn't wait to hand them out. Our excitement was cut short, however, when the nuns very kindly told us of the dangers involved.

*I found such joy in working with the people in India—*

Leprosy is very contagious, especially the wet form which so many of these patients had. They told us that if even one kite broke loose and the public heard where it came from; there would be a major panic. It could result in the leprosarium being closed down by the government. This reality was devastating to consider. It never occurred to us that flying kites could be a problem. We just wanted to bring them a little joy, not realizing we could have made things worse.

*Children and mothers readily respond to kindness*

*To Americans, it's just a cow. In India, it is sacred.*

As Father De Souza waited with us at the airport before our departure, we felt torn about what we had seen. I asked him how God allowed such suffering and cruelty to take place. He said, "It has nothing to do with God, Susan. It's the bureaucracy of this country that is to blame."

When I returned to my comfortable life stateside, I was in culture shock once again. I had little patience when hearing a lady in Beverly Hills carry on about how her hairdresser didn't get her color just right.

I had my hair braided and only felt comfortable wearing very simple clothing at first. Going to lavish restaurants and paying those high prices became difficult for me. It was hard to pamper myself when the images of those who struggle just to survive were so fresh in my mind.

I promised myself and Father De Souza that I would make it back to India. This trip proved to be the catalyst which caused me to leave *Wheel of Fortune* as I shared previously.

After spending a year working with cancer patients at St. Joseph's Hospital in Houston with Dr. Stehlin, my heart still wanted to serve. My thoughts kept returning to all I had seen in India during that first trip.

It wasn't long before American Leprosy Missions invited me to be their overseas correspondent, making documentaries which would highlight the problems in several third world countries. I traveled and worked on location in the summer of 1985 while former U.S. Surgeon General C. Everett Koop and Merlin Olsen presented the issues from the main studio set.

Daddy didn't understand why I wanted to be in India when so many in America needed help. My dad felt like a lot of Americans do about taking care of needs in our country first. This documentary however, was about the devastation of dealing with leprosy in India.

It was my responsibility to be informed and prepared for the on-camera delivery. The producer, Don Baer, was very kind and professional. While I was used to "winging it" on television, that was not how Don operated. That might work on a game show, but not for a leprosy documentary.

As I was going through old boxes recently, I pulled out my journals, thumbing through the pages. Hours went by as I relived so many memories and I found myself quite tearful and disturbed. Tearful because there was so much more to do for the amazing people I had befriended along the way. Disturbed because there were serious questions I had to answer in my own mind. I couldn't help remembering all the babies who died and the faces I would never forget. Their eyes showed such love and hope, knowing we had come to help. Were we able to get the message across? I believe we did, however in situations like this, you <u>always</u> wish you could have done more.

My journals also reminded me of the impossible schedule and the planning it took to make just one of these films. I made the last of the two documentaries for American Leprosy Missions in the summer of 1985, and I tried to keep a journal as we progressed around the world. My brilliant idea was to write during each plane trip and maybe there would be enough material for a book. What a joke! I was either asleep, eating, or discussing with Don Baer, the producer and crew what we were going to film next. There was so much to cover, and we wanted to do it right. So now you know why the entries in my journal are somewhat sparse, but I did try.

June 20, 1985—Flew from Los Angeles overnight to London—a ten-hour flight. Slept most of the way which surprised me as I don't usually sleep on planes. Maybe it was the businessman who sat next to me, talking endlessly about his rubber glove business. I'm convinced that long-distance flying can be the world's most boring and antisocial activity. You're sitting only inches away from someone you've never set eyes on, having to climb over their stiff knees when you spot the Vacant sign on the bathroom door just before someone steps in ahead of you.

June 21—I love London. Stayed at the Gloucester Hotel. Filmed there for close to four hours at the International Center for Diseases. Learned a lot more about leprosy. I discovered that the mother of Moses and her sister were sufferers of the disease, proving that leprosy dates back to the Old Testament. (This was news to me. How about you?) The Brits have a lot of research on the disease. They were actually the leading pioneers on how to deal with it.

That evening, I was too tired to leave the hotel. I lay back to rest my eyes for a few minutes and woke up to the sun streaming in my window the next morning.

June 22—To Africa. British Airways night flight from London to Monrovia, Liberia, Africa. Another long flight. I sat between two men who knew each other and talked all the way. I asked if they would like to change seats so they could sit together. The answer was "No, thank you!" One of them always took a window seat and the other would only sit on the aisle. That's the way they traveled and they weren't going to move for anyone. I was stuck until a steward took a close look and found me another seat. Kindness like that means so very much.

June 23—Arrived in Monrovia at five in the morning, very, very tired. Drove to a leper colony some distance away. Three hours of absolute torture. Weather very hot, plenty of dust. We had to travel as Canadians rather than Americans because in many countries, Americans were so hated. Drove in old medical ambulance for our safety. Even so, rocks were being thrown at our vehicle. It was quite an experience since the ambulance was at least thirty years old with no passenger seats. We kept bouncing around in the back, sliding into each other around every curve.

We shot five rolls of film in the middle of nowhere and worked with a teleprompter that had an automatic speed control which somehow went nuts, going faster and faster until I burst out laughing. At least it broke the tension. We were all getting a little ragged due to the heat and the flies.

Late in the afternoon, we heard the sound of singing coming from the colony's small church. Together with the crew, I walked over to listen and was overcome with the sincerity of the patients as they sang praises to God, thanking Him for allowing us to be there.

I asked a translator for his help and had a long talk with an older patient named Abdul. He was blind and crippled like so many of the older sufferers.

I told him I would like to pray for him and asked, "Is there something special you would like me to pray for?"

He reached out and touched my arm, then, in perfect English, he said, "I can't think of anything. I have everything I need."

I was struck with Abdul's words—he has everything he needs.

After hearing that, I spent several hours in quiet reflection, questioning my own life and purpose. If this man, so badly afflicted with leprosy could be content living in such poor conditions, what did that say about the unrest I felt with such good health and a life of privilege? I found myself quite numb, thinking about these dear people. Just take whatever would break your heart and multiply that seven times and you will have an idea of what I was experiencing.

June 24—Flew from Monrovia, Liberia to Addis Ababa, Ethiopia. Flying across Africa, at least half of it in daylight, one appreciates the overwhelming size of the vast continent. Plane half empty so I was able to lie down across the seats.

June 25—Ethiopia. Immense poverty and malnutrition, worse than India which I didn't think was possible. Spent the day filming at a leper colony and the surrounding countryside. So many children were dying; and since they had no money to buy wood for coffins, we laid the tiny ones in a thin blanket and buried them in shallow graves. I couldn't just stand by and watch. The devastating sights drove me to find ways to help. There was one moment while holding a dying child close, trying to comfort the mother, I found myself asking the age-old question, "If there is a God, where is He now?" It reminded me so much of Houston and Dr. Stehlin's words, "We can only do so much."

I remember a story my friend, Rosey Grier shared with me. Rosey described a large school of fish which had somehow washed ashore. An old man was picking them up, one at a time and taking them back to the ocean. A young man asked him how that could help among so many. The old man held a fish up and said, "It makes a difference to this one." That illustration is so inspiring when we realize that our efforts really do count, even if it's just for *one* person, it matters.

(Rosey played football for the Los Angeles Rams and is called the *Gentle Giant*. The day Robert Kennedy was shot, Rosey was at his side and rushed to tackle the killer, Sirhan Sirhan. Anyone who knows Rosey Grier knows he would have taken the bullet for Robert Kennedy if it had been possible.)

That night, I had dinner with some members of a World Vision film crew who were doing a similar documentary, helping raise money for the cause. Their emphasis was on the starvation issue and the need for basic food supplies.

June 26—Off to Ahmedabad, India. The flight attendants wore beautiful saris. Would love to have one, but where would I wear it? Maybe someday in Hollywood.

I couldn't help reflecting on the contrasts of life. In front of me, colorful fabrics worn by elegant, young women. Behind me, just a few hours earlier, intense suffering and poverty. Zero chance that any of them will experience a plane ride, let alone visit another country. Never had in-flight Indian food before. Stomach is holding up well to all the different foods. They gave us ginger in small amounts to help with digestion.

June 27—Got to see all my old friends and had a precious visit with some of Mother Teresa's nuns including one called Little Mother Teresa, after her namesake. Met with Father De Souza and Rev. Terry Sweeney to prepare for the new documentary, *Land Of Hunger, Land of Hope* which would teach the village people how to build homes that will be secure when the monsoons hit. Very hot and humid.

The director, Bill Riead had just arrived from L.A., explaining a major complication in Bombay. After applying for proper clearance for his cameras, sound and lighting equipment, Customs officials confiscated everything. He was understandably upset and said there was no choice but to go back to Bombay and deal with them. I'll let Bill take the story from here.

*I couldn't believe Customs had taken all my camera equipment and locked it up in Bombay. As I told Father De Souza and Father Sweeney about the situation, all I knew was I had to get to Bombay and back here as quickly as possible. We had a schedule to keep!*

*As we were talking, the most beautiful woman I had ever seen, hands down, walked up to hear the story. I was spellbound by this lady to the point my knees were actually weak. I'm usually a very focused person, but my attention was definitely divided.*

*Right now though, I had to get back to the business at hand. Father De Souza had sent for a rickshaw to take me to the airport and it was just pulling up. As I was getting seated, Susan jumped in beside me. She said "You're not going alone. I'll help you get the equipment back."*

*Now, I'm used to handling things like this myself. I'm a take-charge person, however I soon realized, Susan is too. As she continued to talk, I relaxed a little. I thought, with Susan's charm and beauty, there's not a snowball's chance in hell the Customs agents will deny whatever she asks. I was already gone, having developed an instant crush on Susan.*

*The plane was delayed and by the time we reached Bombay, the Customs office was closed. We would have to wait till morning. I was experiencing jet lag like never before. I was totally exhausted and wanted the security of a hotel with American connections. We went directly to the Bombay Hilton. I asked for two rooms and was told there were none. I didn't have time for this and asked to see the manager. I told him I was one tired American after just arriving in India and having the long ordeal at Customs. "I stay at Hiltons all the time and I know there are always a couple of rooms set aside for emergencies."*

*The manager said, "That is true sir, but all I have tonight is one room. Will that help?"*

*I thought, "Yes, there is a God!"*

*The manager said it was a mini suite, and as I looked at Susan, she agreed we would take it. It was a good size with a kitchen and couch in the main room and a separate bedroom. Besides being exhausted, I was also starving. We ordered room service and had a nice dinner. While needing sleep so badly, I looked forward to bedtime for another reason. After all, we were both single and alone for the night.*

*Susan said she knew how very tired I was and told me to take the bed, saying she would sleep on the couch.*

*I said, "I have a better idea, why don't we just share the bed so we can both be comfortable?"*

*She smiled and said "Not a chance, Bill. Nice try though."*

*I told her chivalry was not dead and insisted she take the bed. I was so tired by now; I lay down on the couch and promptly fell asleep.*

*I was in a dead sleep about 3:00 AM when I felt someone shaking me. I looked up at this vision of loveliness in a little T-shirt who said, "I feel badly about taking the bed, Bill. Come on in and join me."*

*Could I be dreaming? This must be my lucky day. I got up and followed Susan into the bedroom. She slid under the covers and I did too. Lying next to her, I felt hypnotized by those dazzling eyes. Could anything be better than this?*

*The next thing I remember is birds chirping and pans rattling in the kitchen. I looked around and it was morning with the sun shining bright.*

*I went into the next room and asked Susan, fully dressed now, "What happened?"*

*She smiled sweetly and said, "You were so exhausted, you passed out as soon as your head hit the pillow."*

*I couldn't believe it! I ate the breakfast she had prepared and just kept shaking my head.*

*We went on to Customs and thanks to Susan's charm; the equipment was released in no time. We returned to Ahmedabad and shot the documentary.*

*All through that week, I tried again with Susan. She would just shrug her shoulders, "Sorry, Bill."*

—

June 28—During the documentary, we also filmed surgeries at the hospital. Father De Souza reminded me to carry antiseptic towelettes for the germs, Betadine for scratches, and a bottle of drinking water.

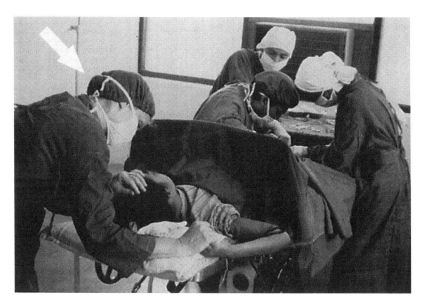

*I'm on the left, praying for a patient during surgery.*
*Amputations are a sad reality for many with leprosy.*

We were working in very cramped conditions, but the crew was wonderful, especially after a delicious lunch of curried tomatoes and rice. (Boy, would I like to have that recipe back home.) Spent four hours at the leprosarium where I talked with some teenagers who were not much bigger than the last time I'd seen them. Just a few years before, I had been touched by their courage and grace. I was so encouraged to see as a result of the medical help, all signs of their disease were gone, and yet they were still confined to the leprosarium because of the stigma attached.

What do you say to people who are whole now but unable to live a normal life? On the way out, I saw a sign that put it all into perspective, "What difference if the world loves us as long as God does."

By the end of the shooting, the crew was really suffering from the heat. They weren't the only ones, and the day wasn't over yet. Father De Souza and Father Terry took me to visit a slum area called "Hollywood". No running water and open sewers were used as a toilet. My hosts felt it important for me to see an example of what needed to be done. We got the crew to do some more shooting. As tired as they were, they realized the contrast between the two Hollywoods would stick in people's minds longer than mere words.

June 29—Air India flight from Bombay to Calcutta. Stayed in a hotel that was a relic of the British Empire. The Grand Hotel on one of Calcutta's main streets, Chowringee. Went for a short walk and had my first taste of Buffalo ice cream, very sweet at the famous Firpos Ice Cream Parlor. Couldn't sleep at all, a combination of the heat, the noise of the old rickety brass fan, and the pesky fly in my room.

June 30—Calcutta, India. Another big culture shock. Got up early and went out onto the Chowringee to watch this great city get into gear for the day. During the night, hundreds of people had slept under the glass canopy which hung over the side of the hotel. Malnutrition is so rampant and a few had not survived the night.

I stood in disbelief as a truck rolled slowly down the street, stopping every so often as men wearing surgical masks loaded bodies onto the tailgate. I was frozen in place, hardly believing my eyes. When I could finally move, I walked into the hotel and dropped onto the first chair I saw, just staring into space, unable to comprehend this new reality. It was so difficult to realize this was a normal part of their everyday existence!

Flew from Calcutta on Thai Airways to Bangkok, Thailand. Departure delayed by three hours. Something wrong with the plane. Great! Arrived very late at night again. (When this is over, I'll have a long talk with the person who worked out this schedule.)

Another long wait at Customs. Must be the norm in this part of the world. We later found out customs officials had gotten tired of waiting for our flight and had gone home. Hotel not too good either—like sleeping in a Turkish bath.

July 1—Bangkok. Don Baer and I spent a long time arranging for our filming permits. Still not used to seeing lepers without noses, ears, feet, hands, etc. It affects me deeply. So do the mental scars from not stopping the disease in time. In Hollywood, everyone has to be so perfect. I should bring some of them to see a leper hospital for themselves. Maybe they'd see how superficial their "perfection" really is.

—

At the leper hospital, we had the usual language problems, but when I looked into their eyes with love and compassion, a different kind of communication occurred. Speaking English didn't mean anything here. Nor did dollar bills or credit cards. It was their faith that kept them alive. Something I had to respect. That was brought home to me by Rev. Bob Bradburn of American Leprosy Missions. We were at a meeting where the spacing was tight, so I lifted a chair high over a few people to make more room. Bob quickly stopped me by saying, "Susan, please don't do that. A man's head is his highest being and you simply don't put anything above it."

Remember what I said about respecting the customs in other lands? Problem is, you don't often know what the rule is until you break it.

That evening, we attended a charity show in the hotel ballroom to raise funds for the leprosy hospital in Thailand. Some of the entertainers were Connie Stevens, Carol Connors, and Jack Carter. I tried a little tap dance with Jack Carter which was really fun. Before turning in for the night, I called Mama and Daddy at my sister Chloe's house in Missouri. They were so surprised to hear about the special evening. So was I when I got the bill from the hotel—312 Rupees to call home. (That was about $17/minute.)

July 2—Singapore Airways to Hong Kong.

In Singapore, chewing gum in public happens to be a serious offense with a heavy fine. I was learning some very important lessons overseas, not just about customs, but about laws in foreign lands. I remember hearing about one of our young American guys who sprayed graffiti on some cars in Singapore and ended up in jail. Maybe they've got something there. The state of our inner cities in America can be quite depressing due to a lack of respect for others.

In Hong Kong, the food and hotel were wonderful. Everything was so clean and orderly. No litter in the streets. Not even a speck of gum on the sidewalk.

July 3—We flew Philippine Airways from Hong Kong to Manila. Another big day of filming ahead of us.

President Marcos and his cronies were in the process of being overthrown by Mrs. Aquino and her followers when we arrived. Don Baer, with his great wisdom, thought we should all get off the streets as quickly as possible. Tension filled the air, and we didn't waste any time checking into our hotel. By the time we got to our rooms, we could hear bullets bouncing off the walls outside! It was also monsoon season, and with the heavy rains, high humidity, and concern for our own safety, none of us got much sleep.

*With a young mother and her two boys in the Philippines*

July 4—America's Independence Day. We visited a leper colony outside Manila. One young man there put the whole trip into focus for me. He was both crippled and blind, his body very shrunken, and yet he whistled the most beautiful songs. I asked him who the woman was in the photo beside his bed.

"That was my wife," he said. "She's no longer here."

"How long have you had leprosy?" I asked him.

"Ten years. I lost my sight two years ago."

Then he began to whistle—"America, America, God shed His grace on thee . . ."

I was overwhelmed with emotion. When I could finally speak, I said, "Thank you very much. That was beautiful!" He said, "Thank you for coming and trying to help. I know it's your Fourth of July back in America." This was without a doubt the nicest Fourth of July gift I have ever received. Lord, please forgive me for complaining about anything!

*This picture was taken in Manila after the monsoon.*
*Such sweet people under these conditions.*

July 5—Philippine Airways flight to Honolulu. Getting near home and at last on American soil. Stayed overnight at a hotel that faced the ocean. I actually managed to get an evening swim and a good night's sleep. I had almost forgotten how good it felt. Tomorrow we're flying home! Back to the USA!

*These girls have "wet" leprosy which is the contagious stage.*

*Close-up of me in the Philippines sharing a story with all the children gathered around. Wider view below.*

July 6—As we took off from Honolulu on American Airlines, I could see Molokai off in the distance. I wish we'd had time to visit the old leper colony, previously known as Father Damien's ministry at Kalaupapa. It's a stunning site, situated on a peninsula, jutting out from the North coast and isolated from the rest of the island by 1,600 foot cliffs. Kalaupapa has a very special meaning to me because when it was still open, Mama and

Daddy helped me box up most of my library on Astrology, Numerology, and Clairvoyance and send them to Molokai. (Daddy was so glad to get rid of these books, he wanted to write on the crate, PLEASE DO NOT RETURN TO SENDER!)

Apparently the old wooden church is still there along with all the buildings. A few people still live on site, keeping the place tidy now that it is a national historic park.

Hundreds of years ago, leprosy was an incurable and prevalent disease in Europe as well as Asia and Africa. You can still see churches in Norway which had windows with special openings so the lepers who could not come in the building, could share in the time of worship. If you can imagine, they could only view the service through a small opening, and I'm sure they were very grateful to at least have that contact.

Looking out the window, I saw the approaching sea of lights in Los Angeles. It would take some time to process the contrast in lifestyle several continents away. In just seventeen days, I had the experience of a lifetime as we visited Africa, India, Thailand, China, and the Philippines.

The enormous suffering of these dear people is hard to fathom from our own comfortable homes. I can still close my eyes and recall those who reached back with their compassion for us. It was a demonstration of the human spirit like I had never known and a real opportunity to give love to those who are considered untouchables. I learned afresh how crucial human touch is and the depth of feeling it can convey.

As a result of screening documentaries like *One Million Children Are Waiting* around the world, just over $3,000,000 was raised for leprosy research. Because they were seen by so many people, public awareness was raised and a cure was actually found for leprosy. If children are given the medicine early enough, they will never develop leprosy, and the cost is only about $150 per person. After the devastation I saw, I'm very grateful to have played a part in this victory.

In America, we're dealing with something just as fearsome as leprosy and that is AIDS. It can cost as much as $200,000 to $300,000 to treat someone with AIDS. That's quite a comparison. The important factor is that something *can* be done, yet like a lot of things in life, it takes serious money to make it happen.

———

*I want to dedicate this chapter to the memory of three very dear friends. Their picture is below:*

*Billie Jean Campbell, Father Herb De Souza and Gov. Pat Brown— from a fundraiser in Beverly Hills for the work in India*

Little did I know when I was in India that I would return home to help care for a dear friend who grabbed the attention of the world with the diagnosis of AIDS. Everything happens in life for a reason and probably no one else could have drawn people together in this special effort as a man who was beloved by all and betrayed by one—Rock Hudson.

*Trust everybody, but cut the cards.*—W. C. Fields

# CHAPTER ELEVEN

# BETWEEN ROCK AND A HARD PLACE

The tight winding road up Mulholland Drive to the Castle seemed longer than usual. I was driving to an oasis high atop the beautiful slopes of Beverly Hills which happened to be the home of a very special and dear friend of mine. He was greatly admired by millions of fans around the world on a not-so-personal level. I'm speaking of the legendary Rock Hudson. What a man! What a star!

All was quiet when I opened the kitchen door. I sat the grocery sack down and began to put things away. Rock's personal assistant and friend, Mark Miller, stopped on his way out to an appointment and thanked me for being there. He said Rock had asked for a cup of his favorite orange lemon tea. We exchanged a hopeful look as he left and I turned the tea kettle on.

I glanced around Rock's smartly styled kitchen where everything was so familiar. When Rock was in town, there was an air of festivity, no matter what the season. His very presence filled the rooms with fun and laughter. Only this time, things were different—I wasn't making my famous double fudge walnut cookies, always a big favorite of Rock's. This time, my dear friend was lying very still in his bed upstairs, reportedly dying of AIDS. Shaking my head to dismiss the ready tears, I chose to fill my mind and heavy heart with fond memories that came in like a flood.

I had the pleasure and I do mean pleasure, of meeting Rock Hudson and we hit it off instantly. It was 1969 when we met through Mark Miller and the late George Nader. I always enjoyed their company. I was doing well around town and was considered "bankable", as the casting directors often said to my agent.

Along with my boyfriend, Clint Ritchie, I was under a term contract at 20th Century Fox with James Brolin and the brilliant Sherry Lansing, who later became president of Paramount. Two of the biggest contract actors at the time were Raquel Welch and the classic Batman, Adam West.

While I was offered a starring role in *Beyond the Valley of the Dolls* which was a great opportunity, it's one I declined due to a nude scene (detailed in chapter 1). I knew very well that agreeing to do that would not make my mother and father proud when they saw it with their friends in Kansas City. Quite the opposite! Remember, in 1969, full nudity or even semi-nudity was considered very racy, and to me, it still is. It's hard enough in the bedroom when you're raised in Missouri.

I learned later on that saying "yes" would have all but destroyed my high five-figure commercials income with BBDO, the largest advertising agency at the time in New York. When Eastman Kodak called me for a major national commercial, one of the first papers I had to sign was a verification that I had never posed nude for photographs or on screen. Thankfully, I was able to say I had not, and that simple fact gave my career a certain credibility for which I have always been grateful.

*George Nader and I
with Mark Miller*

*Sharing a private moment
with Rock Hudson*

Clint Ritchie played Clint Buchanan on *One Life to Live* and was a very good friend of Mark Miller and George Nader. It was Clint who taught me everything I knew about sex and everything I didn't want in a husband. Time takes care of a lot of issues and fortunately, anything negative had long been dismissed by the time we saw each other at George Nader's memorial service. Rev. Terry Sweeney was there as he continues to be through so many crucial times.

Long after Clint and I broke up, Rock, Mark, George, and I remained close friends with an unspeakable bond. Sinatra had his "Rat Pack". Well, this was Rock's own version—three special friends whom he trusted implicitly.

Two or three months prior to Rock's untimely death, George and Mark called to ask for my help. While I had been to Rock's home, the Castle, numerous times before, this was a special request. Knowing his time was short, and with the trust we shared, they asked me to be there for Rock.

I was more than honored that they would call. In addition to being a close friend to Rock, they knew I had ministered to cancer patients in Houston and to leprosy, a.k.a Hansen's disease patients, all over the world. Please understand that after dealing with leprosy victims, the fear of AIDS for me was not as threatening as it was for many. Most importantly, I realized that Rock needed an extra measure of comfort, something beyond what any of us could offer on our own.

Thinking back over the special times with Rock, I flashed back to a wonderful memory. Here is the invitation I received:

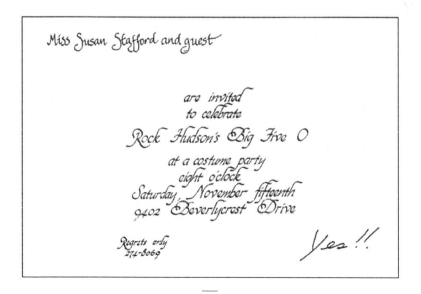

*Miss Susan Stafford and guest*

*are invited*
*to celebrate*

*Rock Hudson's Big Five 0*

*at a costume party*
*eight o'clock*
*Saturday, November fifteenth*
*9402 Beverlycrest Drive*

*Regrets only*
*274-8069*

*Yes !!*

It was Rock's fiftieth birthday party, and being cautious about who to invite, I asked my sister Catherine to be my guest. Mark and George loved Catherine who is such a good sport with a fabulous personality like the rest of my family.

I had returned from working with American Leprosy Missions in Ethiopia and Liberia, Africa, and was excited about attending this special Hollywood party. Catherine was equally thrilled. She had been a fan of Rock Hudson as a teenager, and—like so many—we secretly imagined ourselves in Doris Day's part as his leading lady.

When we arrived at his beautiful home at 9602 Beverlycrest in Beverly Hills, I was a bit nervous after being away for some time. We drove up to the entrance and left my car with the valet. Admiring the new landscaping and fragrant roses, we followed the decorative lighting up the long walkway.

As we rang the doorbell, Rock swung open the massive wooden doors and greeted us with his wonderful charm. Rock was so much fun with an aura that few people on this planet possess.

I introduced Catherine, and Rock gave us both a kiss. He led us into the living room where he announced in a very loud and excited voice, "Hey, everyone . . . she's baaack!" I felt like the belle of the ball, however something was different tonight. I couldn't quite figure it out.

There was a time not too long before when I felt uneasy spending time at Rock's home. As many Christians do, I had judged the gay lifestyle harshly and I know they could feel it. Since that time, I had learned that each person is important to Him and God's love is unconditional. I had written to Rock about this realization which I imagine he had shared with the others.

Mark and George and Kenny Jillson and Al Roberts came over to greet us, and we all started dishing at once as we caught up on the latest. Conversations were always intriguing in this group. There was never a dull moment.

The tables were elegantly set with formal place cards at every seat. Each dark blue card had a personally written note scripted in gold ink. Instead of the person's name, there was a description of each one, which made it fun to read and guess who would be seated there. My card read, "She left, yet returned because she knows the Lord loves all of us." So that was it! Now I understood.

Rock knew how to make people feel very special, and this was no exception. Toward the end of the evening, I heard a roar of laughter and everyone's attention was drawn to the winding staircase. As Sofia on the *Golden Girls* would say, "Picture this . . . Beverly Hills, 1975 . . ." Rock made his grand entrance, wearing only an oversized diaper with a humongous safety pin. On his head was a purple birthday hat with a huge "50" written in bright yellow numbers. Everyone was laughing hysterically; I mean it was off the Richter scale.

What a treat to see this man who literally exuded charm having such a grand time. You had to be there to appreciate it fully. Rock did not take himself seriously and that made the moment a delight for everyone there. We all applauded Rock and said he was the sexiest fifty-year-old we knew. This sight of Rock in the huge diaper will be forever etched in my memory. No press was present for this private party, and no cameras were allowed. This was purely for the enjoyment of his friends.

The whistling teakettle brought me back to the present. I prepared a nice cup of tea for Rock, just the way he liked it with fresh lemon and honey. As I walked to the staircase, I passed the guest bathroom and couldn't help remembering what happened at another fabulous party at Rock's home.

On this particular evening, I'd been drinking quite a bit. As a matter of fact, we were all drinking quite a bit. While alcohol was never my friend, in those days, I didn't let that stop me. Who knew how precious time would be?

The Castle was filled to capacity and the atmosphere was electric with various personalities from actors to the music world. It was literally wall-to-wall people, and it became difficult to move from one end of the room to the other. I was enjoying the excitement when all of a sudden it hit me . . . the urge . . . that uncontrollable sensation . . . I had to tinkle.

I worked my way through the crowd to the guest bathroom. Relief was just a second away, or was it? A lady standing nearby saw the look on my face and told me the bathroom was currently occupied.

She was a little tipsy too and said, "I can't think of her name . . . it's the blonde actress with all the diamonds. Her sister starred in *Green Acres* . . . you know the one."

Of course, it was Zsa Zsa Gabor!

I politely knocked on the chestnut wood door and said, "Zsa Zsa, it's Susan . . . Susan Stafford. Are you almost through?"

With that wonderful Hungarian accent, I heard her say, "Coming dahling . . . just vait . . . it vill just be another moment, dahling." I tried to stand nonchalantly with my legs crossed. I think by this time, my eyes were crossed too.

Finally, in desperation, I could wait no longer. I shouted, Ethel Merman style, "Zsa Zsa, open this door! It's been more than five minutes. Now get your diamond ass out of there!"

Seconds later, Zsa Zsa opened the door, puffed herself up, stared at me and said, "Really now, dahling!"

I rushed past her and slammed the door as everyone nearby started to laugh. Embarrassing at the time, it's humorous now as I remember the stunned look on her beautiful face.

Now, as I reached the top of the staircase, I ever so gingerly opened the door to Rock's room. The shades were drawn, and I sat the cup of tea down on his antique bedside table.

Calling his name softly, I realized that he was fast asleep. His slow, measured breathing gave me a little relief. It was very difficult to see him like this. He had lost so much weight that his body was emaciated, much like the pictures we've all seen of concentration camp prisoners or Holocaust survivors. Rock couldn't get up and walk by himself, even to the bathroom. His immune system was depleted, and he had no energy to take care of himself, much less going to bed as accused.

While his form was not the muscular man I was accustomed to seeing, there was an inner strength about Rock. He still had that same great spirit and tried as much as he could, to smile and make everyone around him feel good. Right now, I was grateful he was able to sleep. My eyes lingered on him another moment as I offered a silent prayer. I stepped quietly down the stairs, looking for a box of Kleenex.

The phone calls had diminished. So many didn't know what to say, they simply stopped calling. The author who had been working with Rock on his book no longer entered the house. She had a young son and there was a natural fear of something so unknown.

Being there when Rock needed his trusted friends the most meant everything to all of us. The word *trust* is so powerful. I can't explain it, even to this day, but I knew I was on an assignment from God. Have you ever felt that way? There was no other reason to put myself in a position of possible jeopardy. So little was known about AIDS at the time—we just knew it was a fearsome diagnosis that conjured up the plague and leprosy. Obviously, someone besides Susan was in charge of my path.

This was a "knowing" that I have experienced only a few times in my life. It's one that can never be taken for granted and one for which fame and fortune can never compete. It was an awesome time, and all of us were dedicated to maintaining Rock's dignity above all. He needed to be surrounded by loving, caring people. George and Mark were crystal clear about this. Rock didn't need anyone asking a lot of questions. When he felt like talking, we let Rock take the lead. I was very aware that I needed exceptional faith and all the courage my Lord could give me for such a time as this.

Touch is ever so powerful when offered by a caring heart, especially when one may feel like an "untouchable" with AIDS. When the need is before you, it's interesting to see what comes forth. Some surprise you with their inability to be present, and others with the depth of character that is revealed.

One of Rock's dear friends whose courage inspired us all, was Elizabeth Taylor. During Rock's final days, it was around 3:00 on a breezy afternoon when Elizabeth came to see Rock. I was standing nearby when Elizabeth entered the room. She simply took her shoes off, slipped into bed next to Rock and cradled his head in her lap. It's a moment I will always cherish.

I quietly left the room, giving them privacy for these tender moments. While they had been great together on camera, this time it was for real. Her friend needed her and she was there. Elizabeth's love for Rock transcended any thought of personal danger, and I honor her courage and compassion.

During Rock's last days, the paparazzi literally swarmed the Castle. It was a media circus. When photographers realized we had blocked every possibility of a photo of Rock, they camped out in the driveway, snapping pictures of everyone coming and going. It was difficult to even get through the gate, but we all worked together to protect his privacy and the dignity which was such a part of Rock.

People sent cards, letters, photos, and flowers to Rock's home. So many truly cared and sincerely wanted him to win this battle. Sadly, he didn't, and on October 2, 1985, we all lost a very dear friend and a legend who had to hide who he really was.

Our dear friends, Al Roberts and Kenny Jillson started ASF, AIDS Service Foundation in Laguna and organized an annual fundraiser they called "Splash". Not only was it popular and fun, they raised money to prevent the spread of HIV/AIDS and improve the lives of so many men, women, and children who were affected. They hosted the event at their home and made sure all the money went to help those who were affected by this dreaded disease.

Elizabeth Taylor championed a private foundation called amfAR, which has raised hundreds of millions of dollars to help find a cure. Rock was right—much good did come from it.

To some, Rock Hudson was the matinee idol with movies we all loved like *Pillow Talk*. Rock told me how very much he enjoyed working with Doris Day. He said they made each other laugh so much that it was difficult to complete some of their scenes.

To others, Rock was the rugged movie star or the admired police commissioner on *McMillan and Wife*, with the wonderful actress, Susan Saint James (who later married my ex-husband Dick Ebersol).

Rock was also a man of great dignity. He was bigger than life; and to those of us who knew him best, he was the kindest, most caring, and fun-loving man who always lived life with a great deal of passion.

It's amazing that while Rock was so well known for over four decades, he was able to maintain such a private life. He had succeeded in keeping the secret of his sexuality hidden from the public, only to have it completely exposed to the world at the end. That became his choice, for the greater good of all. Long before the O.J. case, I saw injustice in the courtroom firsthand while testifying in the Rock Hudson case. Due to a gag order, I'm not allowed to share those details.

After everything has been said and done, after everything has been written about his life, Rock Hudson leaves a wealth of artistry from his films and television shows, which generations to come can enjoy. Most importantly, as a result of the courage he displayed, an entire nation was made aware of AIDS. Many lives have been and will continue to be saved in the process.

I can't tell you how many times I've been asked, "Did you sleep with Rock?" or "Did Rock like women, I mean, to

*My favorite picture of the two of us*

274

sleep with?" Well, folks, I believe there are some questions we would do well to stop asking.

Many years later, Mark, George, and I were still the best of friends which in these days is a miracle. Sadly, George passed away several years ago at the Motion Picture Home in Woodland Hills, California. My godfather John Ford and his lovely wife Mary were among the founding partners. It's a fabulous place that has been set aside for actors and others in the industry and I want to thank them for their kindness. It just goes to show what people can accomplish where their goal is to help others.

*George Nader and I in the early years*

*Walk Of Stars ceremony for Rock Hudson and George Nader. I accepted the Star for Rock and Mark Miller accepted the Star for George whose cousin, Sally Nader is in the middle.*

*Marilyn Monroe and Rock enjoy a special moment after
she received a Golden Globe award.*

*Marilyn Monroe once described Hollywood as* **"a place they pay you $1,000 for
a kiss and 50 cents for your soul."** *She understood all too well how it works.*

*You can only see the greatness of a tree once it has fallen.*
—Anne Morrow Lindberg from *Gifts From The Sea*

# Chapter Twelve

# DON'T BET ON ANYTHING
# THAT TALKS

I've had more than my share of unbelievably encouraging, noble people in my life. And yet, Dan Enright was one of the most incredible people I've ever known. Let me tell you how I met him.

At that point in time, I was going through a period of searching, not knowing what direction to take in my process of education and learning.

As I thought over the choices I had made, they were all quite major. Four years earlier, I left my lucrative position with *Wheel of Fortune* and grew more than I ever thought possible during an unbelievable year of hardship and testing in Houston. Ministering to cancer patients and their families as they faced the end of life's journey was one of the greatest challenges I've ever faced.

I traveled to many third world countries as an overseas correspondent with American Leprosy Missions, making documentaries in the Philippines, Ethiopia, India, Thailand, and Brazil. The rewarding benefits to my soul will probably never be matched.

I've never felt comfortable charging for ministry, however, and now I was back in Los Angeles, wondering if there might be something for me in television in another capacity.

Sometimes life catches you by surprise. Little did I know it was about to take a wide-angle turn. While my life has been so full in every way imaginable, this new season brought something more than I could have ever dreamed.

—

Two friends, Sammy Davis Jr. and Ray Robbins encouraged me to meet Dan Enright, one of the giants in television game shows. Even though I loved his shows, our paths had never crossed. Since he knew so many people in the business, it was hoped he might have some ideas or know of a possible opening in public relations since that had always been my forte. An appointment was arranged for me to meet with Dan Enright at the Barry & Enright Productions office in Century City.

I didn't know exactly what to expect from the meeting; however, they told me that Mr. Enright was one of the kindest men in this town. Even so, I was nervous as his assistant ushered me into the office.

Mr. Enright stood and offered me a diet cola which he poured himself. I took a couple of sips, trying to settle the butterflies. It had been a long time since I'd been in an actual interview. When his phone rang, I was grateful for the momentary distraction.

As he took the call, I relaxed, looking around the office and noticed that he had good taste. When he finished the conversation, we exchanged basic information. He knew of my work and was very complimentary. I could tell that Dan Enright had a special depth to him. My friends were right—he was very kind.

The phone rang again, and I caught him gazing at me as he tried to focus on his conversation. When I became aware, he would quickly look away. As I watched him take care of business, it was obvious that he was very intelligent, paid attention to detail, and loved his work.

Dan Enright was such a legend in the business. I believe that my former boss, Merv Griffin, and successful producers like Goodson and Todman, the King Brothers, and Dick Clark would agree that Dan was one of the most prolific and successful creators of game shows in television history. He seemed like such a genuine person and even during our short conversation, made me feel at ease.

When our time was up, he walked me to the elevator, and somehow I felt like I was walking on air. My spirits had lifted in just talking to this wonderful man. He took my hand and said, "I can't tell you what a pleasure it has been to meet you, Susan."

I had gone for a professional interview, but now my heart was so full as I recalled his kindness. This was not what I had expected. I drove home and since it was on my way, stopped by to see my dear friends, Sammy Davis Jr. and his wife, Altovise.

While enjoying the typical Davis hospitality, I shared the emotions I was feeling. I realized my heart was holding on to his smile and those gentle eyes. I needed help in sorting it all out.

There is one routine in the entertainment business which we all did several times a day—call our answering service. (This was before we had cell phones and can now be reached at a moment's notice.) When checking messages, one always hopes for a great assignment to come your way, yet it seemed that the messages were often from someone needing *my* help.

I excused myself to call the service and was told I had just one message—from Dan Enright, "Please call as soon as possible."

Sammy was sitting on the couch watching me, with Altovise nearby as I put the phone down.

"He called!" I said.

"Who called?" Sammy and Altovise asked in unison.

"Mr. Enright. He wants me to call him back as soon as possible."

"So call him," Sammy said.

They both stared at me as I dialed the number and waited to be put through.

"Mr. Enright, this is Susan Stafford calling. Are you sure, Mr. . . . . all right, Dan . . . if you insist."

At this point, Sammy started to laugh. I shushed him with my other hand.

"Yes, I enjoyed it too. No, I can't, I'm sorry, I have plans. No, Tuesday's not good. Wednesday? No, I have to study. Thursday? That's my weekly volleyball night at Billie Jean Campbell's. Friday doesn't work either. I've been invited to attend a reunion banquet for those who have worked with Mother Teresa at the leprosariums in India. I promised I would be there. I'm so sorry."

Dan was very gracious and said, "Well, call me when you get hungry and we'll get together."

As I placed the phone back on the cradle, the look on Sammy's face was one of disbelief. "Tell me if I'm wrong, Susan. Did you just turn down a dinner date with Dan Enright?"

"Was that not a good idea?" I asked a little sheepishly.

"Not really," said a serious looking Sammy. "I think you should call him back. You'd be a fool not to take time for Dan Enright."

Altovise chimed in, "Susan, didn't we tell you that Dan is one of the nicest men in this town? He's a classy guy."

—

Sammy flashed that big grin of his and said, "Susan, just trust us. You won't be sorry! What's this India thing you're going to on Friday evening?"

"Mother Teresa's people are in town for a few days and I have to be there."

Sammy held up his hand. "Perfect, perfect. Ask Dan to be your escort. It's exactly the right function to invite him to."

With all this encouragement, I couldn't say no. When I called back, Dan answered quickly. "Feeling hungry already?" he asked.

I started explaining, "It's about Friday, the India gathering for Mother Teresa's people." I don't know why, but I started to speak faster and faster, trying to get my message out before he could say "Get lost lady."

I babbled on, "I wonder if you'd like to come as my escort. I didn't ask before because it's not the kind of affair most people would want to attend. I was with a friend of yours, Sammy Davis Jr. and he said . . . Yes, of course, I'll tell him hello for you . . . You will? Oh, yes, fine, at seven then." I gave him the address in Beverly Hills and we agreed to meet there.

I collapsed back into the folds of the couch. "He said he would be honored to join me on Friday and asked me to say hello to you." Sammy and Altovise were both grinning from ear to ear.

On Friday evening, I drove to the banquet and found that Dan had arrived ten minutes earlier so I wouldn't have to look for him. His thoughtfulness was endearing.

As we mingled with the crowd, Dan asked, "Tell me, how did you become involved with Mother Teresa's people?"

"I visited her clinic in Calcutta."

"You did! What were you doing there, may I ask?"

"Over the past few years, I've been helping out at leper colonies around the world. I worked with former Surgeon General Koop and Merlin Olsen making documentaries to raise money to find the cure. I also worked side by side with the missionaries, changing dressings, administering medicine, and looking after the children. It's a devastating disease."

We moved on through the crowded room . . . an introduction here . . . stopping to sample various types of Indian food there.

"How long were you in India?"

"The first time, I was there about four weeks. The next time, it was three months."

"I'm very impressed, Susan, more than you know!" he said. Just then, I noticed one of Mother Teresa's nuns sitting quietly by herself. I introduced Dan to her, and he knelt down beside her chair to talk.

Now it was *my* turn to be impressed. None of the other men I had known would have thought of doing that. I could tell Dan's consideration was genuine.

From watching him, it was obvious that each person was equally important to Dan, whether dignitaries at the function or waiters serving the food. He treated everyone with the same caring attitude. That was just his style.

After talking to some friends of Rev. Terry Sweeney, I turned around, wondering where Dan was. I saw him by the swinging door to the kitchen, helping a waitress who'd accidentally dropped a platter of appetizers.

This was not a typical date by any means, and by the end of the evening, I was enthralled with this man. He walked me to my car, kissed me on the forehead, and wished me a good night.

"I'll call you tomorrow," he said, softly closing my car door. "Thanks for a most wonderful evening."

Dan called five times the next day. My heart was jumping. This was the gallant knight I never expected to actually meet. In the days, weeks, months, and years that followed, we never let a day go by without talking to each other, no matter where we were.

Before moving on, I have to share something about Sammy Davis Jr. and Altovise. Their home was always open to so many in the industry, and we had become very good friends. The social events were fun to share, however our discussions were more on major issues of the day. Sammy even hosted an interview/confrontation show for Dan with celebrities and politicians which was quite wonderful—*Close Up with Sammy Davis Jr.*

When Sammy was so ill with throat cancer, he only wanted to see a handful of people. It became obvious that things were not going to improve, and I'm so grateful I was able to use the experience gained in caring for cancer patients to help during this critical time. When doctors told Sammy the cancer had spread and nothing more could be done, all he really wanted was to be at home in his own surroundings. Altovise had been told this was not possible.

Knowing my way around hospitals by now, I explained to Sammy that he could sign himself out. We handled it very discreetly to avoid photographers and were able to honor his wish to go home. It was a special privilege to be of help when Sammy just wanted to die with dignity in his own bed.

When Sammy passed on, I offered to stay at the house while everyone went to the funeral (Apparently that's when houses get robbed, especially celebrity homes; and besides, I'd been to so many funerals, I needed a break from graveside ceremonies. Too many close friends had been lost).

I tidied up the kitchen and helped lay out food for the returning guests. I made sure each bathroom had extra toilet paper rolls and checked the living room to see that everything was in place. I noticed a coffee stain on the carpet and got a bowl of warm water and a brush from the kitchen. I was on my hands and knees scrubbing away when I happened to look up and saw a crowd of black faces looking down at me. "Things have sure changed," I said as we all enjoyed a hearty laugh.

After my first date with Dan (May 17, 1986) and many, many phone calls later, I asked if he'd go to Hollywood Presbyterian church with me one Sunday. It was a little awkward because I knew Dan was Jewish, however I had to ask because going to church was an important part of my life.

"Sure," he said, "but I haven't been in a church for a long time. I need to ask you a question first." He sounded quite nervous.

"I'm sorry, Dan. One's religion is a very personal matter and . . ."

"It has nothing to do with my religion, but thanks for the thought. It's quite simple."

"Okay," I said, waiting for the bomb to drop.

"Do I have to wear a tie? I'm not good with ties."

We laughed as I told him of course not. I wanted him to be comfortable.

During our second evening together, Dan told me that he was legally separated and all the warning bells went off. For my own peace of mind and my allegiance to God's will, I would have to stop seeing this incredible man. I was already responding to Dan's loving ways and was happy merely to be in the same room.

Breaking it off now would save everyone a great deal of pain. There was no way I wanted to go through another bout of such personal pain. I wanted to say my farewell graciously and make the parting as pleasant as possible. Would that mean saying good-bye to my dreams as well? In this short time, he had already captured my heart.

Dan was living at the Beverly Hillcrest Hotel while the Santa Monica property he purchased was being renovated. He had booked a quiet corner booth for our dinner that evening.

"Dan," I said as softly as I could. "We have to talk."

"About?" he asked gently, surely knowing what was coming.

"You . . . me . . . your wife. We've become so close in the short time we've known each other, but it's uncomfortable to even think about starting a relationship when you aren't really free. It's especially difficult for me because of my Christian beliefs."

There was quite a long pause as we looked at each other.

"Susan," he said, "Stella and I have been apart for a very long time, over twelve years now, and she's a wonderful woman. Sadly, she has Parkinson's disease, for which there is no recovery. She shared in my success and stood by me during the most difficult times after the *Twenty One* game show scandal. She was so loyal, and I will always respect her for that. That's why I never got a divorce. It's a moral obligation I have to fulfill, taking care of her as well as I can."

I nodded, my heart going out to this man who cared so deeply. I felt for Mrs. Enright too, making me love Dan even more for being so honorable toward her. I didn't want to hurt her either.

Dan held my hand and said, "I want more than anything to be with you, but of course, it's your choice as to whether we continue to see each other. I've fallen in love with you and will always adore you, no matter what you decide. If you need more time to think it over, that's fine. If you feel you have to end this right now, I will have to accept that. I just want you to know that whatever you decide, I will love you forever."

There was a long pause. This was not going to be easy. I couldn't help thinking, *I've met the most perfect of men and it's all about to fall apart.*

"Does Stella know about me being in your life?" I asked.

"Yes, we had a long discussion about you a few nights ago."

I hesitantly asked . . . "What did she say?"

"She said she was happy for me."

"She did?"

"Stella truly cares about me, Susan. We've weathered a lot of storms for a very long time. Even though we shared a special love and have two children together, things have changed over time. She admits that. On the other hand, she doesn't want me to be miserable for the rest of my life, and I don't want Stella to be unhappy either."

---

I was stunned. Dan had laid all his cards on the table, face up.

I was very touched, "She sounds like a remarkable lady. I would like to meet Stella if it's okay with you."

He said, "I would like the two of you to meet when she's up to it." (Unfortunately, Stella and I never met until years later at Dan's memorial)

As the restaurant was getting ready to close, we weren't nearly finished with our conversation and Dan asked me to come upstairs. I hesitated only a moment, totally aware of the deep feelings we shared. I was already falling in love with this most wonderful man and I never wanted to be apart from him. It felt like a giant magnet was drawing me to his side and yet I knew I wasn't going to give my body because I wanted Dan forever, not just for a night.

When we entered the hotel room that he called home, he motioned for me to have a seat on the sofa while he sat on a chair nearby. We were both a little nervous, making conversation, but nothing of any importance. I looked at the clock, knowing it would soon be "bed time" and wondering if he was going to be the typical man. A few minutes later, Dan got up and went to the dresser. Opening a drawer, he took out a pair of his long pajamas and handed them to me.

He said, "I just want you to be comfortable. I'm going to the restroom so you can have some privacy. Just yell when you've changed."

As I quickly undressed and jumped into the pajamas, I heard Dan say, "Being close to you at my age is more important than anything, Susan. Go ahead and get under the covers. I won't offend your honor or your faith."

When Dan came in, he was still fully clothed. He smiled at me as he walked around the bed and sat on *top* of the bedspread, placing a pillow behind his head. I have never known anyone more respectful. He pulled the covers up to my chin and began humming "Hush little baby, don't say a word, mama's gonna buy you a mocking bird" . . . He said it was a lullaby his mother used to sing to him which he also sang to his children. And then he held me, just held me, as I realized how very safe I felt in his arms.

Corny as it may sound in today's world, our relationship was not about sex. Dan and I enjoyed a love and devotion, as pure as I have ever known. Dan was the love of my life and we cherished every moment we were together. In previous relationships, I might have had stronger feelings for the man than he did for me or vice versa. With Danny, the feelings we shared were mutual with a level of caring and unconditional

—

love that I have only known from my mother. It was truly the highest *earthly* experience that I could only imagine before. Feeling as I did and knowing how he felt, it was not possible to walk away from the dearest man I knew.

Dan and I had been seeing each other for three months, and I still had not been to his Penthouse in Santa Monica. I felt that once I actually stepped inside his home, a full-time commitment to Dan was inevitable. And when that happened, I would be saying good-bye to my ministry. No matter how right we felt about our relationship, Dan was still legally separated. The bottom line was—he was not free to marry and I could not live with him outside of wedlock.

One Sunday, Dan and I went to services at Hollywood Presbyterian Church before Pastor Lloyd Ogilvie left to become chaplain of the senate. Afterward, we went to Greenblatts, my favorite deli. I love the owner, Jeff, and his mom and dad, not to mention the great food.

*With Dan Enright*

As Dan drove me back to my place, I made a deal with him. I said, "You come with me to Kansas City to meet my folks, and I'll come and see your Penthouse."

Dan, being who he was, turned the car around with a gleam in his eye.

"Where are we going?" I asked, surprised at the sudden U-turn across the double yellow lines.

"To visit your mom and dad. You can call them from the airport as I'm getting the tickets and tell them we're on our way," he said, driving up the ramp to the San Diego freeway.

"Suppose there isn't a flight to Kansas City this afternoon?"

"There will be. And if there isn't, we'll just wait for the next one. Don't worry. We'll get there. I don't know Kansas City very well. Do you think your dad can call to reserve a couple of rooms for us? I don't want to have your parents go to any trouble."

Dan went to arrange the flight, and I called Mama and Daddy.

"Daddy, it's Susan. I have to tell you, I've finally met the right man!" My dad started chuckling. "I think I've heard *that* before."

"No, really, Daddy. We're on our way to see you . . . yes, now! We're at the airport in Los Angeles and . . ."

Dan hurried over, waving the tickets at me. "We arrive in Kansas City tonight at . . ." Dan held up nine fingers. "9 PM. You will? That's great! I have a favor to ask. Can you make reservations at a hotel for us? What? Are you sure? That'll be wonderful! Okay, Daddy, got to go. See you there."

As I hung up the phone, Dan asked, "Everything okay?"

"Yes, Mama and Daddy are thrilled we're coming, and they insisted we stay with them at the house."

As we rushed to the gate hand in hand, there was just time to reach the gate before takeoff. We are all so used to the security measures after 9/11. It's amazing to recall how easy it used to be to catch a plane at the last minute.

We quickly collected our boarding passes and were seated at the back of the plane before it finally sank in. "We don't have any luggage!" I said. "Just the clothes we're wearing."

Dan hugged my arm and began to sing, "We're off to see the Wizard, the wonderful Wizard of Oz. And don't worry about clothes. I'm sure you have something hidden away in an old wardrobe at home."

"What about you?" I asked.

"I'll go into town tomorrow and buy a couple of shirts. Now that the luggage problem is solved, let's eat."

In the rush to get on the plane, I hadn't noticed that Dan had a small paper sack with him. Somehow, he'd found a moment to buy a couple of sandwiches and blueberry muffins. "This will keep us going until the plastic food arrives."

Daddy had always said if my heart went with my head, that would be perfect. This time, even my dad was won over, not by someone trying to impress him, but by Dan's genuine nature. His rapport with Mama and Daddy was immediate, and made my joy even more complete.

We stayed two nights with my folks. Mama was impressed the first morning when she saw Dan making his bed. I was still asleep when he began helping her with the dishes. He didn't just offer, he pitched right in. That kind of consideration really speaks to a mother's heart.

Between going for walks, talking to some of the neighbors, and eating, Dan and my dad had some long discussions out on the back porch about the obvious.

Just as Dan had interviewed me that day at his Century City office, Daddy was now doing the same thing with Dan. He'd seen me get hurt before, usually because I didn't think things through. Now, the man of my dreams was sitting out there in one of the family rockers, and my dad wanted to be sure in his own mind that this "man from television" was going to take good care of his youngest daughter.

Daddy told me later that during his heart-to-heart with Dan, the subject of Stella came up. Dan was very upfront and freely explained the situation. He also said he loved me very much and wanted to take care of me forever. He told my folks they would never have to worry about me again.

Dan must have passed the test with Daddy, because on our last night, they took us to the best restaurant in town. Mama, Dan, and I toasted each other with Diet Coke and Daddy had orange juice. He had been "dry" for almost fifteen years. I was never more proud of my dad than when I found out he'd stopped drinking, and now all these years later, he'd kept his promise not to touch it again. I had tears in my eyes as they wished us well for the future. I had never been happier than that moment; and I knew somehow, the Lord would understand.

On our flight home, I realized it was time to keep my part of the deal. I agreed to drive down to Santa Monica the next day, we'd have lunch together and then the big moment—Dan would show me his Penthouse. As we drove to my place, Dan started to sing one of his Yiddish lullabies and I fell asleep.

The next thing I knew, we were driving into an underground parking garage. As I started to wake up, Dan helped me out of the car. "Where are we?" I asked, trying to clear my head.

"Home," he whispered, steering me toward the elevator. Dan guided me inside and the doors softly closed. He inserted a key in a special slot marked PH and pushed the button.

"I thought we weren't going to do this until tomorrow."

"We weren't," he said. "but you were fast asleep and I decided to swing by here since it was on the way back. It's a little embarrassing. I need a bathroom and I don't think I could have lasted all the way to your apartment."

As the elevator arrived at the Penthouse level, the doors opened and we stepped into the alcove. The rooms were still being remodeled and Dan said, "Let's go and look at the view." He led me through the living room and out onto the balcony. It was the most stupendous view of the "necklace" from Santa Monica. (The "necklace" is the curve of lights that runs all the way south from Malibu to Palos Verdes.)

—

I was so carried away with the magic of this moment in time that I never noticed Dan had rushed inside to the bathroom, until he was on his way out again.

"I have to tell you something," I said softly. "I've been here before."

Dan took a step back, looking at me closely. "You have?"

"Yes. About two and a half years ago. A friend of mine, Bob Marlin, owned this Penthouse. I gave a party for him and on this very balcony; I said a prayer for someone like you!"

"You mean you were here? Right here?"

"Right here on this balcony. It just goes to show that if you pray hard enough, dreams can come true."

I knew this was the beginning of a special life with a man of quality and decency. We held each other close. Two people on top of the world, "our world" now, with breathtaking views in every direction. I knew in my heart that I was meant to be with this man, even if it would not be in the conventional way I had hoped.

*With Dan on our Penthouse deck*

We discussed the fact that Dan was not legally free to marry me. While that was difficult to face, the compassion we both felt for Stella superseded any selfish desire on our part. She was older now and dealing with Parkinson's. While it would be wonderful to marry the man I loved, I could not in good conscience make her life more difficult. I realized there would be problems to face down the line, but they could wait for now.

As we attended many professional and social dinners together, Dan noticed that I was contributing not only some good ideas, I was also helping bridge the gap with clients and his staff as well. Networking was a natural for me and Dan hired me as vice president of Public Relations for Barry & Enright Productions. I would have gladly helped him without the title or position, but it was also nice to have my abilities acknowledged.

When I decided to get my Ph.D., this is a portion of the letter of recommendation Dan wrote on my behalf—*At Barry & Enright, Ms. Stafford's primary function is the liaison with our clients, writers, directors and performers; for the most part, they are people who bruise easily and whose egos are somewhat frail. Thus, her work requires the constant exercise of enormous tact and delicate sensitivity. She has performed flawlessly, always with unflagging zeal and drive.*

*When I received my Ph.D. in Clinical Psychology, we had a special celebration.*

*L-R My personal asst., Tammy; Sandy Martin; Dan Enright and Stevi Goetz.*

Sandy Martin is undoubtedly one of the smartest women I've ever known with a personality similar to Ellen DeGeneres. When Dan offered her a job working with him, Sandy said she could never leave her home in Kansas City. I've always felt that true friends like Sandy remain in your heart forever.

One of the most attractive things about Dan Enright was his humility. He was not at all pretentious. As I looked closely at one of his framed pictures, I was astonished. "Danny, that's Golda Meir! Who is the man with her?" He told me matter-of-factly, that it was his father.

"Long before she was well-known, her name was Golda Mabovitch. She grew up in Russia and lived in Milwaukee. When she moved to Palestine, that young lady was my father's secretary."

*Golda Meir with her boss who happened to be Dan's father*

"But, Danny, why didn't you tell me?"

He said, "You never asked."

I also learned that many years later when Golda Meir was prime minister of Israel, she contacted Dan and had him come to set up television programming for the state of Israel.

A few months after Dan and I started seeing each other, I moved to Unit 203 in his building so we could spend as much time together as possible. My parents came to visit us in Santa Monica in 1987. Dan was wonderful to them and they adored him. They knew how happy he made me, and Mama told me she could die in peace now because I had finally found the love of my life. She was certainly right about that.

One of Mama's favorite actors was Dick Van Patten. We invited Dick and Patty, Jimmy Hawkins, and my sister Catherine to join us for dinner at a Chinese restaurant called Genghis Cohen one evening. We were having such an enjoyable time when all of a sudden, Mama slumped over in her chair and started to fall. She was sitting beside me, and I immediately eased her to the floor and felt for a pulse. Dan told the waitress to call 911 while I started CPR. Jimmy was beside me trying to tell me how to hold her nose. When the paramedics arrived, they ripped open her blouse to work on her. Catherine and I looked up to see a crowd around us and quickly got a tablecloth to hold around her. Mama had always been very modest. I rode with her in the ambulance while the others followed.

Although she was pronounced dead on arrival, they kept working with her. Danny talked to Dr. Geft, her Jewish doctor in Hebrew and I could tell from his expression that things did not look good. We spent the night at the hospital and were told her chances were very slim.

I knew Mama would have to die someday, but I wasn't ready to let her go, not then. I pleaded with God to give her more time with us. Mama was my best friend, and I counted on her unconditional love. The Lord answered that prayer, and the doctors were able to do a quintuple bypass. My brothers and sisters all came, and it was a special bonding time for all of us. What a gift it was when Mama woke up and saw all seven of her chicks standing at her bedside.

My friends were very kind as well. Murray Schwartz made a special visit to bring Mama a new pair of tennis shoes. He knew it was important for her to have good support when she started walking. We were all touched by his thoughtfulness.

*Mama*

When Mama was released from the hospital, she was very weak, and Dan and I arranged for them to stay in a cottage at the Miramar Hotel across the street from us. It meant so much to be able to see her and Daddy every day and talk about all that had happened in her life. A couple of months later, when she was strong enough, they went back to Missouri, and she continued to take things easy. Daddy was good to her and she had my sister Chloe and my brother Georgie living nearby. They came to see her often and her next-door neighbor Pat Gaskin was always willing to pick up groceries, fix her hair, and help with whatever she needed.

About six months after her surgery, Dan came to my apartment one morning about 10:00. Dan always left about 5:30 every morning for work, and I didn't see him until dinnertime. When he walked in the door, I knew something was wrong. He didn't say a word, just looked at me with sad eyes.

I asked, "Is it my mother?"

Dan just nodded his head.

After seeing the look on his face, I dropped to my knees, thanking God that she was now with Him.

Dan took me in his arms as I realized the day I had been dreading was finally here. My brother, Georgie had called Dan to tell me so I didn't have to hear the news over the phone. Mama had been very tired the night before when she went to bed. Her heart gave out and she never woke up. While I was grateful she went peacefully, I missed her so. For a long time, something would happen that I wanted to share and I automatically reached for the phone to call her. I knew I would see her again in Heaven, but not being able to hear Mama's sweet voice with that Boston accent was so hard for me.

Daddy was depressed living in Missouri without Mama. They had been married for over fifty years and had survived some rocky times and loved each other very much. Dan and I decided to have Daddy live in my apartment and I moved to the Penthouse guest room. Daddy made friends with Ralph and Viola Ives and Milton and Ruth Firestone in our building, talked politics, and wrote brilliant letters to the editor and to congressmen. It meant everything to have him with us, and it gave him a new lease on life as well.

We had a couple more years together before Daddy got liver cancer. My brothers and sisters came so we could all spend quality time with him. A special thanks to Diane Weissburg for donating blood to my dad during this crucial time.

*With Dan and my dad celebrating Chanukah*
*at the home of my friend, Stevi Goetz*

We knew the time was short. My dad was always thinking ahead to the future. I remember three things he told me on his death bed that he believed would happen in my lifetime. 1. Social Security would run out (that's certainly been in the news a lot). 2. The twin towers in New York would be attacked. 3. We would eventually have a Hispanic president.

When he died in 1991, it was the middle of the night with me holding him in my arms and Dan close beside us, getting a little sleep on the couch before work. Catherine was on the other couch and Tammy was resting in the recliner.

Dan was such a comfort during these most difficult times. He always knew what to say. There were times I needed to be alone with my thoughts and other moments when I just needed him to hold me.

Dan was very supportive of my charity work, and together we became co-presidents of the Chabad Chai Circle which was a special honor for us. We also worked in Mid-East Communications along with Casey Kasem, trying to improve relations among those who had a common heritage. There has been such division because both groups claim the Holy Land of Jerusalem as their own. It was a real education for me and stimulated my thinking even more as I've had the privilege of working in Israel in recent years.

In 1990, one of Dan's greatest thrills was winning an Emmy as executive producer of the Hallmark Hall of Fame movie *Caroline?* which was produced by his son, Don and his partner, Les Alexander. Accepting the Emmy was such a *wonderful* highlight for him.

*Dan Enright and I, Mr. & Mrs. Les Alexander, Mr. & Mrs. Don Enright*

The day we learned Dan had lung cancer, October 7, 1991, was a devastating one. When we were given the news late that afternoon, we looked at each other and Danny said, "let's enjoy every minute we have left. It will be a great party tonight." We were hosting a fundraiser that evening and never thought once of canceling. The benefit was to honor Sammy Davis, Jr. and raise money for kidney research.

I've found that everyone handles this life-changing news in their own way, and we were determined to make the most of each day we had together. Dan's wonderful attitude was more than uplifting to me. His concern was always to give me the care and protection he had provided since the beginning of our relationship. We didn't tell anyone right away about his diagnosis and that evening, no one had any idea. It hardly seemed real to me. I watched him a lot that night, thinking how I could never, ever let him go and then reminding myself how truly blessed I was to have had him at all.

Dan always had boundless energy and he wasn't going to let this defeat him. His courage was remarkable! He was still the first one out on the floor to dance when he heard Israeli folk music. Dan found so much joy in life. Someone once said, "Don't die until you're dead" and Dan was a wonderful example to all of us. Each weekend, as long as he was able, Dan continued his 50-mile bicycle trips from Santa Monica through Venice Beach to Marina Del Rey and back.

I served as President of the homeowner's association in our building. Anyone who has been involved in an HOA knows what a challenge it can be. It was difficult to go through the lobby or get on the elevator without someone sharing a complaint. The board meetings got heated at times, especially when I mentioned a concern that there may be two sets of books and we needed to clean house. At the end of that meeting, someone spoke up and said that I had no business serving as President since I wasn't really a homeowner. I said goodnight with all the grace I could muster and went upstairs to the Penthouse. I didn't want to bother Dan with this. I was having enough trouble processing it myself.

The next morning as Dan was leaving for work; one of the board members saw him in the elevator and said, "It's too bad about Susan."

Dan asked, "What do you mean?"

The man said, "Didn't she tell you about being dismissed as President last night? While Susan lives in the Penthouse, she has no ownership here."

Dan went to the office and within an hour, he came back and handed me the deed that he had drawn up 4 years earlier, giving me half of the Penthouse. Not only was I surprised, I felt so honored that he would do this. Dan was proud of my being President and knew I took it very seriously. It gave me such satisfaction to make copies of the deed and distribute it to all the board members. I can't tell you how much I loved Dan for his consideration and for vindicating me in this way. I resumed my position without any further discussion.

During the last year of Dan's life, the business started to lose ground and he needed more funds to stay in operation. It was a joy to deed my half of the Penthouse back to Dan so he could refinance and have what he needed. I think he appreciated that decision as much as I did his generosity.

Up at 4:00 a.m., Dan was the first patient scheduled each morning for radiation at St. John's, where he always brought muffins for the staff. After his treatment, he went straight to his office to work a long, full day.

*One of the few times Dan wore a tie*

The riots hit Los Angeles right after the Rodney King verdict, followed soon afterward by an earthquake. It was a frightening time, and I remember so clearly running to Dan's room. As we held each other, we talked about how much easier it would be if we could go together right then.

---

Facing the imminent loss of someone you love so dearly has to be one of the most unbelievable challenges on this earth. Each day was so precious. Dan lived eight months after the doctors predicted it could be three. He showed me what true courage is in the face of our last enemy, death. I want to say a special thanks to the doctors who were so very kind and caring to us—Dr. Chuck MacElroy, Dr. David David, Dr. Emil Soorani and Dr. Don Ha. How I thank the Lord for allowing me to spend the last years of Dan's life with such an amazing man.

In today's world, it seems the public has learned to wink at scandal. It has become so commonplace that we tend to accept the abnormal as normal. A headline in 1954 caught everyone's attention: *Crooked Producer Cheats With Quiz Show*. You might be interested in some facts that are not widely known about that story.

Dan Enright was born in New York to Russian Jewish parents and raised in British Palestine. As a young man, he rode for miles, transporting guns on his bicycle for the Haganah, the Jewish underground army. After returning to the United States and graduating from RCA Institute, he worked as an engineer for Westinghouse. At the company's exhibit at the 1939 World's Fair, Dan was among the first to work in the new medium of television. After marrying Stella, the girl next door, he enlisted as a lieutenant in the U.S. Army during the Second World War and was stationed in Dover, England, where he commanded a radar station.

In 1947, Dan met Jack Barry at WOR Radio in New York and with fearless determination; they became legendary radio and television producers. In the 1950s, they created and produced very successful shows like *Tic Tac Dough, Joker's Wild, Juvenile Jury, Bumper Stumpers,* and *Winky Dink And You*, the first interactive show on television. (I'm currently working on a revival of *Winky Dink* with Ed Wyckoff and my friend, Ron Schneider. I know Dan would be pleased.) By 1953, Barry & Enright Productions had six network shows on at the same time.

Unfortunately, Dan is remembered not as much for those accomplishments as for the quiz show scandal involving *Twenty One*. The show became a sensation as families were glued to their television sets to see what would happen next. In 1957, *Twenty One* became the first regular series to beat *I Love Lucy*.

As Dan explained the situation to me, the show actually started out with low ratings. Since making money for the sponsors and networks is key to any show's success, something had to be done. Geritol and the NBC president ordered Dan to "do whatever it takes" to make the show more exciting. Dan was very creative and he found a way to send the show over the top. Thanks to Dan and his close friend, producer Al Freedman, the success of the show exceeded all expectations.

During contestant interviews, Dan selected a working-class man who was very bright, but unknown to the public. Dan made Herbert Stempel into an exceptional character on-screen. He became an overnight celebrity, however the fame carried a price tag.

As the plans were laid out, Dan told Stempel he would be a big winner; but eventually, he would have to miss a question and lose. Herb agreed to the arrangement because winning money on the show would help him out of a financial difficulty. Dan said he gave Stempel $100,000 in cash up front which was a fortune in the fifties.

To build excitement for the audience, Dan turned the air-conditioning off in the soundproof booth so that the contestant's sweat was real! He coached Herb to use certain mannerisms, patting his forehead with a handkerchief, looking up at the ceiling, or closing his eyes as he struggled to come up with the right answer.

Dan choreographed dramatic pauses while the audience held their breath, week after week, waiting to see if Stempel could answer correctly. Since Dan had gone over the questions and answers with Stempel, he was able to win each round. Dan even went to Stempel's home and chose a crumpled brown suit from his closet to make him look a little eccentric.

The show was a big hit, and it changed *everything* for Stempel on the home front. Not only was he becoming rich in the process, his wife had come to admire him once again, and he bought her the mink coat she had always wanted. Neighbors who had basically ignored him prior to the show now called out his name and waved when they saw him on the street. Stempel was enjoying every moment of his newfound success.

But Dan knew he had to implement his original plan. To continue the drama and keep people's attention for the long run, it was time for the audience to cheer for a new winner.

When contestant, Charles Van Doren entered the scene, Dan knew he had his man. Van Doren was the opposite of Stempel. He was a handsome, Ivy League professor from one of the most prominent literary families in the country. His father, Mark Van Doren, won a Pulitzer Prize for poetry and his late uncle Carl, won the Pulitzer Prize for his biography on Benjamin Franklin. Dan knew that having someone of this caliber as the new winner would boost the ratings even more.

Dan called Stempel into his office and told him the time had come for him to lose as they had agreed. With his newfound fame, it's not surprising that Stempel was resistant. Even though he tried to convince Dan to let him win a little longer, Dan's focus had to be on the ratings. Unfortunately, the question Stempel was instructed to answer incorrectly had to do with his favorite movie, *Marty*. He was angry about knowing the answer so well and having to act like he didn't.

When Stempel reluctantly gave the wrong answer and Charles Van Doren won, the audience went wild. Van Doren was in the limelight now and drew unprecedented fan mail as the tension mounted each week with challengers trying to top him. Van Doren was very knowledgeable and coaching him on the answers was hardly necessary. The eligible bachelor, Van Doren, received countless marriage proposals and ratings skyrocketed.

In the meantime, it didn't take long for Stempel's world to crumble. His wife and family were upset with him. How could he miss such a simple question? He heard them say that he wasn't as brilliant as they had thought after all. He was no longer his wife's hero. The neighbors were ignoring him again, and the fall he had agreed to take became too much to bear. We've all heard that "what goes up, must come down", and that is just what happened.

Stempel called Dan, asking to come back on the show once again as a contestant. Dan tried to gently dissuade him. When Dan did not comply with his request, Stempel asked for a job on the show. Dan had been very good to Herb and yet he knew there would never be a *good* time for him to leave. When he realized Herb was not going to let it go, Dan arranged and paid for him to see a psychologist to help with the transition. While Dan did what he could to help, he had the television network by the tail and needed to keep building the ratings.

For Stempel, *nothing* could match the fulfillment he had achieved on the show. Dan had befriended Herb, spent time in their home, and lifted him to national prominence. Now he had been shown up by someone who already lived a privileged life. The *only* thing that would have satisfied Herb was another shot on the show.

As his phone calls went unanswered, a disgruntled Herb Stempel wanted revenge. All of the financial help Dan had given was quickly forgotten. Herb went to the authorities and told them what was going on behind the scenes. He revealed how contestants were coached and given answers before the show. One of Dan's favorite lines became, "Don't bet on anything that talks."

At first, a deaf ear was turned to Stempel's allegations. Then, a contestant from *Dotto*, Edward Hilgemeier Jr. reported that one of his opponents had been given answers before the show. Another contestant, James Snodgrass, had mailed registered letters to himself about the outcome of the shows along with the answers. This proved that the shows were fixed . . . not just Dan's, but several others as well. Game show scandals became headline news and were the topic of discussion both in boardrooms and at the water coolers.

Dan had felt great pressure to take the show to the top and keep the edge of excitement going. Only a handful of people knew what was going on. Even though the host, Dan's business partner, Jack Barry, had been kept in the dark, I'm sure he felt the pressure and tension.

When the story broke, the shockwave caught everyone in its path. *Twenty One* was cancelled with NBC and Geritol pointing the finger at Dan Enright while they denied any knowledge of his actions.

Charles Van Doren went down in disgrace and his distinguished family suffered great embarrassment, which as I understand, they still do. Under the appearance of truth, with all the presumed safeguards, the trusting public realized they had been duped.

A grand jury in New York was assembled to investigate. No actual *law* had been broken, so there was no legal punishment. At the time, there were no official rules against giving answers to contestants or prompting them. The resulting uproar, however, led to the establishment of "Rules and Compliances" which we later took very seriously on *Wheel of Fortune* and all the other game shows did as well.

The agony of being involved was tremendous; and almost all of the contestants including Van Doren, committed perjury by saying they did not cheat. Later, during the congressional hearing, Van Doren admitted to participating. The result is that Congress made fixing game shows a federal crime.

Dan never forgave himself for the hurt he had caused. His focus with great pressure from the network and sponsors had been the ratings—first and last. Dan now realized he had taken a man's life and molded it for certain purposes, only to pull the rug out from Stempel when he was at the pinnacle of private and public acclaim. Dan accepted full personal responsibility for the fiasco, thus shielding several highly respected people who should have shared the blame.

Dan's valiant wife, Stella, stood staunchly by him during the uproar, while their son and daughter had to endure their own trials from mocking schoolmates. Dan told me that Don and Erica went from being some of the most popular kids of the top television producer, to being outcasts among their friends.

Here's the grim irony—when Congress investigated the "crime" of coaching quiz show contestants, the committee members met with Dan before his testimony. Why? To guide him in giving the "correct answers" during the hearings. There is something terribly wrong with that scenario which was of course, not public knowledge. Will someone please tell me how that is different from what Dan did on *Twenty One*?

After the humiliation of being forced to leave Hollywood, Dan still needed to make a living for his family. For the next fifteen years, he produced many shows in Canada and Australia, one of them the popular *Sea Hunt* with Lloyd Bridges which we all loved.

When he was finally able to return to the United States in 1975, Barry & Enright started production again. Dan was associated with 240 game shows, reality shows, and movies. They were once more very successful with the game show format and also movies of the week. They moved their headquarters from New York to Los Angeles. And when Jack Barry passed away in 1984, Dan kept the Barry & Enright name out of respect for his partner and the success continued.

I was in the studio with Dan 25 years later and saw his sincere remorse as he freely admitted his role in the scandal on *Larry King Live* and *Memories*. Larry couldn't have been nicer during the interview.

Dan's exile and return is not the end of the story by any means. Even though almost forty years had passed since the game show scandals, they waited until Dan was no longer alive to make a movie about it.

Enter Robert Redford, a fine actor and director whom I had always admired. It was 1994, two years after Dan died when I heard about his plans to direct *Quiz Show* about the *Twenty One* game show scandal. I sent a letter by FedEx to Mr. Redford on May 27th at his shooting location in New York, with a copy to Sundance Studios in Idaho. Here is what I wrote:

*Dear Mr. Redford,*

    *I am delighted to hear that you are directing the feature film, Quiz Show. Your project deals with a gentleman who I had the joy of sharing my life and love with during the last six years of his time on earth. I am speaking of Dan Enright.*

    *Knowing you are a man who is interested in both sides of a story, and above all, the truth, I am enclosing a few obituaries and bios which appeared in the media following Dan's death. I also have the last notes dictated by Dan before he passed away, stating his involvement with the Quiz Show scandals, the Congressional hearings and his life after the ordeal when for 15 long years, Dan could not get a job in America.*

    *To say I am eager to see this film come to the screen is an understatement. It is my hope that the truth behind the scandal and the lives of everyone involved, will be presented in the most honest and realistic manner.*

With Dan no longer alive to defend himself, all I wanted was a disclaimer so the film would not misrepresent the Dan Enright I had come to know and love. He was not a heartless manipulator who cared little for the contestants, he was a man of decency and compassion who in his lifetime, helped infinitely more people than he hurt.

The people on the show who willingly went along with his scheme ended up with a lot of money in their pockets. Wasn't their integrity compromised like Dan's?

When *Quiz Show* opened, Charles Van Doren refused to give an interview, even when approached by Barbara Walters, "The New York Times," and *60 Minutes*. He took a job at Encyclopedia Britannica as a fact checker and has never spoken about it publicly until recently I've been told.

The truth is that in the industry, Dan Enright was known for his supreme kindness and generosity. So many have told me that in this town noted for giving attention and applause to whoever is hot at the moment, Dan took time for those who were down on their luck.

—

He provided second chances to some whose careers were faltering and extended generous loans which he readily forgave when friends and associates were unable to repay. Dan was tireless in his desire to provide good entertainment and was the most creative man I have ever known.

Unfortunately, Redford never replied and the slant of *Quiz Show* only revealed the negative aspects. Apparently, facts don't matter as long as you can sell tickets. Dan's son, Don, got his viewpoint on public record in the *Los Angeles Times* on September 19, 1994, in this letter about Redford's film:

> *When the quiz show scandal broke, my sister was 10 years old and I was eight. Almost overnight, our lives changed. As the producer of the wildly popular Twenty One—and five other network shows—our father had been the toast of the industry. As his bright, well behaved children, we had enjoyed a modest school yard notoriety. But now our father had become a villain, excoriated everywhere as the living symbol of all that was wrong in this country. And many kids were no longer allowed to play with me.*
>
> *Many other kids—and many adults—were for years, just casually nasty. Of course, watching my father go down, I was taught more about social cruelty. Among many other things, I learned to have a healthy skepticism for the official story. Yes, Dan Enright fixed his quiz shows, but shows had been fixed since the beginning of quiz show history. As I saw my father take the fall—and watched so many others, equally culpable, scurry away free—I learned much, since confirmed about public executions and more about sanctimonious hypocrisy.*
>
> *And now life has brought us Quiz Show, the movie. Written by a former film critic, who calls it his "revenge on television" and based on the memoirs of its hero, a young congressional investigator, the film is explicitly intended as a morality lesson. It was produced and directed by Robert Redford. "The film raises the question of ethics," he told the New York Times. "Are they going to keep the concept of ethics, or will it disappear from the language, like* **'shame'**?" *Someone needs to give the answer to Mr. Redford.*
>
> *While in interviews, Redford admits to changing some facts, on the screen, Quiz Show is explicitly represented to be a true story. It*

*uses real names in its promotion and it uses real faces. At the same time, the movie carries none of the fictional content disclaimers. Not even at the very end in tiny letters. No, Redford hands down his movie as revealed truth, re-created. But it's not.* Quiz Show, *the movie, is rigged. Fixed. Just like its counterpart. And for precisely the same reason. Played straight, the story would be much more dramatically complicated and much more morally convenient.*

*The truth is that Redford has sacrificed truth—not to say decency—to make his show more dramatic, more compelling and ultimately a more successful product for mass entertainment. Precisely the same offense for which they once, quite properly, condemned Dan Enright. But the irony is lost on Robert Redford.*

*His fix is in the opening titles—a flamboyant sequence portrayed as part of* Twenty One, *but actually lifted from a rival program. People will ask, "Does it matter? Does that really change anything?" I don't know. Maybe not. Perhaps it doesn't matter that Redford creates scenes from whole cloth, drastically alters the sequence of events, forever transforms my father and his associates into maligned caricatures, offensive and unrecognizable. The man who, as deputy district attorney, really investigated* Twenty One *has told the New York Times that this film is a "tawdry hoax" and that much of its portrayal of Dan Enright—bribing the court to suppress evidence, tricking a contestant into rigging—is wholly fictitious. Yet apparently, as a media certified public moralist, Redford qualifies for an unrestricted license. Because though I have video tape in my office of the actual show episode that Redford dramatizes in his movie, so far, nobody has asked to see it. Maybe truth only really counts when scandal is in season.*

*"The concept of shame," Redford lamented to the New York Times, "carries no weight any more," Yet shame sure weighed heavily on Dan Enright. He lived in his shame until the day he died, trying for years to make amends, haunted by his history in everything he did. At his funeral, hundreds of people mourned him. But oh, how my father's great shame now rests so lightly, on the broad shoulders of Robert Redford.*—Don Enright is an Emmy Award winning producer of movies for television. He lives in Los Angeles with his wife, Cheryl and daughter.

———

How I wish Dan could have read his son's letter which is such a fitting tribute! A response which also touched my heart was written by the well-known movie critic, Rex Reed:

*October 10, 1994*

*Dear Susan Stafford,*

*It was wonderful hearing from you after so many years but very disturbing too. I am just a gullible movie critic who has seen so many bad movies, I tend to over-react when I see a good one. I did like* Quiz Show *but the epilogue is very misleading. I had no idea Dan Enright and Jack Barry had passed away, and the movie makes no attempt to say so. I cannot be the only member of the audience misled by the assumption that they continued prosperously without retribution and continue to do so to this day. You cannot imagine how foolish I feel for not knowing the facts. Don Enright's letter to the L.A. Times as well as the other article you enclosed are very revealing and thought-provoking and now I wonder if all of Mr. Redford's moralizing isn't strangely manipulative. Popular success seems to be a bigger gauge of ethics than the truth. I worked for Dan Enright on a few occasions when he was trying out various celebrity panel shows in later years and I liked him a lot, so I was horrified to see him revealed as a monster in the film. I did not know he had passed away and I did not know how untruthful the film's epilogue was until you pointed it out. I apologize for any personal grief you've been caused by reviews such as mine and hope you'll forgive my naiveté.*

*Sincerely,*
*Rex Reed*

Dan felt immense guilt over his part in the scandal and what his family had to endure, and he learned much through this difficult experience. He dedicated the next thirty five years of his life to producing quality television programs.

Dan gained the respect of people like Ralph Nader and Jack Anderson due to his integrity and the risks he took. Dan accompanied Jack to Palestine at his own expense to interview PLO leader, Yasser Arafat. For a Jewish man, that venture was either insane or extremely brave. I believe it was the latter.

It seems to me there should be a law to protect the reputations of those who have passed on when lies and half-truths distort and destroy their memory, especially when they are no longer here to defend themselves and set the record straight.

*One of Dan's favorite photos of the two of us*

None of us have a guarantee of tomorrow. To live in the moment is a real art, and well worth it. This life is *not* a dress rehearsal. Sometimes I need to be reminded of that fact.

Meri Hillier shared a story with me about Dan's ability to stay focused on his countless projects. One afternoon, Meri knocked on his door at Barry & Enright and Dan looked up, waved his arm and said, "Not now, in a minute." Meri waited and when she knocked again, his answer was, "Whatever it is, it will have to wait." She finally walked in and put this note in front of him—**We've had a bomb threat and everyone else has already left the building!** Dan thanked her for her persistence as they quickly went downstairs to join the others waiting outside. Fortunately, it was only a threat and no one was hurt.

When Dan Enright passed away, the industry lost one of the most creative producers of all time. Dan's friends lost someone who truly cared and was always there for them. I lost someone irreplaceable. Dan was truly the love of my life.

Our dear friends who shared at Danny's memorial are listed below. Again, thank you all for affording Dan the tribute he so richly deserved.

| | | |
|---|---|---|
| Dick Van Patten | Fr. Herbert De Souza | Michael King |
| Rev. Terry Sweeney | Casey and Jean Kasem | Dr. Don Ha |
| Michael Colyar | Marilyn McCoo | Sybil Brand |
| Wink Martindale | Billy Davis, Jr. | Buddy Rogers |
| Don Enright | Chris Sohl | Dr. Bill Evans |
| Cantor Jay Frailich | Stan Rosenfeld | Howard Leitner |
| Mrs. Bernice Brown | Gary Jonke | Sandy Martin |
| Helena Buscema, who sang "Amazing Grace" | | |

—

I used Dan's game show bell to limit everyone to two minutes of sharing. If I hadn't, we might still be there. It was upbeat and fun as Dan would have liked. A somber ceremony would have brought no honor to a man who loved life so much. We came together to celebrate a man who touched countless lives.

After Marilyn McCoo spoke, her husband, Billy Davis Jr. joined her and they lifted our hearts in song.

Among those listed above are Sybil Brand (founder of the Sybil Brand Institute for Women). Sybil was such an icon in Los Angeles and on a personal level, a strong supporter of our relationship. She adored Dan and from her own experience, knew the courage it takes to stand up for what you *believe*. Sybil very kindly wrote this quote on my behalf when I was getting my master's degree in psychology. "Susan has a special desire to serve her fellow man and has found several avenues to accomplish this goal."

Others who spoke are Fr. Herbert De Souza with whom I worked in India, Michael King of King World Television, who syndicated *Wheel of Fortune and* Bernice Brown (Gov. Pat Brown's wife and mother of Gov. Jerry Brown and former State Treasurer, Kathleen Brown).

Anyone who knew Dan, knew how much he disliked wearing a tie. In one of the lighter moments of the service, Buddy Rogers stood up and said that in memory of Dan, all the men could remove their ties . . . and they did, gratefully.

Close friends in the medical profession such as Dr. Emil and Edlyn Soorani and Dr. David David and his wife, Dr. Vera David, closed their offices for the day.

Following the service, as everyone went outside, Casey Kasem and his wife Jean released three white doves. What an honor it was to truly *celebrate* the life of the most wonderful man I have ever known.

Another dear friend who shared how much Dan meant to him was Michael Colyar. Dan rode his bike fifty miles each Saturday; and one day, he stopped to hear a comedian who performed right on Venice Beach. It was Michael Colyar and he really made Dan laugh. Every weekend after

*With Michael and Brooks Colyar*

that, Dan would stop to hear him and began staying afterward to talk. As Dan befriended him, he began to encourage Michael and helped boost his career. Michael competed and won the top prize on *Star Search* and Dan was so proud of him. Michael has continued to grow and thrive in his profession. When he found the love of his life, Brooks, Michael brought her to meet us. It was our special joy to host their wedding at the Penthouse.

When my Mother passed away, four years earlier, I asked Dan what he would like on his headstone. Dan asked me to make the decision when the time came. For a Jewish man whose favorite song was "Amazing Grace," it seemed only fitting to use the Star of David and the cross. They represent one Bible.

At the top of the headstone is a replica of *Tic Tac Dough*. Here is the full inscription:

|   |   |   |
|---|---|---|
| O | O | O |
|   | X |   |
| X |   | X |

*DANIEL ENRIGHT, BORN EHRENREICH, WENT TO OUR LORD*
*MAY 22, 1992. DAN WAS A WINNER OF THREE EMMY AWARDS,*
*A MAVERICK OF GAME SHOWS AND A LEGEND WAY AHEAD*
*OF HIS TIME. AT GOLDA MEIR'S REQUEST, DAN HELPED START*
*TELEVISION IN ISRAEL AND ALSO INTERACTIVE TELEVISION.*
*DAN PLAYED A MAJOR ROLE IN THE HISTORY OF TELEVISION.*
*THE FILM "QUIZ SHOW" WAS WRITTEN ABOUT OUR DAN*
*ONLY STOPPING SHORT OF REVEALING ALL*
*HE LEARNED AND THE LIVES*
*HE ENRICHED AS A RESULT OF THAT EXPERIENCE.*
*DAN SUPPORTED ALL FAITHS AND RESPECTED ALL HUMANS.*
*DAN WAS KNOWN FOR HIS WARM GLOW AND SUPREME KINDNESS.*
*DAN WAS MARRIED TO STELLA FOR 50 YEARS AND*
*THEY HAD AN ENDURING BOND.*
*DAN ENRIGHT HELPED MAKE ALL HIS FRIENDS' DREAMS COME TRUE.*
*SUSAN STAFFORD WAS DAN'S COMPANION AND WAS WITH HIM*
*AT THE TIME OF HIS DEATH. DUE TO THEIR BELIEFS,*
*THEY WILL BE TOGETHER FOREVER.*
*DAN ENRIGHT WAS NO ORDINARY MAN.*
*I SHALL BUT LOVE THEE BETTER AFTER DEATH.*
*HERE LIES A HEART OF G-D*

What greater thing is there
   for two human souls
Than to feel they are joined . . .
   To strengthen each other . . .
To be at one with each other . . .
   In silent, unspeakable
     memories.
—George Eliot

*A visit to Dan's grave*

As I scanned the horizon from our beautiful Penthouse in Santa Monica, the loneliness was almost unbearable. The person I had loved so deeply was no longer there to share it. I sat shiva seven days for Dan out of the deepest respect. Unfortunately, there was little time to grieve because of having to deal with all the vultures coming out of the woodwork. I can't tell you how many used the phrase "Dan said" for their own benefit. I've never seen anything like it.

After Dan's funeral, lawyers went through his will with a fine tooth comb. They discovered that Dan owned or had a financial interest in more than 120 companies, with many of his deals agreed to with nothing more than a handshake. Legal discoveries with such an incomplete paper trail became a complication.

I was talking with my friend Bob Marlin recently about legal issues on a certain property investment. As I tried my best to explain it to him, he said, "Susan, I believe what *you're* telling me. It's the other guys you have to watch out for."

When he first met them, Dan told my parents he wanted to provide for me so I never had to worry about finances and his will was very clear. During one of their meetings, his lawyer noted this memo: "Dan Enright specifically stated that if Susan Stafford wanted to give the money to an Indian Maharajahi to float down the Ganges River, that would be permitted."

How in the world did that come about? All my life, with sincere anticipation before each of my marriages and following their demise,

I looked for someone to share my dreams. I prayed there would be a mutual admiration, accepting each other and bringing out the best in them, someone with whom I would want to spend the rest of my life. Dan Enright was that person. As Dan's assistant, Scott DeShong remembers, he always closed his letters "With a warm glow" and signed his name in green. Dan's sincere heart touched so many lives.

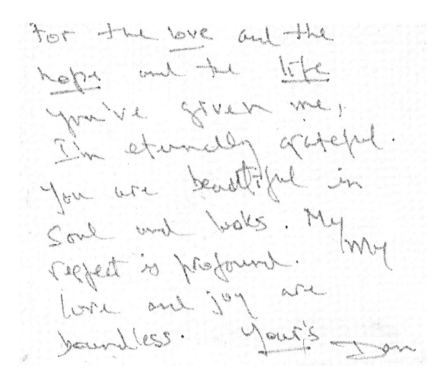

*A favorite love note from Dan which I cherish*

*[It says – For the love and the hope and the life you've given me, I'm eternally grateful. You are beautiful in soul and looks. My respect is profound. My love and joy are boundless. Yours, Dan]*

When the big earthquake hit Los Angeles in 1993, no one wanted to buy the top story of a high rise condominium that showed cracks all over the front of the building. Who could blame them? So just a year after Dan passed away, I had to walk away from the Penthouse we had enjoyed so much.

Was I wrong to live with Dan out of wedlock? Yes, I know that to be true. My life would have been much different both then and today if we had been able to marry. Do I regret it? Well, from a spiritual standpoint, I wish it could have been different. However, the Lord is the only One who knows the *whole* situation and I trust Him to judge my heart.

It's fascinating to me how the lives of people we've never even met can become so important to us. I have to admit there are times that even I fall prey to this curiosity, which I think most of us did following the passing of Michael Jackson. My friend, Seth Riggs. who was Michael's voice coach of over 25 years, could share the real story. The media is obsessed with reporting all the details of the lives of celebrities and the public never seems to get enough.

*As you climb the ladder of success, check occasionally to make sure it's leaning against the right wall.*—Author unknown

# Chapter Thirteen

# CELEBRITY STATUS: WHAT'S IT ALL ABOUT?

In making the decision to write this book, I realized that being honest about my experiences was the only way to serve a higher purpose. A watered down version would miss the mark. If just one person can be helped, it will be worth it.

I loathe drugs and have no empathy with those who have gotten hooked, and yet I fell into so many traps myself. That's why I know there is an enemy who wants to destroy us. I'm not in a popularity contest or running for election. I'm simply a person who cares about others and hopefully, some can learn from my mistakes. When we are willing to take our masks off and be real with each other, we see that everyone has some skeletons in their closet that they would rather not reveal.

Little did I know the anxiety and insecurity I felt since early childhood, not knowing where I belonged, would set me on a collision course of self-destruction. That was an excellent breeding ground for a life of inner turmoil. Many who knew me thought I was having a grand time, they just weren't aware of the struggles I kept to myself. There was an enemy within, clamoring for attention, and I believe that is true for many of us, especially in the celebrity world. If you're going through a tug-of-war in your life, it's important to know you're not alone. That's why a fellowship group like MFI is so important, to have the support you need with media people.

While I've always liked living in the moment; I haven't always stopped to think how those decisions would affect me. Despite what this generation thinks, "If it feels good, do it" is not a new philosophy. I

—

remember just wanting to enjoy life without any restrictions and frankly never thought I would live past the age of twenty-one.

A lot of people tend to think if you're a celebrity, you have it made. In reality, nothing could be further from the truth. Just look at the tabloid headlines and the mug shots they love to publish of the stars of this generation. People seem to revel in celebrity meltdowns played out across our TV screens. Our country is going through a major crisis and yet the breaking news is more often about Paris Hilton and Lindsay Lohan or the Kardashian girls than the soldiers fighting to keep our country free. Something is very wrong with this picture. As Glenn Beck, a well known radio and television host said, "It seems that fame and money have become the new God."

I happen to love a great story which shows celebrity in a positive light. When a son was born to Dr. Don and Dr. Ping Ha from China, they named him David Elvis Ha. As Don explained it to me, Elvis Presley was not only popular, people genuinely loved him. Don also knew that coming from China, his son might need a little edge in being accepted in America. He named his son Elvis because he believed the very name would bring a smile to people and a joy to their hearts and it certainly has.

Try not to be so hard on celebrities. They're learning as they go along, just as I imagine you are. Let's be patient with each other. With the economy and pressures we're all facing, none of us need to be judged harshly when for the most part, we're all doing the best we can.

The truth is that a lot of celebrities often have *more* problems because they were never taught how to handle success and all the trappings that go with it. Often, paranoia creeps in after dealing with a lot of rejection along the way. The competition is unbelievable in the world of entertainment. They can be on top one month, receiving the highest accolades possible. In just a few months, they are knocked off that pedestal before they know what hit them.

We are definitely not immune to troubles. After not being paid for my work on camera by a high profile Christian man, I was devastated to find I was losing my home. Although forgiving him was not an automatic response, I've learned that by choosing to forgive, it doesn't fester into bitterness and I can move on. Someone gave a great description of resentment—it's like taking poison yourself and hoping the other person will die. That's not healthy for either one. And guess what, by taking the high road, we stop holding on to something we never had control of anyway.

As celebrities, we have our ups and downs just like everyone else. We try not to complain because frankly, no one wants to hear it. That has never been more true than today. Literally everyone I talk to is having a difficult time with the economic crisis. More than ever, counting our blessings is not just a phrase—it's a necessity! I think we are all taking stock of our lives and realizing what is most important.

There is nothing more beautiful than a tree that is windblown. During the storms it endured, the roots had to reach deeper so it could remain standing. That's true for us also because whether we like it or not, hardship builds character. We may not have a choice in what happens to us, but we *can* choose how we respond and that, my friend, makes all the difference.

When celebrities make it big, relatives and friends often expect the celebrity to bail them out of problems, buy them a car or home—you name it, there's no limit. In many cases, the family becomes jealous or resentful. It can be difficult for everyone involved.

Even lottery winners tell us that a huge windfall brings challenges and headaches they never dreamed would happen. Just because someone is rich and successful doesn't mean they have the vaguest idea about how to deal with newfound fame or how to keep the money from flying out the window.

Some who are on top and successful at the moment remember all too well those days of struggle, sitting in a restaurant with a cup of coffee, waiting for the guy next to them to leave so they could finish whatever was still on his plate. When they *do* make it, many never learn how to handle the huge paycheck. If that level of success doesn't continue, they often find themselves in the worst financial condition of their lives.

Some celebrities have great advisors and business managers who help them invest well and save for the future. Others have professionals who "help themselves" to the money that has been entrusted to them. No names will be mentioned here, however I've had huge stars share their horror stories.

We need to allow celebrities to be what they are—talented people who happen to be very human like the rest of us. Even though fame and fortune sound exciting, no one can be fully prepared for it. They run the gamut of being so impressed with themselves to thinking it will all be gone tomorrow and no one will want them again. Is it any wonder they try to live it up while they can?

---

It can become an obstacle in relationships when you begin to wonder why someone wants to be with you. Celebrities often feel insecure and unable to trust, questioning the motives of those around them, rightfully so.

What happens when a career goes down the tubes? Are your friends riding the wave of your success just through the high times or are they willing to stand beside you in the unemployment line? I was surprised to learn that even actor Walter Pidgeon stood in that same line.

The truth is, a celebrity is no better nor worse than anyone else. While I have never murdered anyone, I have killed a few with my tongue, which I'm ashamed to say, can be cutting at times. The tongue is more powerful than we realize.

I learned that the longer you're in Hollywood, you find yourself rubbing shoulders with people who later become headline news. I first met Robert Kardashian (later to become O.J. Simpson's attorney) through his sister-in-law, Joan. She was Miss Missouri (from my home state), and I'm very proud of her. She was once married to Joe Esposito, Elvis Presley's road manager and later, married Robert Kardashian's brother, Tom, all terrific, decent people. Joan and Tom lived on the same street as my friends, Buddy and Beverly Rogers who invited me into their hearts and were so loving to me.

When O.J. and I met years earlier, he was an all-American hero. He was so popular and charismatic—on the A-list of all the parties. As I shared before, O.J. and Nicole had been to our Mandeville home when Dick Ebersol and I were married. Nicole was beautiful, really breathtaking. Who would have guessed that years later, she would die so tragically along with Ron Goldman? Our world seemed to stop with this news, much like it did with the '69 murder of the lovely Sharon Tate when we all learned the name, Charlie Manson. It's such a relief when justice is done as with Phil Spector. Fortunately, he will be locked up for a long time, but even justice can't restore the life of a beautiful actress like Lana Clarkson. Her friend and publicist, Ed Lozzi worked so hard on her behalf, even after telling me that Spector had threatened him. I really admire that courage to stand up for your convictions.

Although Rosey Grier (the Gentle Giant) is a personal friend, he has never spoken about O.J. to me. He's a minister, and I honor his integrity in keeping a confidence. I have a lot of respect for Rosey and his wife Margie. We go back a long time and have worked together for several charities.

I'm sure we've all done things we wish we hadn't. However, when I was on top, on the number 1 show, *Wheel of Fortune*, I made sure our young people didn't see me promote smoking in a commercial. I never encouraged drug use or performed nude as would have been required on *Beyond the Valley of the Dolls* and I'm proud of that.

I believe Madonna made a huge impression on the young girls who came after her. Britney Spears watched and imitated Madonna in many ways. Madonna happens to be very talented and has begun to clean up her act and has written several children's books. Britney has had a very hard time dealing with the notoriety. I'm scared for the kids and teenagers today who look up to people who are not setting good examples. Their actions influence so many.

Miley Cyrus, the star of *Hannah Montana,* is one of our most successful young talents today at 17. She recently said everything she's doing "is just for now." She's enjoying this special time because it will never be quite the same again. She seems to have a maturity beyond her years.

When I was growing up, the ladies I admired and wanted to emulate were Loretta Young, Rhonda Fleming and Doris Day. These ladies were always gracious when dealing with the public and the press.

As a young actress, I remember enjoying a conversation with a man at a lovely dinner and upon leaving, someone mentioned that was George Murphy. I had no idea! There should be a course for young entertainers so they can recognize those who have perfected the craft before them. The great films come alive again as they are presented by Robert Osborne, the dapper host of Turner Classic Movies and Nick Clooney on American Movie Classics. Both men are such professionals and teach us a lot about the history of these great films as well as the actors.

It used to *mean* something when you were considered a role model. The lack of character being instilled in our young people concerns me because it will be felt for generations to come. The impact is major.

I realize no one's life is perfect, we all make mistakes, however when a celebrity makes one, the news media plasters it over the TV, internet and newspapers. Today, flaunting bad behavior seems to be acceptable and I find that pathetic.

Every one of us can use our talents to help others or to harm them. The choices we make, each one building on the one before, determine our destiny. We can't rely on what happened yesterday because *today* is all we have. We are *all* somebody, and no matter what our station in life, each of us should strive for a measure of dignity.

Watching people interact with celebrities is a real study in human nature. Several years ago, I went with a group to minister to prisoners in Chino, California. The women in the group were told to be most careful to dress like ladies that day. I understood the necessity and even wore two slips under a dress that was very modest.

As much as you may be shocked by the behavior of celebrities, others do outrageous things just to see how a celebrity will react. During the service, it was hard not to notice a prisoner nearby who unzipped his pants and started playing with himself. He was staring at me, waiting for my reaction. If he was trying to startle or impress me, he certainly didn't. The reason doesn't matter. I motioned to the guy next to him, "Hey buddy, tell your friend to knock it off. We've seen all that before." The prisoner quickly looked away and put it back in his pants. Since we're never certain what we may encounter, I try to be alert and as ready as possible to handle any situation. I'm always grateful when it turns out well.

In today's society, it has unfortunately become open season as the paparazzi delight in finding celebrities at their worst, without makeup, or with a few bulges showing at the beach. The next time you have to run to the store for a loaf of bread, just think what it would be like if photographers were camped outside the door, waiting to capture your every move. When there is not always time for makeup or styling hair, maybe you can understand why they wear bulky clothing and pull a cap low over their eyes.

We sometimes hear of a celebrity grabbing the camera pointed at them or their kids and knocking a photographer down. While that is a bit extreme, so is not respecting a person's privacy.

I heard about one successful lady who was at dinner, minding her own business when she noticed someone watching her. Feeling flattered, she waited politely for the person to speak, only to hear this question, "Hey, didn't you used to be somebody?"

Being a celebrity is not for the faint-hearted. They have to be prepared for rejection, often as a steady diet until finally being discovered as an "overnight" sensation.

All too often they're given a political platform just because of their celebrity status. No one seems to care that their knowledge may be limited. Somehow having a "name" makes their opinion noteworthy.

After *Wheel of Fortune* and working with cancer and leprosy patients, I co-hosted the *700 Club* with Pat Robertson and Ben Kinchlow. I sat with Pat and Dee Dee Robertson on the dais at a Republican fundraiser and Governor Ronald Reagan was on the platform as well.

I walked over, kissed Gov. Reagan on the cheek and said, "I want to be the first to congratulate you on being the next President of the United States." He turned to me with that great smile and twinkle in his eye, "Are you sure?" I said "Absolutely!" He wasn't even running for the office at that time. I just sensed something so special about this man and it was a delight to me when he actually became our President.

My dad was not a celebrity or a politician. He owned and operated a café and later managed a commissary on military bases. Of all the people I've known, he was extremely well-read and informed on the issues, challenging others to think for themselves.

As a young actress and the original hostess of *Wheel of Fortune*, the number one daytime television show, I experienced celebrity life for myself. There were a lot of interviews and photos taken, but not like today, thank goodness.

I share this part with hesitation, knowing that my nieces and nephews may one day read this book. It is my wish that this axiom will be heeded by them and other readers as well—"Learn from the mistakes of others. You can't live long enough to make them all yourself." If I had it to do over, I would have realized I didn't know as much as I thought I did and saved myself from many heartaches.

While I'm still alive to tell the story, too many have had their lives cut short before they could learn the lesson. Others cause accidents, never meaning to, but when you can't think or see straight, you should *never* get behind the wheel of a car. The results of those decisions are on the nightly news far too often.

If what I experienced can keep those reading my story from destructive behavior, we all win. Perhaps it can help a young celebrity who thinks no one understands. I'm here to tell you I know what a difficult path you're on, however you can make it easier for yourself by taking a step back and realizing how the choices you're making will affect your life.

Many times I felt like a social misfit in Hollywood and tried to blend in by adopting the behavior of those who seemed to have it all. In this business, being seen with the right people is crucial. Being invited to a black tie event sounds glamorous and it certainly can be. There are times though, when you would rather just go home, take off that girdle, slip into comfy pajamas, and pop some popcorn.

Try taking a deep breath in a dress that's too tight and sit at a meal when there's no time to enjoy your food because of all the interruptions. Try not to blink when they want "just one more" photograph and you can still see spots in front of your eyes from the last picture. For the next four hours, keep smiling until your jaw literally aches. Finally, make sure you keep everyone entertained. Even though it sounds like an exaggeration, the expectations are all too real.

Growing up as the child of an alcoholic, I never wanted drinking to be a part of my life. I remember calling Mama one time and she said, "I'm so upset with your father!" When I asked why, she said "He's out watering the lawn." I told her that didn't sound so bad to me and she said, "Susan, it's raining!" Mama was sure the neighbors were watching and talking about it among themselves.

To my dad's credit, he never missed a day on the job, always working hard to provide a living for our family of nine. I'm proud of my dad and realize people can maintain a certain amount of control.

When I first came to Hollywood, drinking looked glamorous, and it seemed that I was the only one *not* drinking at parties. I was very hesitant and yet in time, I eventually joined in. Although I didn't like the taste, it did make me feel more witty. My shyness seemed to disappear and I could talk to people I didn't have the courage to approach before. This felt pretty good after all, and I just knew it would be different for me. I had seen other people get drunk and not know what they were doing, but that was them—I told myself I would never let things get out of control.

After awhile, I began drinking more than was good for me at these affairs. It's called *escape*. One excuse is as good as another, however like an earthquake, there were always aftershocks. One time I was so out of it, when I woke up, everything was a blur. As my eyes began to focus, I saw a name stamped in pretty letters—American Standard. That was it, I must have married someone named Standard. Looking around, I was horrified to realize I was lying on a tile floor and those letters were spelled out on a familiar white tank in the bathroom. That realization made me sick all over again.

One night after a party, I knew I was in no shape to drive. I left my car right where it was parked and decided to walk home. I was having a great time, singing loudly as I went along. A police officer stopped beside me and asked why I was walking in the middle of the highway. I told him I didn't want to get a ticket for drinking too much, so just to be safe; I started following the yellow brick road. Trying to reason with someone who's been drinking is not easy; however, he finally convinced me to accept his offer of a ride so I didn't get hit. (If you're reading this, sir, I sincerely thank you again for your kindness.)

After many years of going in this circle, I kissed my mother in her coffin and with all the sincerity of my heart and soul, I promised never to drink again. Years later, this demon raised its ugly head again. It was a shock to my system and still is to this day.

Long ago, I drank too much at a party hosted by my agent, Fred Wostbrock and he wouldn't let me drive. I called a dear friend, Maria Comfort to come and pick me up and she was kind enough to let me sleep on her couch which I appreciated so much.

It caught me by surprise once again at a birthday celebration for Billy Davis, Jr. of the original "5th Dimension". He and his wife, the beautiful Marilyn McCoo, continue to be such great talents. Marilyn is also my prayer partner and asked me to share at the party. It was a wonderful group in a beautiful setting. I was having a good time that night and throwing caution to the wind, decided to just enjoy the evening. That old familiar thought crept in and I said to myself, "*one* glass of wine won't hurt." Remember I'm the one who always thought a little vino made me charming and fun. Before I realized it, one glass became two and by the time I got up to speak, I made a fool of myself. I'm very grateful that Marilyn and Billy love me unconditionally (it's called Agape love) and were willing to forgive my behavior.

The problem is that drinking can be so deceptive. If you still think it makes you more charming, have someone take a video of you at the time and watch it when you're sober. It can be pretty embarrassing to see yourself like that. Drinking sometimes made me sick to my stomach, and often sick of myself.

I've gone in and out so many times and while I'm grateful today that it doesn't control my life, it's still a conscious choice I have to make. As alcoholics, we have to remember not to get too hungry, too tired or too angry. I've learned that you can always start over and get on the right track and I'm so grateful I have.

Through the years, I've taken the Bill W. route several times (they are the best!) and received three cakes. (It takes a whole year of sobriety to receive just one cake and it truly is an accomplishment. Just ask anyone who's done it.) My sisters, Catherine and Chloe even came to one of the "birthday" celebrations.

It's difficult to admit that you're dealing with darkness. When you're not even *aware* of what you're saying or how you're behaving, you are out of control. While alcoholism is a disease, it can also be a selfish decision when you care more about escaping for a short time than how it's affecting those you love. I was grateful when my friend, Ron Schneider, took me aside at a party and said, "Susan, you're beautiful, but tonight, your actions are ugly and I know you don't want to be like that." He was right.

When I recall the days with Sammy Davis, Jr. and Altovise, they are very memorable. Hospitality was the order of the day for Sammy and he always went beyond being a gracious host. I used to walk around their home, admiring the glass showcases with gifts from famous friends. There was a stuffed llama from Kim Novak, Judy Garland's red slippers which she wore as Dorothy in the *Wizard of Oz,* paintings by the well known artist, Ernie Barnes and beautiful crystal decanters from Frank Sinatra filled with the finest liquor one could desire. They had one of the most tremendous bars in the world.

Drugs were not really my issue, in fact I was convinced they would not even be a temptation for me. But being in the wrong place at the wrong time with a little peer pressure and a lot of curiosity, can change the best resolve. While cocaine used to be offered in the back rooms at parties, because so many wanted to indulge, it was placed in plain sight where anyone who wanted to could sniff a line of coke. That's something I told myself I would *never* try!

Sammy was most generous with his guests and had bowls filled with coke for their use. The A-list people came to these parties and you can probably read those names in another book. I was too naïve at first to realize why Sammy had such a long fingernail on his pinkie finger. I finally got the picture when he used it to dip cocaine from a humongous bowl.

One night, I waited till everyone left the party and decided to see what all the fuss was about. I tried "just a little" and ended up gritting my teeth for days. I was so wound up, I had to keep jogging until I came down. It was awful! That was my first and last time with coke. As they say, DON'T TRY THIS AT HOME! (or anywhere else for that matter.) That was enough for me.

———

Dr. Emil Soorani taught a Substance Abuse class at Antioch University and showed dramatic presentations of the fact that serious users of crack cocaine will never get the drug out of their system. It's called the drug of no return.

My high school friend, Vicky is one of the few who were finally able to escape the choke hold of crack. It took twelve years until she was able to crawl her way back to the land of the living and she's grateful every day that her nightmare ended. I'm so proud of her.

Although I had seen the result with friends like Freddie Prinze and John Belushi, somehow all of us seem to think we're immortal, especially when we're young. The truth is that a **natural high** is the best high of all. It's such a shame we keep searching for something else.

It's amazing the memories that surfaced when I began thinking about the past. On my honeymoon with Gordon in Acapulco, unbeknownst to him, I was offered PCP (Angel Dust). It took me days to feel normal again as I ricocheted into the pool and out of the pool—I was so uncomfortable in my own skin. It was a terrible way to learn that you don't need it at all. I would *never* want anyone to try it. Just don't!

Now we have Meth which grabs people from the very first time and takes them on a trip. That train is way down the track before they even know they left the station and their lives become a living hell.

Some celebrities have too much time on their hands, too much money in their pocket and too many "friends" who can't wait to show them the next high. I promise you, these people are *not* your friends. The surprise is not how many of the Hollywood crowd is involved, but how many have *escaped* it. It's a deadly situation because alcohol and drugs make you feel invincible.

Drinking was always my weakness. Then came the blackouts. You hear about judgment being impaired—there isn't any! Am I proud of it? No. Do I remember it? Noooo! I would sometimes call friends in the middle of the night and not remember the conversation, or even the fact that I had called.

The sad part is when people know you have a problem and keep offering you a drink anyway. Some of them find it very entertaining to see you out of control and those people are not real friends. You see others who seem to handle it well so you take "just one glass" to be sociable. That may work for some, however you need to know yourself and if you can't stop, you have a problem.

—

Before his last marriage, Larry King called me when I was in Washington, D.C. with our L.A.D.I.E.S. group. (It stands for Life After Divorce Is Eventually Sane.) I was so freakin' drunk, I don't have any idea what I said to him. All I know is, he never called me back. I'm sure sorry, Larry.

Parked cars seemed to jump out in front of me, and it was only the Lord's grace that saved me when I crashed into the back of a gas tanker that had just been filled late one night. Having friends to call who were great attorneys saved me from spending any nights in jail, but I know down deep, it wasn't luck, it was God's mercy.

I have to tell you that in recounting these stories, it has even been shocking to me. Who *was* that person? While my memory is all too vivid about certain experiences, at times it seems like I'm sharing about someone else. I lived the fast life for a long time and am amazed I'm still here to talk about it. So much of this seems like another lifetime, however those who knew me during those days know it's all too true. Although I never thought it could happen to me, I've had to realize that no one is exempt from making bad decisions.

Why do we think there will be no repercussions as a result of those choices? Einstein once said, "The definition of insanity is doing the same thing over and over and expecting different results." Duh, do you think?

One beautiful tree in Santa Monica was sacrificed in a crash that almost took my life and finally woke me up. I don't know if you've ever been hit in the face with an air bag and I hope you never are, but it's pretty forceful. My head bounced off the side window just before the air bag hit me; and three days later, I appeared on the *Oprah* show where a skillful makeup artist did her best to cover my black eye. I was wearing Sammy Davis Jr.'s sunglasses which not only looked very stylish, they also helped cover the bruise. (One of the all time great announcers, Casey Kasem and his wife Jean and I had gone to Sammy's estate auction. We were all trying to help Sammy and

*Susan is wearing Sammy Davis, Jr.'s sunglasses*

Altovise with their big tax problem. Casey and Jean bought Sammy's sunglasses and gave them to me. It was such a special gift!)

Little did Oprah know that I almost didn't make it to the show that day. I asked my assistant, Tammy, to fly to Chicago with me. Her background is in nursing and I didn't feel stable enough to make the trip by myself. I was still dealing with a concussion from the wreck and my training as an actress helped carry me through the interview. I even told Oprah on the show that drinking was *not* my friend. It never has been. It's an intense craving that becomes a mental obsession. You know it's destructive, but feel powerless to stop yourself. Can you imagine waiting for years to do the *Oprah* show and almost blowing the opportunity?

So many times I thought I could handle social drinking. While some can, I had to admit I'm an alcoholic and for me, it's destructive. After a bad scene, I promised never to drink and drive again, and I have kept that promise. I'm so grateful to be sober and I know not to take that first drink. Addiction is a lifelong battle for so many of us. Problem gamblers know they can't roll the dice even once. Shopaholics can't allow themselves the freedom to use credit cards instead of cash. For food addicts, just one delectable brownie will never be enough. I'm no different. Not lying to myself or others anymore is the key to my sobriety and realizing it's truly one day at a time.

We wonder today why so many young celebrities hit the party scene right after being released from rehab. Unless you've been there yourself, you have no idea the pressures they are under and what it takes to change neighborhoods and find new friends.

It seems that celebrities are fair game to the press and even when they're making difficult choices for the greater good, you can count on some people to be critical. When Tammy Faye Bakker Messner appeared on *Larry King Live*, no one knew it would be a matter of hours until she passed away.

My dear friend, Deborah Keener enjoyed a thirty-year friendship with Tammy Faye and was by her side for the last seven weeks of her life. Deborah's life was filled with diversity and dynamic living. Hugh Hefner was once her brother-in-law and as Debbie Hefner, Deborah composed songs for many recording artists including Dale Evans and Tammy Faye. Deborah also received a Grammy nomination and performed for millions. I thank God for people like Deborah who are willing to put their own lives on hold to give of themselves in this way. Deborah said it would have been much easier for Tammy Faye to stay in bed during those hours when her strength was almost gone and just speaking took all the energy she could muster. However, true to Tammy Faye's character, she wanted to use every opportunity to let people know how much Jesus loves them and assure them she knew where she was going. While it was hard for us to watch her in such an emaciated condition, it demonstrated her deep spiritual conviction to the ultimate degree. How can your heart not be touched by that?

When Deborah was helping her get dressed for *Larry King Live*, she offered her beautiful necklace to Tammy Faye to wear on the program. It was a solitaire heart-shaped diamond necklace. Tammy Faye said, "Thanks, Deb, I've wanted to wear this heart for years." It symbolized the close sharing which was such a special part of their heartfelt friendship and sisterhood.

Due to the misconception that surrounded Tammy Faye's passing, wrong information was shared. People seem so eager to hear things that are detrimental while good intentions are overlooked or even dismissed. One day, Deborah will write a book about Tammy Faye, sharing a story that has never been told. I can only hope that when my time comes, I will be blessed enough to have someone like Deborah by my side.

My favorite actress growing up was Rhonda Fleming. I always admired her beauty and later learned that beauty came from the inside as well. Getting to know her and enjoy the sweet fellowship we share is one of my most treasured gifts.

*Rhonda Fleming*

One morning on her way to high school, Marilyn Louis was discovered and soon became the glamorous Rhonda Fleming. Her career began with a featured role in Alfred Hitchcock's *Spellbound*. She went on to star in forty films and become one of the legendary actresses of our time.

I know it would be more popular in today's world if I embraced new age beliefs and followed the Dalai Lama whom I happen to adore.

But when I fell in love with God and then Christ, my soul found the completion I was seeking. Nothing else has come close.

The richest days of my life have been those in sobriety with absolute clarity. I don't know why I took so long to get there, but it's thrilling to know that God above has spared me from my own destruction. I always endeavor to make up for my failings, and when I do, it allows growth in my character.

There's a new film which was produced by Matt and Laurie Crouch from TBN called *The Cross* that I would encourage you to see, regardless of your faith or even if you don't have one. It's about our friend, Arthur Blessitt, who walked around the world for 40 years carrying the cross. This man was willing to leave his comfort zone and in the process, survived countless dangerous situations. It's the story of purpose and destiny, one step at a time. If you see this film and are sorry you went, please let me know why. I would love to discuss it with you.

I want to focus on what is really important in life and touch people's hearts. I don't think I'll ever get used to seeing those I care about leave this earth. We're never quite ready to say farewell, no matter how old the person is. When my good friend, Altovise Davis (Sammy's widow) died a few days after suffering a stroke, she was young, just sixty-five.

Her funeral was well attended and it was a very religious service with five pastors sharing. Among them were the pastor who opened his church on short notice, Pastor Jon Barta; my pastor, Pastor Bob Rieth and Rev. Jesse Jackson. Jesse had performed the wedding for Sammy and Altovise and had come to say goodbye. The paparazzi seem to follow wherever he goes. If it had been a supermarket opening, he would be there and they would cover it. As I shared that day, Altovise and I had been friends for over 30 years and I only wish she had known how much talent she possessed, how charming she really was and how many truly loved her. Unfortunately, she was her own worst enemy as many of us have been.

The sweet comical genius, Dom DeLuise, also left us, long before we would have liked. I can't begin to tell you the joy he brought to everyone around him. As his wife and my dear friend, Carol said, "It was a beautiful passing." Dom waited until Peter arrived from Canada and once Carol and their three sons were at his bedside, he wrote a note to the Doctor, asking for the life support to be removed at 6 p.m. It was a sweet time for them to be together and 20 minutes later, he passed from this life into the very presence of God. What a wonderful example of courage and grace, by Dom and his entire family.

Dom did not want people to weep at his memorial—he wanted the day to be filled with laughter. Dom would have been so pleased. Their sons Peter, Michael and David and his wife, Carol, honored Dom's memory in grand style. I have attended a lot of memorials, but *never* one that was more uplifting and hilarious. Between Mel Brooks, Ruth Buzzi and Carl Reiner and the family, it was a brilliant tribute to a man who truly loved others and is remembered so fondly by us all. I can assure you that I'm a much better person today because of Dom and Carol.

I think we were all impressed with the class and courage demonstrated by Farrah Fawcett. I met Farrah through Jay Bernstein and Patty Van Patten and even adjusted her back a few times because I'm good at that. Farrah Fawcett was best known for *Charlie's Angels*, and her acting ability was incredible as she continued to grow with each role. Jay told me that when he was her manager, he came up with the famous poster of her in the red bathing suit. Farrah enjoyed so many years of great success and later, when she saw all the articles in the tabloids claiming she was on her deathbed, she ripped them up and let everyone know how she felt. Her determination to fight with everything she had was alive and well as the documentary was filmed to tell her story, her way—with dignity.

Saying good-bye to Fred Travalena was difficult because I adored him so. He was like a brother to me. Fred was born to entertain and even when his voice was weak after all the chemo and radiation, he still tried to keep everyone laughing. Fred showed all of us what it meant to keep the faith when you're no longer able to live out your dreams. His wife, Lois and sons, Cory and Fred, Jr. are determined to get his last dream to the Broadway stage. So many admired Fred including Shirley MacLaine who spoke at his memorial and offered her help to get this wonderful project to the stage.

When I need some time to think, I like to go where I won't be bothered. Through the years, I've found a lot of solace in cemeteries. I don't find it morbid at all, in fact, it can be quite fascinating. One of the quiet places I've retreated to since I came to Hollywood is Westwood Memorial Park which is tucked behind a theatre on Wilshire Blvd. in Los Angeles. I went to Merv Griffin's grave to pay my respects and the engraving on his headstone is just the same as he told me many years ago, "I won't be right back".

Farrah Fawcett is buried beside Merv and nearby are dear people like Natalie Wood, Mel Torme and Walter Matthau along with Ross Hunter and Armand Hammer. Hugh Hefner bought the crypt next to Marilyn Monroe and I understand that the crypt above her is for sale starting at $500,000. The interesting part of that story is that this man with a good sense of humor, asked to be buried above Marilyn, with his body face down. Now, his wife needs the money and wants to move her husband elsewhere. Such is life.

I've been blessed beyond grace and believe that life goes on after death. Living life to the fullest is the key. It doesn't matter whether you're a celebrity or a janitor, giving of yourself to make life better for someone else is so rewarding to your own soul.

What keeps entertainers pumped is the response of the audience. For a comedian, laughter is the greatest sound of all. When actors, singers, dancers, musicians and athletes hear an audience cheer, their energy is renewed to give even more than they thought they could.

It was such a privilege to work with great talents like Robert Young; Jim Brolin; Bill Bixby; Burgess Meredith; Stuart Whitman and Raymond Burr and I will always appreciate their patience in teaching me. I truly value those who took me under their wing with such kindness as they guided me through the maze of Hollywood. People like Rock Hudson and "the Duke", John Wayne; Lucille Ball; Beverly and Buddy Rogers; Joanne Dru; June Haver MacMurray; Anne Jeffreys and of course, Rhonda Fleming. John Ford's group also included great stars like Harry Carey, Jr., Maureen O'Hara and Joel Macrae. People have been so good to me and just listening to their sagas was a thrill.

Even though the greats from Hollywood's heyday like Humphrey Bogart; James Cagney; Broderick Crawford; Henry Fonda; Jack Lord; Spencer Tracy; Katherine Hepburn; Randolph Scott; Lucille Ball; Bob Hope; Joan Crawford; Jack Lemmon; Walter Matthau; Jack Palance; Dudley Moore; Zero Mostel and Rock Hudson are gone, their films will be enjoyed for generations to come. George Nader is still considered an icon in Europe where his *Jerry Cotton* series started, similar to the 007 character made so popular by Sean Connery (isn't he the cat's meow?)

———

I'm grateful we still have so many good actors. Even today, Mickey and Jan Rooney have more energy than I do. Mickey has made more films than any other actor, and yet he's even more grateful that he was able to serve our country and is so proud to be a Veteran. Surprising, isn't it?

Movies have always been an enjoyment for me, depending on the content of course. In recent years, especially, I've had to walk out on a few of them. That would have been unthinkable when watching Doris Day; Liz Taylor; Cary Grant; Andy Griffith from *A Face In The Crowd*; Charlie Chaplin; Audrey Hepburn; Robert Mitchum; Gene Autry; Bette Davis; Helen Hayes; Gregory Peck; Ingrid Bergman; Spencer Tracy; Raquel Welch; George Peppard and Lauren Bacall. I've always been told Ms. Bacall developed that distinctive low voice by going to a hilltop to scream which changed the pitch of her vocal cords. Ruta Lee has had a great career in films and television. She recently spoke at her friend, Rona Barrett's star ceremony in Palm Springs. She was impeccably dressed as always and her sharing was flawless and funny.

Content is so important in films. It took me at least seven years to feel comfortable in taking a shower after seeing *Psycho*. A bath had to do. I'm sure I'm not alone in having that reaction. Janet Leigh was incredible.

I have great respect for Sidney Poitier and the dignity with which he has always conducted himself. Jimmy Stewart was an icon in films and *It's A Wonderful Life* will always be a classic with my dear friend, Jimmy Hawkins who played little Tommy Bailey. He was only four at the time. He later started the Donna Reed Foundation and I met Shelly Fabares, Joey Heatherton and Deana Martin through Jimmy. After so many years of acting and producing, Hawk *knows* Hollywood, yet he doesn't *play* Hollywood.

In meeting Liv Ullman who studied with Fellini, I found a soul with such depth and warmth—I love her. Tom Selleck is as good as you might think and his mother and father were the very same. Clint Eastwood is well respected as a director by the actors in his films. He's so bright and is always striving for perfection. When I met and spent time with Clint at our ranch in Texas, I learned that he is just as down to earth as he seems. Clint first caught our attention as Rowdy Yates on *Rawhide* and went on to star in Spaghetti Westerns. After coming in the back door in Hollywood, I applaud Clint for his great career in films as he continues to "make my day".

I've known Jon Voight a long time and have always admired his acting ability as well as his willingness to stand up for what he believes. While that can be hazardous in Hollywood, it becomes even worse when people go against their own principles.

I tend to favor older men like Clark Gable, Claude Rains and Maurice Chevalier. I don't think we will see their likes again.

*With Beverly Rogers, Patty and Arthur Newman and Paul Newman*

Paul Newman has always been a class act. I had the privilege of sitting with my dear friend, Beverly Rogers, Paul and his brother Arthur and sister-in-law, Patty for dinner. We were at the home of Jim and Jackie Houston for a special fundraiser. They are the most generous philanthropists in Palm Springs. Paul was so tired after just flying in from Connecticut and I remember being quite concerned for him at the time. We all keenly felt his loss.

In thinking of actors I enjoy, Scott Wilson, who co-starred in Truman Capote's *In Cold Blood* is most talented. Ed Lauter is one of the best character actors around and I never tire of seeing his work. Buddy Hackett and his wife, Sherry were one of the most popular couples in Hollywood. She is quite a lover of cats and a person as *real* as they come.

Charlize Theron is one of our most talented actresses and isn't afraid to go outside her comfort zone. As I continue to follow her work, Charlize is one I would like to see play my life's story. She knows how to incorporate all the nuances and gives such depth to her characters.

Danny DeVito and his wife, Rhea Perlman are as strong as a couple as they are actors. Henry Winkler, a graduate of the Yale School of Drama was such a joy to watch as the "Fonz". Out of all the characters on television, I miss that character the most. Ron Howard is not only a good actor, he has become a great director as well. Mike Henry was my favorite "Tarzan" and two of my favorite comedies are *The End* with Burt Reynolds and Dom DeLuise and *Birdcage* with Robin Williams, Gene Hackman and Nathan Lane. A close third is Mel Brooks with Gene Wilder, Cleavon Little and my gal, Carol Arthur DeLuise in *Blazing Saddles*. Let's not forget our movie critics like Rex Reed and Leonard Maltin. Their reviews were always informative and more than fair with no payola in sight.

I believe that Tom Hanks is one of our best actors today, one I certainly admire. Meryl Streep continues to re-invent herself from portraying a harsh nun to a woman who doesn't know who the father of her daughter is in *Mamma Mia* to bringing Julia Child back to life. She is equally believable in each role. I always enjoy Sandra Bullock, but never more than in *The Blind Side*. What a wonderful story and example to us all. Meg Ryan and Reese Witherspoon are always entertaining and Drew Barrymore is refreshing. Cameron Diaz has one of the best bodies, similar to Jane Fonda who has gone through many transformations from Vietnam and Tom Hayden to Ted Turner. As an actress, she has always been superb.

Michael J. Fox is courage personified and shows us what it means to stay committed to your craft just as Kirk Douglas did after his stroke. Goldie Hawn and Kurt Russell are true professionals and so much in love. I tend to want the whole world to be like that.

It always makes me happy when a person I've prayed for finds the right mate such as Jim Brolin did after his wife passed. Barbra Streisand is in a class of her own and I'm glad for the happiness they have found together. His son, Josh, is a darn good actor as well.

Mickey Rourke and Robert Downey, Jr. have fought the fight and won. My hat's off to them. No one knows how difficult it really can be to escape that entrapment.

Stars of today like Leonardo DiCaprio and Brad Pitt from my home state, Missouri, talk about being inspired by Jimmy Cagney, while others studied Marlon Brando and James Dean. I'm proud to say that Ed Asner and Jack Carson are also from Missouri. We produced some pretty talented people I have to say.

Some of my other favorites are Robert DuVall; Jason Robards; James Mason; James Coburn and Ernest Borgnine who starred in *Dirty Dozen* with my friend, Trini Lopez; Charles Bronson and Lee Marvin who is buried in Arlington Cemetery. Warren Beatty and Annette Benning have had wonderful careers. I remember when Warren was the only actor people talked about. I have to add Glenn Close; Sir Anthony Hopkins; Brenda Vaccaro; Ed Harris; Lena Horne and Tippi Hedren who we can never forget in *The Birds*. Her daughter Melanie Griffith is a wonderful actress and Melanie's husband, Antonio Banderas is always a box office draw. We have Sean Penn; Sophia Loren; Gene Wilder; Martin Sheen; Harrison Ford; Michael Douglas and his beautiful wife, Catherine Zeta Jones. Bill Cosby is pure charm. Billy Bob Thornton is very talented. I love his boys who I met through his ex-wife, Pietra. Peter Sellers; Helen Mirren; Gary Sinese; Christopher Walken and Denzel Washington are all top talents and of course, Bruce Willis. (Bruce, I would love to have your mother, Marlene, get back in touch with me.) Robert De Niro and Al Pacino are amazing in every part they have ever played. I often wonder how Kevin Spacey grew up to get to where he is now.

My goodness, where do I stop? Certainly not before mentioning Jennifer Aniston; George Clooney; Kelsey Grammer; James Gandolfini; Cate Blanchett; Will Smith; John Schneider; Michelle Pfeiffer; John Travolta; Angelina Jolie; Beau and Jeff Bridges; Johnny Depp; Ben Affleck; Matt Damon; Bo Hopkins is a great actor who really knows how to have fun; Andy Garcia; Philip Seymour Hoffman, David Hyde Pierce; Jim Caviezel; Mark Wahlberg and George Hamilton, whose youngest son, G.T. is my godson. (His mother is Kimberly Blackford.)

John Malkovich never misses in grabbing hold of his character and he continues to mistify me. John, Hector Elizando and Burt Lancaster are actually my three favorite actors.

There are many newcomers like Lisa David Dean who is an actress and a super mom who you will be hearing a lot more about in time. Dick Van Patten's sons, Vince and Jimmy are coming up right behind their dad and I'm really proud of them. Dick and Patty have three sons and Nels happens to be the favorite tennis instructor for most of the stars and athletes. In real life, three was just right.

———

You may wonder why I mention all these names. It's because this generation of actors is superb and hard as I tried, it was difficult to find a stopping place. My tastes are very eclectic and every time I thought the list was complete, several more came to mind and I just couldn't leave them out. We are all ONE and I believe if we understood that, we wouldn't be so hard on celebrities. I'm proud of Hollywood. It has given much more than it gets credit for. While there are a lot of mixed up people in Hollywood, guess where a big percentage of them came from—the Midwest and Brooklyn! I'm so proud of our industry for getting class back into the scripts and integrity back into the characters.

In television—Jon Hamm from *Mad Men* is right on the mark. I've always enjoyed Debra Messing's comic timing which reminds me of Lucille Ball. That is a huge compliment. My friend, the unbelievable comic impressionist Louise DuArt, is the only who has been given permission by both Carol Burnett and Cher to portray them. Louise and her husband, SQuire Rushnell do an act together with her impressions and readings from his book "When God Winks" that is tremendous.

So many others make me laugh like Dick Van Dyke; Carl Reiner; Mary Tyler Moore; Valerie Harper; Dick Van Patten; Jay Leno and David Letterman. They have all proven that "Laughter is still the best medicine". Betty White is one smart cookie, totally opposite of her character on *Golden Girls*. It takes real talent to make a character that believable. I remember seeing Betty when her husband, Allen Ludden was hosting *Password*. They were so in love and it made me happy just to see them together. Talking about quality entertainers, Shirley Jones and Pat Boone are right at the top of the list and their voices are still strong. They've come a long way since *April Love*. A real life love story which has endured through the tests of time is Pat and his wife, Shirley whose dad was Red Foley.

As I watch the Academy Awards, I often think it would be a more valid contest if the nominated actors or actresses could play the same part to see who gave the best portrayal. I've always been amazed to see the different slant each actor can bring to a character.

Julia Roberts and her brother Eric both have such talent. I met their mother, Betty in Atlanta, Georgia at a luncheon which my author friend, Susan Wales gave for me. Betty was Julia and Eric's acting coach and deserves a lot of credit for their success.

*Pretty Woman* was such a beautiful movie which hit close to home and it brought Julia to our attention. Richard Gere is a great actor and one of the best followers of the Dalai Lama who uses his stardom as a platform to share issues of importance.

After 111 years in business, the William Morris agency has merged with Endeavor and we're all waiting to see what Mark Itkin will do. I first met Mark when he was working with Dan Enright on a few projects. He's a darn good agent with honor. Imagine that.

Groups like Ted Baehr's Movie Guide Awards, honor clean films and quality entertainment for all audiences. MFI (Media Fellowship International) founded by Pastor Bob Rieth, also honors celebrities, actors, directors and producers who have chosen to maintain high standards. These are the people in the limelight, but we all like to know an honest mechanic, used car salesman, contractor, electrician, plumber or a doctor who doesn't do unnecessary surgery or prescribe medication you don't need. It's inspiring to see integrity in *every* field.

Even though Walter Cronkite passed recently, he remains to be my favorite newscaster of all time. He and his wife, Betsy were from Missouri where I was raised. The only time I ever crashed a party was one given for this incredible man whom everyone seemed to respect. My friend, Barbara Valentine and I were in New York and we were out one evening with Andy Kunkle who worked with Dan. We were dressed to the nines that evening and stopped by Tavern on the Green. As the Maitre d' welcomed us, he quietly asked, "Are you here for Mr. Cronkite's 75th birthday celebration?" I didn't hesitate a moment, responding, "We certainly are." As we circulated through the room, there were a number of people I knew. The highlight of the evening was when I noticed that the guest of honor had just finished his dinner. I walked over and said, "Let me take your plate, Mr. Cronkite." He looked up at me and said, "You don't look like a waitress." I kissed him on the cheek and said, "For you, Mr. Cronkite, I am."

A dear friend of mine and a great New Yorker, Dick Levy, introduced me to Ernie Anastos a number of years ago. Next to Mr. Cronkite, Ernie is my favorite anchor. He is such a professional with genuine warmth and a caring heart. In addition to being a wonderful family man, I almost agree with Regis Philbin who said, "Ernie may be the nicest guy I ever met in this business." In my opinion, Ernie is the nicest guy in this business.

—

Because celebrities are in the limelight, they have a real opportunity to share something meaningful when so many want to hear their views. When people hang on your every word and action, you carry a heavy responsibility and no one is quite prepared for that. As we've seen with Susan Boyle on *Britain's Got Talent*, the talent may be *exceptional*, but few are prepared for all that comes with "celebrity status".

Instead of pointing the finger at others, I believe we all need to take responsibility for our own choices. If we're complaining about someone whose life is going down the tubes, why do we give that kind of behavior so much attention? It's my belief that they may be acting out because of a hurt or need and they're not sure how to handle it. Even though they may look good on the outside, we can't see what they're dealing with on the inside. What they really need is love and guidance from people who truly care.

Shouldn't we be applauding those who stand above the crowd because they are helping others be all they can be? The most successful people I know are those who find something they truly enjoy and take pride in doing that job to the best of their ability.

When Dan Enright and I were in Washington, D.C. for the National Prayer Breakfast, we took Natalie Cole to see the Vietnam Mermorial Wall. It had just started snowing as we walked up and began to silently read the names. Dan wept and Natalie and I were speechless. It was such a sobering time as we were reminded that these very soldiers gave their lives to keep our land free. That's why I support our Veterans and want to do much more for them in the future. Trudy Andes Campbell wrote and narrates a new DVD called "A Friend's Prayer", giving tribute to our men and women in uniform. We can never forget the sacrifices they make for us.

It feels like I've come full circle because when I first went to India, it was with Billie Jean Campbell who was married to Glen Campbell. Their oldest son, Travis is married to Trudy, who is the U.S. Ambassador to the Troops. The scars of leprosy victims were so visible and it was not difficult for me to reach out and care for them. When our veterans return from battle, many are missing arms and legs, and others have scars we cannot "see" that affect them deeply. I want to help as many of them as we can.

Right now, our world is in crisis mode like never before on all fronts, from the economy to serious healthcare insurance issues. At one time, the world feared Black Death when an outbreak of bubonic plague killed 30-60% of Europe's population. Recently, we were all put on alert to prevent the spread of Swine Flu.

When President Harry S. Truman gave the order to drop the bomb, I'm sure he thought that was the most crucial time of all and the only way to go. I can't imagine making a decision of that magnitude. Our world is rapidly changing today with milestones our forefathers never thought possible. Many of these changes are applauded. We have the first black president in our history and the first Hispanic Supreme Court judge. We are a land of great diversity where every group is encouraged to express their religious beliefs. I have no problem with that as long as the Judaeo Christian principles and expressions of faith like the Ten Commandments and prayer that our country was founded upon, are not banned. Why are our beliefs so feared? Amendment I of the Bill of Rights states "Congress shall make no law respecting an establishment of religion, or prohibiting the free exercise thereof;"

While we were in Jerusalem in November, several of us started talking about Bob Dylan. What a talent! He at one time confessed to becoming a Christian. He was still a Jew of course, but one who accepted Christ as his Messiah. He even spoke about his faith during his concerts—"Years ago they said I was a prophet. I used to say, 'No I'm not a prophet.' They said 'Yes you are, you're a prophet.' I said, 'No it's not me.' They used to say 'You sure are a prophet.' They used to convince me I was a prophet. Now I come out and say Jesus Christ is the answer and they say, 'Bob Dylan's no prophet.'" From the little I understand, between the pressure of the music world and disappointments with Christians, Dylan may have become disillusioned. I would sure like you to know, Bob, there are a lot of Jewish believers in the industry who you would admire. You might want to give the Lord and us another chance. The Jewish people are still G-d's chosen ones.

It is the right of every American to worship as he or she wishes. A lot of people navigate their lives by astrology, graphology and clairvoyancy. As my father used to say, "It's fine if *you* want to kiss a cow, just as long as you don't ask *me* to kiss that cow." We all have choices in life and that is what America is about—the freedom to choose. If we could only learn to love each other, how perfect that would be.

Johnny Ray Watson is a dear friend of mine who sang in the various Billy Graham Crusades. We jokingly call each other Chocolate and

335

Vanilla. Johnny told me of a personal experience which is so dear. He was sharing with a group of children and asked them this question, "What color do you think we will be when we get to Heaven?" After a few moments, a little girl raised her hand and said, "I think we will all be CLEAR." Out of the mouth of babes. I love this concept, because what God sees is our heart and soul. He sees beyond the outward appearance.

## MY STORY WILL BE CONTINUED

and guess what, so will yours . . . as long as the world doesn't blow up . . . and if it does, then we'll all go together. If you've never thought about it before, remember that Eternity is forever, it just happens to begin on earth.

## WHAT WILL MATTER

(Written by Michael Josephson and shared with me by Suzi Wehba)

Ready or not, some day it will all come to an end.
There will be no more sunrises, no minutes, hours or days.
All the things you collected, whether treasured or forgotten, will pass to
    someone else.
Your wealth, fame and temporal power will shrivel to irrelevance.
It will not matter what you owned or what you were owed.
Your grudges, resentments, frustrations and jealousies will finally
    disappear.
So too, your hopes, ambitions, plans and to-do lists will expire.
The wins and losses that once seemed so important will fade away.
It won't matter where you came from or what side of the tracks you lived
    on at the end.
It won't matter whether you were beautiful or brilliant.
Even your gender and skin color will be irrelevant.
So what *will* matter? How will the value of your days be measured?
What will matter is not what you bought but what you built, not what
    you got but what you gave.
What will matter is not your success, but your significance.

———

What will matter is not what you learned, but what you taught.

What will matter is every act of integrity, compassion, courage or sacrifice that enriched, empowered or encouraged others to emulate your example.

What will matter is not your competence, but your character.

What will matter is not how many people you knew, but how many will feel a lasting loss when you're gone.

What will matter is not your memories, but the memories of those who loved you.

What will matter is how long you will be remembered, by whom and for what.

Living a life that matters doesn't happen by accident.

It's not a matter of circumstance but of choice.

Choose to live a life that matters.

Albert Camus said, *I would rather live my life as if there is a God and die to find out there isn't, than live my life as if there isn't, and die to find out there is.*

# EPILOGUE

## by Tammy

I first met Susan Stafford when she was the original hostess of Merv Griffin's *Wheel Of Fortune* and have had the privilege of serving as her personal assistant for twenty-five years. After reading her story, I think you can understand why I say that working with Susan has been exciting and unpredictable, but *never* boring.

Through the years, many have found it difficult to imagine how Susan could *choose* to leave a life of fame and fortune on the #1 daytime television game show in America. While there's no question that Susan was one of the fortunate ones, the brass ring had lost its luster.

After working alongside Mother Teresa's nuns with leprosy patients in India, Susan returned to the show with an indelible imprint on her soul and a burning desire she could not ignore. She left the show to fulfill a "calling" to work with cancer patients, realizing the decision was no longer hers to make

As you read about Susan's childhood, you saw that she had a very early start being pulled in different directions. The adults had no idea how difficult it was for her as she quietly dealt with the uncertainties and confusion. This began a lifelong quest to know *where* she belonged and *why*. Susan said she often felt like a chameleon, trying to adapt herself perfectly to each environment and that has continued throughout her life on many levels.

Susan's divorces and her struggle with alcohol were evidence of a life out of balance. While she was determined to rescue others, skillfully guiding them through difficult situations, she continued to make poor choices in her own life. Wanting to find love and really belong to someone, Susan kept skating along the surface without being able to put roots down deep enough to take hold.

Long before it was fashionable for celebrities to be concerned about the plight of people in Third World countries, Susan had already proven

339

herself as a true humanitarian. Today, many have found a way to maintain their careers while reaching out to those in need. For Susan, it was an *all* or *nothing* proposition which she took very seriously.

From the beginning, Susan's life was unconventional and she is the first one to admit that she's still learning. Because of her positive attitude, some may think Susan has never gone through hard times as an adult. Early in her career, Susan was training on a trampoline for a segment on *Circus of the Stars*. Her lower back was fractured when she struck the frame and she had to lay in a body cast for two months. Thirty years later, she had surgery for a severely ruptured disc in that same area. That was followed by what should have been simple cartilage surgery in her right knee, however the doctor scraped too deep and she was seldom without pain. Susan was not able to drive for several months and a wonderful young man named Jaime was kind enough to be her driver during that time. This summer, all that changed with the wonderful stem cell treatment she received.

Susan often says she would rather have her problems than those of someone else. She continues to choose to meet life head on and learned long ago to work *through* her fears instead of running from them.

You've heard people say, "I'm doing pretty well under the circumstances." One thing I admire about Susan is that she refuses to live her life *under* the circumstances. When people ask Susan, "How are you?" she has adopted the best answer of all, "I'm grateful." Whatever she is dealing with on a personal level, she continues to reach out to help others who are dealing with their own difficulties.

One example of this is Susan's first fiancée in California, Clint Ritchie. You may remember him as Clint Buchanan from *One Life To Live*. They had kept in touch through the years and when he first became ill with congestive heart failure, Susan was one of the first people Clint called.

When his condition worsened and he went to the hospital, Clint's neighbor, LeRoy Sherer called Susan to let her know. Susan made the trip that very day, Thanksgiving, 2008. After canceling dinner plans in Palm Springs, Susan flew to Sacramento and got a cab to the hospital in Roseville, CA. Because of the holiday, very few drivers were on duty. The cab driver happened to be a Muslim from Pakistan. He gave Susan his number and told her to call him. She didn't know how long she would need to stay, but he said no matter how late, he would make sure she got back to the hotel.

After spending many hours at Clint's bedside, Susan called the driver. He knew she hadn't been able to enjoy a traditional Thanksgiving dinner and brought along a hot meal prepared by his mother. Before sharing the delicious lamb and rice dish, Susan gave thanks to her Lord while the Muslim driver thanked Allah. She found the driver's act of kindness especially touching in light of the disharmony and conflict in our world today. No matter what the question may be, Susan believes love is still the answer.

Susan and Clint kept in close phone contact after she returned home. Little by little, Clint began to regain his strength and doctors cautioned him not to drink or smoke. He was doing better, driving his truck around the ranch to see the 40 horses he loved so much. Everyone was shocked when he suffered a heart attack late in January. After he was rushed to the hospital, doctors told his sisters and LeRoy they would insert a pacemaker and he should be fine. Unfortunately, during that surgery, a blood clot went to his brain and Clint never recovered. Susan was so grateful she made the trip to see him. Someone said "you can never do a kindness too soon, because you never know when it will be too late." None of us knows what tomorrow may hold.

*Mother Teresa and Pope John Paul II*   *Susan spent a month inside the Vatican walls where few are privileged to visit*

When Pope John Paul II died, Susan noted the final act of <u>his</u> personal assistant was to cover the Pope's face with a veil. My instructions are a little different. Susan made me promise to put socks on her feet to keep them warm. Anyone who really knows her would never describe Susan as having "cold feet". God has given her a special courage and determination which allows Susan to reach out during times when others step back.

Susan is a member of the Emergency Crisis Team with Media Fellowship Intl. led by Pastor Bob Rieth. She was called to Columbine following the devastating high school shooting and provided counsel and guidance for the survivors and families of those whose lives were cut short. When the students were shot at Virginia Tech, Susan again dropped everything to go there to help. I have always admired her devotion and caring heart. In my opinion, no one does it better.

One of the mothers from Columbine wrote to Susan, "We watched many turn their lives around in the wake of that fateful day in April 1999. I believe that because of people like you who cared enough to just show up and cry with these kids, many lives were saved. Thank you! Thanks for all you've done and all that you continue to do! May you be richly blessed in life and every endeavor you undertake!"

The mind of this amazing lady never stops as she takes care of so many in her ever-enlarging world. As long as Susan has breath, she will care about those who are hurting. With all the demands on her time, this book has been a bit difficult to complete, but we finally made it!

When Susan was honored with a star by the Palm Springs Walk of Stars, each speaker heard the one before them describe Susan as their best friend. They started saying, "Wait a second, I thought *I* was her best friend." That came as no surprise because I have seen this exceptional gift Susan has of making *each* person in her life feel special. I hope you've enjoyed this fascinating journey with *your* new best friend—Susan Stafford.

Please check her website *www.SusanStafford.org* for dates and locations of book signings where you can meet Susan in person. We will also list guest appearances on television and radio where she will share more stories from behind the scenes.

Susan is available for seminar speaking as well. For scheduling, please email her agent, Fred Wostbrock at *Fred@ksrtalent.com*.

# ACKNOWLEDGEMENTS

More than a special thank-you to Amy Freeman Cohen for suggesting the title for my book. Isn't it great? You're a doll, Amy.

When you work with someone in the midst of all the pressures life brings, it can be a real challenge at times. No one knows that better than my personal assistant of twenty-five years, Tammy. The grace and mercy of God has kept us working together for a common goal and I am most grateful. Without her faithfulness, this book would have never been written.

How could I have ever gotten through this without my prayer partners who never stopped praying for this book to be completed?

Beyond doubt, the friend who pushed me the most is Jimmy Hawkins who was forever asking "Where's the book? Where's the book?"

Then there's my agent and more importantly, my friend, Fred Wostbrock whose wise counsel and encouragement each step of the way, helped make this book possible.

Special thanks to "Risee the niece" for her help with the family history.

Maria Comfort was wonderful to take time she didn't have to assist with some of the early editing which was most helpful.

Kudos to my exuberant publicist and friend, Doris Bergman, the most flamboyant redhead you've ever seen. Her enthusiasm is contagious.

Thanks to my sister, Catherine, for her kind assistance and encouragement with the final editing.

I'm more than grateful to Barbara Valentine and her son Todd for their true caring and expertise in assisting with the technical quality of the photographs.

So many people have helped me in countless ways during difficult times in my life. You know who you are, and rather than risk missing someone, I decided not to list the names here. Please know I hold you in my heart as we continue to find our way.

—

# HOLLYWOOD BEAT

## by Marci Weiner

### Honoring Merv Griffin on the Beat

My connection to Merv Griffin was through Susan Stafford, the original hostess of Wheel of Fortune. I met this gorgeous lady when I first moved to L.A., and she has come a long way since then. Her book, "Stop The Wheel, I Want to Get Off!" shares her eclectic life of service to patients with leprosy, cancer and AIDS. She has also been chosen as Ambassador of Entertainment for the Walk of Stars in Palm Springs, Las Vegas and Anaheim and the Motion Picture Hall of Fame, founded by Bob Alexander.

*With Merv Griffin*

—

345

Dr. Susan's escort at Merv Griffin's memorial was Dr. Mark Karalla, who delivered Merv's two grandchildren and Dick and Patty Van Patten's grandkids. She was happy to reunite with Fred Hayman (Giorgios), who is charming and never slips up. Everyone related how creative Merv was and how he loved life.

# ODDS AND ENDS

*My favorite television hosts and hostesses:*

Monty Hall—the most humble
Pat Sajak—the wittiest
Chuck Woolery—Brother, you're still my favorite to work with
Peter Marshall—the warmest charm
Wink Martindale—besides having such a faithful wife, Sandy, who's
    adorable, you're a great host with the best smile
Ellen DeGeneres—her dancing is so fun—she's cuter than a bug's ear
Ryan Seacrest—darling yet professional
Christiane Amanpour—one of the most professional in the business
Howie Mandel—confident and more than fair
Meredith Viera—she's one classy lady
Anderson Cooper—so professional and caring with a great laugh
Rick Sanchez—the people's host without an ego
Jim Hill—my favorite sports announcer in L. A. He keeps it interesting.
Glenn Beck—who knows what he will say next? My hat is off to Glenn.
Kathie Lee Gifford—I love her. She is so natural and honest with a big
    heart as well as being my friend.
Tom Bergeron—who thinks on his feet better than anyone
Charlie Rose—a man with such style who I would love to meet. He
    <u>always</u> does his research.
Robert Osborne—so casual, yet he brings depth out of each person
Lou Dobbs—He only delivers the truth.
Matt and Laurie Crouch—with wit and caring, they are genuinely
    interested in their guests
Alex Trebek—he's the best. The one show I could never play because of
    the extensive vocabulary and high intelligence is *Jeopardy!* I learn so
    much from the show. It's la crème de la crème

—

And naturally, our Oprah—no words are sufficient. You always take the high road!

*My mentors*—while some may have two or three, my world is so eclectic and full that I've been blessed with many. Since it's not possible to list them all, I will share just twenty-five of them for now:

My beloved mother, Louise Vignone Carney    Mama Shirley Boone

Eleanor Roosevelt    Golda Meir    Ruth Carter Stapleton
Mother Teresa    Rhonda Fleming    Suzi Wehba
Laura Davis    Beverly Blitzer    Mother Placid
Bonnie Green    Sybil Brand    Peggy Ebersol
Dr. Marianne Dunn    Mandy Evans    Diane Weissburg, Esq.
Ruth Mollott    Colleen Keene    Mrs. John Ford
Dr. Vera David    Bette Hawkins    Beverly Rogers
Peggy Goldwater    Mrs. Billy (Ruth) Graham

**Remember playing *Twenty Questions?* Here are my answers:**
**If you want to send me your answers, the email address is**
*StopTheWheelBook@aol.com*

1. What is your greatest fear? *Losing my eyesight.*
2. What trait do you most deplore in yourself? *The words I have spoken and cannot take back*
3. What trait do you most deplore in others? *Rudeness*
4. What is your greatest extravagance? *Spending money on creams and bath salts which I love. I could open my own store.*
5. What is your greatest regret? *The waste of my drinking days.*
6. What are your favorite foods? *Mama's spaghetti and Hungarian goulash and the scalloped corn made by Tammy's mother, Edna*
7. What or who is the greatest love of your life? *Jesus Christ*
8. Which talent would you most like to have? *Mastering the piano*
9. What would you change about yourself? *Have a flat stomach again*
10. What do you consider your greatest gift? *Knowing how to read people*
11. What are your most treasured possessions? *My faith and health*
12. What are the qualities you most like in a person? *Kindness, humor and faith*
13. What do you most value in your friends? *Loyalty*

——

14. Who are your favorite writers? *Dominick Dunne, Ayn Rand, Max Lucado, C.S. Lewis and Leo Tolstoy*
15. Which historical figure do you most identify with? *Eleanor Roosevelt*
16. What are your favorite songs? "Kokomo" *by the Beach Boys, the* "Vienna Waltz" *and* "Jesu, Joy of Man's Desiring"
17. What is your motto for life? *Life is not a dress rehearsal.*
18. What's your favorite color? *Aqua*
19. Where would you most like to vacation? *At my friend Gerdta's farmhouse near Salzburg, Austria, the hills of Missouri and Pagosa Springs, Colorado*
20. Who are the men you most admire? *Dave Loftus; Martin Luther King, Jr.; Dr. David David; Rev. Terry Sweeney; David Rockefeller, Jr.; Bill Gray; Pat Boone; President Harry S. Truman; Rosey Grier; Rev. Billy Graham; Steve Burns; Rabbi Mendel Itkin; Charlie Rose; Ed O'Sullivan; John Wayne; Billy Davis, Jr.; Leo Normoyle; Gov. Pat Brown; Israeli Prime Minister Itzhak Rabin; George Carney, Jr.; Casey Kasem; Ed Asner; Dr. Buzz Edelburg; Abraham Lincoln; Dr. Bobby Carney; President Ronald Reagan; Al Kasha; Walter Cronkite; Dr. Don Ha; John Walsh; Michael J. Fox; Dr. Thom Mintz; Dick Levy; Pastor John Hagee; Ron Schneider; Pastor Bob Rieth; Michael Reagan; The Dalai Lama; March Schwartz; Seth Riggs; Dr. Richard Mouw; Manfred Cieslik; Steve Ozark; Roger Lee Harrison; Mahatma Ghandi; Grandfather Clyde Carney; Ed Lozzi; Hal Sloane; Robbie Robertson; Rudy Giuliani; Gavin MacLeod; Fr. Mike Manning; Matt Crouch; Bill Greene; Ralph Nader; Anderson Cooper and . . . Dan Enright.*

*Specialist Fred Brewer*

I'm so grateful for soldiers like Specialist Fred Brewer who served with Delta Force in Afghanistan and was awarded a Purple Heart. As we remember all the soldiers who have fought for our freedom in every generation, it reminds us that FREEDOM IS NOT FREE.

I have met so many in various cultures who have shown me kindness and the value of being a responsible human being, even if I never knew their names. One thing that's great about America is we are a nation who knows the value of sharing what we have with those in need. There is no shortage of groups and individuals who can use our help and yet sometimes, people aren't certain where to give. I would like to share the charities that have touched my heart and ones I like to support.

Media Fellowship International
Human Trafficking programs
John Wayne Cancer Foundation
Ryan's Reach
P.A.T.H. (People Assisting the
Homeless)
MAOZ—a Messianic ministry in Israel
A Friend's Prayer Foundation with Trudy Andes Campbell for Veterans

ASF—AIDS Service Foundation
Soldiers of the Second Coming
United Negro College Fund
Friends of the Orphans (Spanish)
Rona Barrett Foundation

I have learned to trust certain people from a great CPA to a skilled photographer, hearing aid specialist, etc. I highly recommend each one and you can find them on the Links tab of my website at *www.SusanStafford.org* as well as my favorite charities listed above.

I love this poem by a man who spent 8 ½ half years in a Nazi Concentration Camp and it has greatly influenced the way I live my life:

**In Germany, they first came for the communists,**
**and I didn't speak up because I wasn't a communist.**
**Then they came for the Jews,**
**and I didn't speak up because I wasn't a Jew.**
**Then they came for the trade unionists,**
**and I didn't speak up because I wasn't a trade unionist.**
**Then they came for the Catholics**
**and I didn't speak up because I wasn't a Catholic.**
**Then they came for me—**
**and by that time, there was nobody left to speak up.**

(by Martin Niemoller, German Protestant pastor, 1892-1984)

# INDEX

# Y

*While I was the original hostess of Wheel of Fortune when our show began in America, there are now 42 countries televising Wheel of Fortune. I recently enjoyed a wonderful evening getting to know the former hostess of the show in Germany, a beautiful lady named Maren Gilzer. She left the show to pursue a career as an actress and is married to a charming television tycoon in Berlin named Egon Freiheit.*

The music CD inside the back cover is a gift to the first 1500 people who buy my book. Many people are going through difficulties, some minor, some major. It's my hope that we can heal us all.

*Animals are special gifts in our lives
and can teach us so much.
Their unconditional love is
a great example of healing
grace and my beloved dog,
Butcherman, was one of the best.*

**HEAL US ALL**
**by Paul Hampton**
(Lyrics for the CD)

The clouds keep hiding
The sun from view
The mood of the country
Is American blue
Outwardly smiling
Inwardly in pain
Our voices intertwining
In the same refrain
Like a siren's call

See us, Hear us, Feel us, HEAL US ALL

God only blesses
He wouldn't damn

Sweet innocent children
That's not part of his plan
We don't understand it
Angrily we grieve
So who does the allowing?
Is the only cure
Letting teardrops fall?

See us, Hear us, Feel us, HEAL US ALL

Heal the fallen
So again they
Will be able to stand tall
Heal the aching heart whose sorrow
Never seems to end
Hear their silent call

See us, Hear us, Feel us, HEAL US ALL

Made in the USA
Middletown, DE
24 August 2024

59664042R00203